SPORTS
PROFILES

SPORTING PROFILES

—

Sixty Heroes of Sport

Michael Parkinson

To Keith Miller and Alistair Cooke,
both great all-rounders.

This paperback edition first published in Great Britain in 1996 by
Pavilion Books Limited
26 Upper Ground
London SE1 9PD

First published in hardback in 1995

Text copyright © 1995 by Michael Parkinson
The majority of the articles in this book were originally published in
the *Daily Telegraph*, and the author and publisher acknowledge the co-operation
of the Editor in compiling this collection.

The moral right of the author has been asserted

Text designed by AB3

Jacket designed by Nigel Partridge. Jacket photograph by Douglas Robertson.

A CIP catalogue record for this book is available from the British Library.

ISBN 1-85793-878-X

Typeset in Garamond 3 11/13.5 pt by Texttype Typesetters, Cambridge
Printed and bound in Finland by WSOY

2 4 6 8 10 9 7 5 3

This book may be ordered by post direct from the publisher. Please contact the
Marketing Department. But try your bookshop first.

CONTENTS

	Preface	7
1	Graham Gooch	9
2	Gary Lineker	13
3	Naseem Hamed	17
4	Tom Finney	21
5	Dickie Bird	26
6	Allan Border	30
7	Brian Clough	34
8	Angus Fraser	40
9	Rory Underwood	44
10	Derek Randall	48
11	Greg Norman	52
12	Denis Compton	56
13	Peter Thomson	60
14	John Emburey	64
15	Steven Rhodes	68
16	Laura Davies	72
17	Michael Holding	76
18	Martyn Moxon	79
19	Ellery Hanley	83
20	Bernard Gallacher	88
21	Ray Wilkins	92
22	Tony Greig	95
23	David Leadbetter	99
24	Martin Crowe	103

25 George Best   107
26 Keith Miller   111
27 Graham Thorpe   115
28 Nick Faldo   118
29 Roger Taylor   122
30 Darren Gough   126
31 Philip Don   130
32 Brian Barnes   134
33 Mike Gatting   137
34 Steve Redgrave   141
35 Mark McCormack   145
36 David Lloyd   150
37 Nat Lofthouse   154
38 Don Bradman   158
39 Jackie Stewart   164
40 Alistair Cooke   168
41 David Gower   173
42 Dale Gibson   177
43 Michael Atherton   182
44 Geoffrey Boycott   186
45 Brian Close   190
46 Robin Smith   194
47 Gary Player   198
48 George Pope   202
49 Sir Matt Busby   205
50 Bobby Moore   207
51 Cec Pepper   211
52 Fred Perry   213
53 Danny Blanchflower   217
54 Gavin Smith   220
55 Jimmy Baxter   222
56 Cec McCormack   225
57 Skinner Normanton   227
58 Harold Larwood   229
59 Wilfred Rhodes   235
60 John William Parkinson   239

PREFACE

—

THE WORLD is divided between those people who would donate a limb to spend their working life watching sport, and those who believe that being a sports writer is not a job for a grown man. Having written about sport almost all my adult life I have a sympathy with both points of view. Indeed, being a journalist for 44 of my 60 years on this planet has placed me in daily confrontation with the situation, because nowhere is the dichotomy more apparent than in a newspaper office.

I once worked for a national newspaper whose editor referred to the sports desk as 'the toy department'. When I was interviewed for a job on the *Manchester Guardian* (when that was its name and I was a very young man) I was warned that the editor had no time for young journalists who wanted to write about sports or the arts. 'I suppose, young man, you want to write about cricket and the theatre,' he said, regarding me with a wearily cynical smile. 'No sir,' I lied. 'Good,' he said, 'because fools write about one and dreamers the other.'

I was in both categories, but I got the job. However, I never did write about sport for the *Manchester Guardian*. What I really wanted to be was a mixture of Keith Miller and Neville Cardus. There were other heroes too. H D 'Donny' Davies was one, the *Guardian*'s 'Old International' and a superb stylist and wit, both as a writer and an observer on radio. Other heroes were John Arlott, who later became a friend, and that supreme journalist Alistair Cooke, whom I also came to know and who once defended his love of sport by writing: 'I have come to feel a deep, unspoken pity for people who have no attachment to a single sport, almost as sorry for them as I am for teetotallers.'

I learned much from those journalists of my youth. When I was late-duty reporter on the *Guardian*, whiling away the hours with calls to the police and fire brigade around Manchester, hoping for a pub fight or a chip-pan fire to reduce the boredom, I would invade the newspaper's library and read as much as I could find written by my aforesaid heroes. It was then I began to realize that, despite rumours to the contrary, some of the very best writing to be found in our newspapers is on the sports pages. All the journalist needs is an editor who gives him reassuring support and a decent space to fill. I have been lucky. I started writing about sport because the journalist and author Richard West, with whom I had worked on the *Guardian*, encouraged me to write about the sporting North in the now defunct *Time and Tide* under the pseudonym 'Jack Braithwaite'. A delightful eccentric called Clifford Makins, who was the sports editor of the *Observer*, picked up on the idea (under my own name) and then Harry Evans and John Lovesey at the *Sunday Times* gave me a home for 15 years.

There have been distractions. It was difficult while interviewing Raquel Welch to remember that your first love was writing about sport; almost impossible having become a 'television personality' to be a fly on the wall, observing but rarely observed; awkward to persuade hard-working colleagues in the press box that you are more than a dilettantish observer.

New readers who were more used to me being attacked by emus than writing about Gower's cover drive were similarly confused. One of the first letters I received after joining the *Daily Telegraph* in 1991 was addressed to 'Michael Parkinson, Sports Writer and TV Personality, If They Be The Same Person'. It's a good question, but not to be answered here. Except to say that since joining the *Telegraph*, and with the substantial support and encouragement of Max Hastings and David Welch, I have come to understand further why my ambition to be a sports journalist was a sensible one.

What follows here are meetings I have had with heroes. Rereading them I was tempted on occasions, because of hindsight, to alter the text. Also there were changes I wanted to make because since the interview significant events had overtaken the sportsman concerned. For instance, my interview with Michael Atherton came long before the traumatic experience of alleged ball tampering that could have ended his career as England captain. I resisted the temptation, because what we people who write about sport understand is that our task is to tell you what it was like in a certain moment of time and not to rewrite history.

My father, being a proper Yorkshireman, went to his grave believing that his son, by not playing cricket for Yorkshire and England, had denied his birthright. All I can tell you is that by writing about sport for a living instead of playing it, I did the next best thing.

Michael Parkinson, 1995

·1·

GRAHAM GOOCH

—

I JOURNEYED to Cambridge on a chirruping, blossoming spring day and saw Graham Gooch give a master class to the eager young pups of the Combined Universities, his bat echoing like a bass gong around Fenner's. He scored a century.

Two days later at Chelmsford against Worcestershire he almost scored another. His last three trips to the crease have yielded 317 first-class runs: he might have finished with Test cricket but no one should doubt his determination to defend his reputation as our best batsman.

Anyone who watched Gooch on the last tour of Australia could be in no doubt that he was right to announce his retirement. It was, as he admits, a tour too far. Nonetheless I have no doubt that there will come a moment during the summer with Ambrose and Walsh on the rampage when we would all feel much better with Gooch at the crease unflinching, resolute and proven in the heat of battle.

The circumstances leading to Gooch's retirement had nothing to do with a fraying of technique or nerve, nor lack of appetite for the encounter. In the end his body told him to quit. There was a time in cricket's history when Gooch, at 42 with 22 seasons behind him, might still have been a force in the international game. That he has lasted this long as the game became faster, fitter and younger is a tribute to his determined and relentless pursuit of excellence.

In a new book about his life written along with the excellent Frank Keating, Gooch says that when he came into the pavilion at Perth having played his last Test match he was content with the thought he could always look in the mirror and say: 'If I did nothing else I know I always did my best.'

If you find the statement simplistic, even mawkish, then you fail to understand the man. Gooch believes in the solid virtues of hard work and dedication. This is a man who carries dumb bells in his suitcase to exercise with, who would think nothing of running a few miles from hotel to ground and back again, who in the chaos of a dressing room had his own controlled space with everything in its place and in apple-pie order. He left nothing to chance.

If this meticulous preparation was the cornerstone of his success it was also one of the reasons why his public reputation was of a dour, even dull, man. In the famous dispute with David Gower, Gooch was cast as the Black Knight and it was Gower who rode the white charger, the sunlight dappling his golden hair.

With his sloping shoulders and world-weary manner, Gooch was easy meat for the media whenever it felt like blaming body language for the problems of our cricket team. Nor did he help himself. He has always been wary about opening his mouth in public. In the book he recalls an early incident in the Essex dressing room when, as he sat in the corner trying to avoid the attention of the captain 'Tonker' Taylor, Keith Fletcher nodded over in his direction and said: 'Does it talk?'

Well it does, and very fluently when it has to as we shall soon discover. But Gooch is not a soundbite cricketer. He doesn't feel the need to underline his achievements with words, preferring people to make up their own minds about what they have witnessed.

This was most famously demonstrated after he had scored 333 runs against the Indians. We asked how did he feel and awaited, pencils poised, to report the torrent of words from a man who had just scored a triple century in a Test match. 'All right, I suppose,' said Graham Gooch.

But he is not a sourpuss. Quite the opposite. He has a sly, but deep, sense of humour. He is, as Keating observes, 'the most companionable of men'. After reading his book I am also prepared to shortlist him as the most forgiving of men. What strikes you as you read this painstaking account of his life is the lack of malice, the way he side-steps paying back old grievances.

Ted Dexter, before he became chairman of selectors, once wrote that Gooch's captaincy had the effect on him of 'a slap in the face with a cold fish'. All Gooch has to say about that insult is to observe that Mr Dexter is entitled to his opinion.

Indeed the book is so short on hair-raising, headline-making sensational revelation that an interview published the day I met him at Fenner's concentrated on the break-up of his marriage and asked the question: 'Is he the sort of man who needs a woman to look after him?'

We sat at Fenner's on a bench, near the wall at the back of the pavilion. Earlier I had watched him bowl, an unexpected pleasure brought about by Neil Williams pulling a hamstring and Gooch, ever the willing workhorse, taking over in an emergency. After every over as he trudged away to his position in the deep, slope-shouldered, slightly knock-kneed, head bowed, he looked for all the world like a ploughman returning home after a back-breaking day in the fields. At such moments you would have a hard job convincing the stranger to the game that Gooch was one of the most glorious batsmen of modern times, someone who could make even the best bowlers seem accommodating.

Nor would it prepare you when you met him for the attractive mien, the frank and humorous blue/green eyes, the agreeable, easy manner.

I asked him if he had been tempted when writing the book to answer the critics, to rout his enemies. It had, after all, been a controversial career. The Gower affair and the Dexter observation were nothing compared to the abuse he took after the rebel tour to South Africa. The team was labelled 'Gooch's Dirty Dozen'. He tells the story that upon his return he heard a father say to his son: 'That's Graham Gooch.' The son replied: 'Dad, isn't he the man you call "the traitor"?'

Gooch said: 'I was interested in putting the record straight but not in paying back in kind. That's not my style. When I was writing the book all I could think about was how lucky I was to play cricket for a living and to play with and against such a good bunch of blokes. I have enjoyed the game for 22 years. Why get angry about that?'

He was lucky in his apprenticeship. The Essex team of his youth was a lively mixture of hard-nosed professionals like Keith Fletcher and sometimes barmy individuals like 'Tonker' Taylor. It was Fletcher who had the most profound effect on Gooch's career. Gooch repays the debt by calling him 'a genius'. 'Tonker' Taylor, who played his cricket as if he was batting on Clacton beach, once reported umpire Cec Pepper for 'over-excessive and noisy farting'.

During his time Gooch has seen the first-class game change almost beyond recognition. He said: 'Gone are the days when you could come on a cricket field and just swan about. There is a new athleticism in the game, there are new standards of fitness to be met. Australia was the latest example.

'They have a strength of purpose, a desire to succeed that we must learn from. Will we? Good question. We didn't alter the tour of '91 and the lesson was there then.

'What drives me mad about our cricket is the lack of consistency. We play well for one Test match and then perform like idiots in the next. I think our young cricketers have got to look inside themselves and ask how much they want the job. They have to realize that they have to do the important part themselves, that no one can hand it to them on a plate.

'They must understand that to succeed at the top level in any job involves sacrifice. Too much of our young talent is lost in a mire of mediocrity. There's a lot of dead wood in county cricket and it must be got rid of.

'In the end it's all about self-motivation. Daley Thompson once told me that he wanted to show his rivals that he was the first to arrive for training and the last to leave. He wanted them to be aware that he was prepared to work harder than they were at being the best. People often laughed at me and my attitude towards training. But I didn't do it for fun. What I know for certain is I never saw a fitter, stronger cricketer ever become a worse cricketer,' he said. One or two of our young players who went to Australia last time should take that advice to heart.

So, in the final analysis who would he, the perfectionist, choose as the best 11 players he has played either with or against? Boycott was his favourite opening partner but he doesn't get in the team. Barry Richards and Sunil Gavaskar are the openers. Then: Viv Richards, Allan Border, Javed Miandad, Ian Botham, Alan Knott, Malcolm Marshall ('the most brilliant fast bowler of my time'), Wasim Akram, Shane Warne and Curtly Ambrose.

How long will Graham Gooch remain playing for Essex? 'A couple of seasons I should think. Just so long as I enjoy it and can play to the required standard,' he said.

Then he went out to bat and face the young men from Cambridge, Oxford and Durham who were either unborn or in nappies when he made his first-class debut.

They ran in with great vigour, the chance of bowling a legend lending them extra ambition and strength. In the end a surfeit of testosterone was not enough. The ardent young men were given a tutorial.

It was reassuring watching Graham Gooch bat on a lovely, dreamy English day. There was a beguiling serenity about the occasion, a sense of time standing still.

A new cricket season, a great player in full flow. Let it last forever. If only.

6th May 1995

·2·

GARY LINEKER

—

I HAD this fab idea. Instead of interviewing Gary Lineker face to face, why not do the job on the golf course? I could see the headline: A Round With Gary Lineker. But why interview Lineker in the first place? His cuttings file would sink a fair-sized cargo ship and he is no longer playing the game.

Well, for one thing there is the new career outside football to talk about. He has just completed his first 100 days as a BBC TV pundit and – more significantly and taxingly – as host of a live weekend sports programme on Radio 5 Live. There was also talk he wasn't up to the job, that he would be too bland, and his voice too boring. How does he think he has done so far? More to the point, are his bosses at the BBC happy?

Also, I wanted to talk to him to be reminded that the game of football is still capable of producing men in the tradition of Finney and Charlton; real and proper heroes who proved that being a good sport, a modest man and a well-behaved member of society was not incompatible with becoming a great player and a stern competitor.

In other words I am sick of the ugly side of football, of the in-your-face skinhead, foul-mouthed, yobbish, violent aspect of the game. I need the antidote and what better than a round of golf with the man who was never booked in his entire career and who has been called: 'The Queen Mother of football' (*An Evening With Gary Lineker*), 'The nicest man on earth' (Spurs fanzine) and 'One of nature's Boy Scouts' (Hunter Davies).

If honest to Mr Lineker, I have to say he cringes at the mention of these descriptions and much prefers the assessment made by Joe Kinnear, the feisty manager of Wimbledon. After Mr Lineker had said that he preferred to watch Teletext than Wimbledon play, Mr Kinnear was asked his opinion of the former captain of England. 'He is,' said Mr Kinnear, 'an arsehole.'

We came together on the first tee of Woburn's Duke's Course, a piece of golfing terrain nearly 7,000 yards long snaking through a forest of trees in glorious countryside near Milton Keynes. Since 1985 it has been the home of the British Masters and has sorted out many a great player.

The first hole is a 514-yard par five. As we surveyed what we had to do the sun was shining, a light breeze trembled the very tips of the slender pine trees and there were yellow flowers on the gorse. During Mr Lineker's practice swing I positioned myself behind and slightly to his right. It was as if I was fielding at gully. Had I been positioned at old-fashioned deep point I would certainly have been in with a chance at catching his tee-shot, which remarkably flew at right angles from his club into the forest.

'Mmmm,' said Mr Lineker, which is not what I would have come out with had I been in his position. During our round I was to marvel at his iron control and limitless patience. It wasn't until much later in the game that he snapped, which is more than can be said for your correspondent. After much hacking in the pines Mr Lineker finally hit his ball out of bounds and settled for a blob.

The second hole is a 384-yard par four. Again we were both unconvincing off the tee and I began to see a problem emerging. I am a left-hander with a slice, he is a right-hander with a tendency to hit the ball left to right. That being the case our natural game was designed to take us to different parts of a golf course. Normally this wouldn't matter. However it is difficult to conduct an interview when both parties are in dense undergrowth on opposite sides of the fairway. When we did finally meet we were sharing a bunker. This was neither the time nor the place to discuss the state of the modern game or Mr Lineker's views on the influence of French philosophers on the career of Eric Cantona.

'We're crazy. We came on the course without warming up and expect to play well. It's silly,' said Mr Lineker. I didn't tell him that I hated practice and that my idea of warming up was a double egg, sausage, bacon and fried bread breakfast which I had managed to scoff that morning. I did the decent thing and sympathized.

I told him that when I once complained about playing badly, the golf pro I was with said: 'It's your own fault. You walk on to a course without preparing yourself. You never see a pro do that.' I said something sarcastic like that was because pros had nothing else to do. He said: 'Let me ask you a question: when you do a show on television do you rehearse?' I said we did. 'That's exactly what we do,' he said.

Mr Lineker managed a wan smile at my homespun wisdom. At the time he was knee-deep in sand looking at an impossible shot on to a sloping green and thinking he would settle for a double bogey. Could it be I am losing my sense of timing?

The third hole on the Duke's course is one of the most photogenic in British golf. It is a 134-yard par three across a valley to a green far below. The hole is surrounded by trees and rhododendrons. It was here that Gary Lineker showed his mettle. He hit a high, soft nine-iron to within 15 feet but left the ball above the pin.

When the sun shines and the greens are running this is a bit like putting down a glacier. He nicked the cup with his first putt and holed from six feet coming back for a par.

We can now talk golf. He played first as a teenager but gave it up when he became a professional footballer. He started playing again when he went to Japan. He hasn't got a handicap but thinks 20 or 22 might be fair at present and hopes to get down to single figures. No reason why he shouldn't. He's got a slow, rhythmic swing, a calm temperament and a self-belief that comes with being a top-class professional athlete.

His problem will be finding the space in what has become a full-time occupation with the media. In addition to radio and television he also writes a column for the *Observer*. It is typical of the man, and the wise counsel offered by his agent Jon Holmes, that Lineker chose to grind out his own thoughts for a broadsheet rather than take the easier, ghost-written and more lucrative option offered by the tabloids.

When we recommenced our round we played quietly and without much incident until the eighth hole when there was a most remarkable occurrence. Gary Lineker hit his drive into the trees. He called that he had located his ball and the next sound I heard was a ball hitting timber followed by quiet. More scuffling in the undergrowth and then terrible clatter as a ball seemed to strike four or five trees before silence descended once more.

As I waited on the fairway, my ears as sensitive as tuning forks to any indication of what might be happening to my opponent, there came the crack of ball on tree followed this time by an anguished cry of 'Shit!' It is the moment Gary Lineker lost his claim to sainthood. It was so unexpected I'm thinking of sponsoring a commemorative plaque on a tree at the spot where it happened.

I only mention the incident because it does Gary Lineker a disservice to portray him as a sickeningly perfect goody-goody with a halo and whipped cream for blood. Any athlete who gets to the top has to be tough, mentally and physically. Lineker's self-control and patience are part of his physical toughness, just as his ability to learn quickly using a mind which is not befuddled by either booze or fame is an indication of his mental strength.

One of Lineker's new bosses, Bob Shennan, who is BBC Radio's Head of Sport says: 'He's single-minded, intelligent, works hard, takes nothing for granted and, most important of all, wants to succeed. Our only worry was the voice. It sounded flat and monotonous. We sent him for voice training. He knows what he has to do and is improving all the time.

'But most of all he's a star. He has a quality people like. He improves the ratings because he attracts kids who normally only listen to radio if it's playing music. He's close to becoming the finished article.'

In BBC execspeak this can be taken as meaning that Auntie is very much taken with Gary Lineker, and the feeling is mutual. Lineker is heading off down the media superhighway on yet another episode in an extraordinary career. Will it end there? Will being a witness to events be as fulfilling as becoming a shaper of the future? He would love to help decide the direction his sport takes in years to come and thinks it sad that soccer tends to ignore its great names.

As we approached the final hole on a day when we had been soundly beaten by the course, he said: 'Sometimes I hate this game and sometimes I love it. Today I think I hate it.' Then he knocked in a 15-footer for a par and changed his mind.

As I walked off the course a man who must have thought I was Mr Lineker's minder or, alternatively, possessed a kindly face, asked me if I could get him the star's autograph. I said he should make a direct approach as Mr Lineker was not renowned for assaulting autograph hunters. 'Where's he off to?' the man said. 'He's going up to Leicester,' I answered. 'Why?' the man asked. 'He's going to be given the Freedom of the City in order that he might graze his sheep near the town hall,' I said.

'Quite right, too,' said the man as if it was the only sensible thing to be done for the likes of Gary Lineker. Which it is.

22nd April 1995

·3·

NASEEM HAMED

—

I F PRESSED, good judges of boxing will tell you that Naseem Hamed might one day be recognized as the best fighter we have produced. Without any urging and nary a second thought Hamed will tell you the same thing.

Indeed he will volunteer the information to anyone within earshot and without regard for the possibility that they might not know what he does for a living. For instance, we met in the cool, high ceilinged dining room of a London hotel. He was finishing his breakfast and I had a coffee. The waitress, an attractive Scandinavian girl, gave him the bill.

'Excuse me, love, but this is not mine,' he said. Love, by the way, is luv. He was born in Sheffield.

'But it is your room number and you have had breakfast,' she said. I think she was new to the job.

'But there are two breakfasts down here and I've only had a bit of toast and my friend only had coffee,' he said.

The girl started to explain that if he had taken anything from the buffet he would be charged for a full breakfast. Things were becoming very complicated. She was also getting flustered.

'Please don't worry,' he said to her. 'I will sign the bill and you will get the money. You see money is no problem. I am going to be a multi-millionaire.'

The girl smiled gratefully.

'And a legend,' he said, as he signed with a flourish.

You will not be surprised to know that Muhammad Ali is his hero. They share the same love of the pantomine of boxing, have the same outrageous self-confidence, worship the same god. Hamed's parents came to Sheffield in the Fifties from Yemen.

His dad worked in the steelworks, saved money to buy a couple of shops, raised nine children.

When his sons began to be bullied at school he took them along to Brendan Ingle's gymnasium and asked the trainer to teach them how to look after themselves. You could say that Ingle did a good job.

Ingle says that the first time he stepped into a ring he could see the kid was a natural. For his first amateur fight they stuffed his shorts with lead so he could make the weight. He won the Yorkshire championships. The respected editor of *Boxing News*, Harry Mullan, remembers their first meeting.

'He was an amateur and he came up to me and said: "You ought to write a story about me. I am going to be world champion."' Mullan smiles: 'He was 12 at the time,' he said.

Ingle has no doubt that his man is special, a once-in-a-lifetime fighter. He once said: 'He's a one-off. He has moves that other fighters can only imagine. He's got everything a boxer needs: timing, co-ordination, balance, agility, mobility. He also hits hard. He makes them wince. He's learned the hard way. If you broke his arm he'd kick you. If you broke his leg he'd bite you. And if you took his teeth out he'd nut you.'

If you were relying on this description to find Hamed in a crowded room you would never pick him. He is an attractive, slight young man with neat, small hands, slightly hooded eyes and a calm, watchful manner. You sense that by the time he has observed you walk across the room he has all the necessary information stored away in case he needs to do a job on you. Boxers cannot help measuring people they meet, literally weighing them up. Undertakers do the same thing.

Hamed was once accused by an interviewer on television of trying to stare her out before they went on air. He explained he was inspecting her for signs of nerves so he might know what to expect when they were in the studio.

'How was I?' asked the interviewer.

'Cool,' he said.

Cool is what he admires, what he tries to be until he steps into the ring. Then there is a change. The polite, softly spoken, amiable young man is transformed into one of the most destructive fighters we have produced. He taunts and jabs and snarls and hooks with a ferocity that has already lifted him into the élite list of the world's top 10 pound-for-pound fighters, and might, in the summer, take him to his first world championship.

He thinks he can win four world titles, from bantamweight to superfeatherweight. 'I might even win five. People say that if I went to lightweight height it would be a problem. But I've seen Tyson flatten men taller than him. In the end it's talent that counts. I want to set records. No one in Britain will achieve what I achieve. I will become world champion this year. I won't go berserk. I have the speech ready. I will tell them that I expected to be world champion and that my only concern is retiring in many years' time undefeated.

'I want to be a legend. A rich legend. I believe that God has given me a gift. I don't abuse it. I cherish it. I don't drink or smoke or gamble. I train six hours a day, seven days a week, every day of the year. When I spar I go on for two hours or more. I never want to leave the ring. I spar with anyone, bigger men, older men. Sometimes I see it in their faces that they think I'm a kid. I say "cool" because once they are in the ring they are mine and nothing can save them.

'It's the same when I'm fighting. Opponents are disrespectful, make remarks about your manhood or whatever. I wait until I get them in the ring, then first I destroy their confidence, then I go to work.

'I hate them so much I destroy them mentally. I'll look at their feet and hit them. If I see an opponent's feet I don't need to look up to hit him. When I look in their eyes I see the hurt and the despair. I can see the tears. They know they can't win,' he said.

I said there had been criticism of the way he taunted opponents, humiliated them. 'I don't do that. I try to break their concentration by doing unorthodox moves, but that is not humiliating them. Ali did it to all his opponents. If you break a fighter's concentration then you've won,' he said.

I said that if Ali was his hero, hadn't he better make sure that he did not end up like the great man?

'It wasn't boxing that did that to Ali. God did that to show he was mortal after all. Nothing bad can happen to me. I believe there is a script. That it is written down. I think I am blessed. Being a Muslim gives me a guideline for living which helps me as a boxer. I am only 21 but I have been preparing for this all my life. I've been learning for 14 years. When other kids were off smoking and drinking I was going round Britain with Brendan, watching and learning.

'Then I come from this very close family. My parents have always loved and supported me. When I become a millionaire they are going to be millionaires, too. I am proud to have been born in Great Britain but I am an Arab. I am proud to be an Arab. When I get in the ring I am fighting for two nations. In Yemen the entire country prays for me night and day. How can I lose?' he said.

I asked him if he felt he was a Yorkshireman.

'I don't know what a Yorkshireman feels like. But I am proud to represent Sheffield. When I was boxing as an amateur we'd go down to London and the smart guys would say: "This lot can't be any good because they're only from Sheffield." They didn't say that when we'd finished with them. They had more respect. Just imagine, when I become world champion it will be like Sheffield winning the World Cup,' he said.

He was just about to leave for a trip to Yemen. The last time he was there a grateful president gave him a Rolex watch worth £10,000. He showed it to me. Those criminals who prowl London at present looking to snatch expensive watches from their owners had better not make the mistake of trying to nick Hamed's Rolex. Not unless they fancy spending a life in traction.

He was off that day to buy some clothes. 'That's all I spend my money on. After every fight I go out and spend four or five thousand quid at Armani. A nice gift to myself. I've been told that on this trip to Yemen the president might give me a Mercedes sports car. I've heard he might give me three,' he said.

Why three? 'One for me, one for my dad and one for my brother,' he said. 'Anyway, I've found the car that I am going to buy when I am world champion. It is in a showroom in Park Lane,' he said.

'What is it?' I asked.

'A McLaren Formula One. A wicked car. Flash, quick. Suits my image.'

'How much?' I asked.

'Two hundred and fifty thousand quid. But it will be mine. I shall laugh and pose in it. But that is a little goal. The main aim is to be a legend. A very rich legend. It will happen. Do you know I don't have off nights. God's on my side. I can't lose.

'When I am very rich I think I'll buy an island in the sun. That Richard Branson's got one so why shouldn't I? Someone asked me the other day what I might do when I finish boxing. I can't imagine ever finishing. I mean I don't get hit or hurt in the ring so I could go on for a long time,' he said.

I asked if he'd ever been knocked down. He looked shocked. 'That's not possible,' he said. Why, I asked, 'Because it's not in the script,' he said.

If you happen to meet him outside the ring Hamed is a funny, engaging and pleasant young man. One day, and not too far off, he might make us all very proud of him. So far it has been plain sailing but it is going to be much more difficult and complicated from now on. His voyage takes him into shark-infested waters where, as his hero, Ali, discovered, the scripts are written by people who prefer counting to writing and who worship different gods from those to be found in Heaven.

25th March 1995

TOM FINNEY

—

TOM FINNEY resides in a quiet cul-de-sac near Preston. The bungalow where he lives with his wife Elsie glows with elbow grease and the pale winter sun glints on the silver-framed photographs of loved ones. Mrs Finney had been to the optician about her glasses and was fussing with a tea tray in the kitchen. Her husband – going on 72 but still a strong and purposeful figure – was telling me that generally he is in good nick except that his left leg gives him a bit of gyp now and then.

A stranger peering through the window at this vignette of suburban life would not know that he was watching one of the greatest soccer players of all time talking to yet another fan masquerading as a journalist. Tom Finney wears his eminence lightly; indeed, it could be argued that he does his best to hide it. Yet there is no denying the special place he has in the hearts and minds of those fortunate enough to have seen him play.

Trying to find his house, I became lost on the outskirts of Preston. He drove to show me the way. Two cars having a conversation on a suburban street was too much for one householder who decided to investigate. When he saw Tom Finney, he almost stood to attention. Had he been wearing a hat, he would have doffed it.

That evening, sitting in a hotel lounge in Manchester, I was engaged in conversation by a group of shrewd, hard-headed businessmen. When I mentioned I had just returned from interviewing Tom Finney, they became like teenagers seeking news of a pop idol. It might seem silly, middle-aged men reacting like this, but if you had seen Tom Finney in his pomp you would have understood the reason for our hero worship.

Stanley Matthews, George Best and Tom Finney were the best British wingers I saw play, Best and Finney the most complete attacking players. Only Best, of the moderns, could match Finney's range of talents: the ability to operate on either wing, the capacity to play in midfield and mastermind attacking strategy. They shared two other priceless assets: they loved scoring goals, and they were fearless.

Tom Finney took a lot of stick. Nowadays, his bad leg reminds him of it. He remembers his persecutors well. 'Do you recall Stan Willemse at Chelsea?' he asked. 'Took you and the ball. Tommy Docherty and Jimmy Scoular could dish it out a bit, too. You wanted shin pads on the back of your legs playing that lot. Then there was dear dear old Tommy Banks at Bolton. His brother, Ralph, played in that Cup final when Stan Matthews gave him a terrible time. The first time Tommy played against Stan, he said: "Tha' might have made a mug out of our kid but tha'll get no change out of me." Hard man. Had a great sense of humour. You needed one when you played against him, too.'

Finney played with Tommy Banks in the England side under Walter Winterbottom. Walter was a bit posh, Tommy salt-of-the-earth Lancashire. During the preparation for Tommy's international debut, Walter took the team talk and paid particular attention to Banks's opponent. 'Your winger is a good player, Tommy. Two-footed, cuts inside well, likes going outside the back, too. He's quick, crosses accurately and is a good finisher. I feel you must impose yourself on him as soon as possible,' he said.

'Can I say something, boss?' asked Tommy.

'Certainly,' Winterbottom said, not knowing what to expect.

'Well, I'd like thi' to know that this winger tha'rt goin' on abart will nobbut go past me once than I'll have him up in t'air, on to t'dog track and gi' his arse a reight good grittin'. Is that what tha' wants, Mr Winterbottom?' Banks enquired.

'Er, something like that,' said Winterbottom.

Tom Finney played 76 times for England and scored 30 goals. In 565 appearances in first-class football, he scored 247 times. These statistics become even more remarkable when you consider that it wasn't until his mid-thirties that he started playing centre-forward.

As a child he worshipped Alex James, who lorded it at Deepdale before moving on to Arsenal. He still treasures one of the wee man's medals given to him by his widow. He joined Preston as an amateur when he was 15. The club offered him pro terms of £2.50 a week but he decided to complete an apprenticeship as a plumber so that if he didn't make it at soccer he would have a proper job to fall back on. Even genius has its uncertainties.

Finney wasn't the only one with doubts about his ability to make it as a professional footballer. He first played for Preston at inside-left, like his idol. One day the outside right of the youth team was injured. Finney was instructed by Bill Scott, the trainer, to play on the right wing. Scott then uttered the immortal line: 'Don't worry, son, we're not expecting too much from you.'

It wasn't too long after that the two best-known players in the world played for Preston and Blackpool. The media exploited the rivalry between Tom Finney and Stanley Matthews for all it was worth. According to Finney, it was a fiction. 'There wasn't any rivalry. He was simply the best ball player I ever saw in British football,' he said.

'His close control was remarkable. I never saw anyone work so near to an opponent. He'd literally give the defender the ball and at the last minute flick it away. They say he would have been a luxury player in the modern game. Some luxury. He would win a game for you in 10 minutes' play. He would play in any company at any time and do that. They say he didn't score too many goals. Didn't want to, that's why. Preferred to lay them on for others.'

Matthews, Mortensen, Lawton, Mannion and Finney formed an England forward line to rank with the best of all time. It is some indication of the influence Finney had on the international scene that when he played his last season for his country he was in the company of the likes of Bobby Charlton and Johnny Haynes. He looks back fondly at the calibre of his team-mates but remains very clear-eyed about their appearance on the field of play.

'They had one size of shirt for everyone in the England squad,' he said. 'So if you were six foot two it strangled you and if you were my size it came down below your knees. Same with the socks. When you put them on, they reached to the top of your thighs. Then those boots. Remember? Stiff leather, up over the ankles, bulbous toe caps. Felt like diver's boots. When it rained and the shirt collected the water and the socks were soaked, we must have weighed a ton apiece. Don't know how we moved.'

For his 76 internationals Finney was paid between £20 and £50 per match. When the team travelled by train, they went second class. It was a time when footballers, even those of genius like Finney, were kept firmly in their place. Nowadays, he watches the game avidly on television and is depressed by what he sees.

'We have to get back to grass roots, be prepared to learn,' he said. 'If you watch Italian football you invariably see intelligence and skill at work. The defenders mark close and are good on the ball. We don't have players like that. Gazza, on form, is such a relief. Tremendous ability, but the rest are very predictable.

'When the Hungarians came in 1953, I was injured but I went to Wembley to watch. Up until that point we had thought we were the best players in the world. We were beaten 6–3 and the nation was shocked. That Hungarian side was the best national team I ever saw. They did things that day that were new and wonderful. I played against them in Budapest when we lost 7–1. It was like being an apprentice all over again.

'I think that the gap is as big now as it was then. The lessons are as obvious now as then. There's too much football. It's played at too great a pace. It seems to me that players arrive on the international scene without having served an apprenticeship. It also concerns me that talents such as Bobby Moore possessed aren't used by the FA.'

In the everlasting debate about players from one generation fitting into another, there is no one I have ever met foolish enough to doubt that Tom Finney would have slotted perfectly into the modern game. Indeed, there is a strong case to make that he would have been an even better player because his range of skills would have given him a freer role than any allowed by Preston and England during the time he played.

When he first joined Preston, he came under the wing of a tough half-back called Bill Shankly. It was the start of a friendship and mutual admiration society that was to last until Shankly's death. Bill Shankly had no doubt that Tom Finney was the greatest player who ever lived and never tired of telling people. The story goes that one day, after extolling the virtues of Kevin Keegan, one of the Liverpool team asked him if he was as good as Tom Finney. 'As things stand at the moment, Kevin is as good a player as Finney, but you have to remember that Tommy is 64,' said Shankly.

Shankly believed Finney could have played in his overcoat and still have been great.

Finney smiles at the memory of the man. 'I served my apprenticeship with men like Bill. He'd been down the pits like many of them. Proper men. He would say: "This football is a simple game, Tommy" – and that's the most profound observation to be made about it.

'One of the problems with our game at the present time is that coaches talk gibberish to children, teaching them systems, denying them the joy of playing with the ball. You hear them shouting "get rid" when they should be encouraging the lad to dribble. They murder talent with organized football.'

Tom Finney is not a regretful man. He is glad he played when he did, even though, nowadays, he would likely be living and working in Italy and gaining more in one week than he did in 20 years as a player at Preston.

He nearly went to Italy in 1952 when he was offered £10,000 to sign for Palermo, wages of £130 a month plus bonuses, a villa and a car. At the time he was earning £20 a week.

Preston turned the offer down. 'Tha'll play for us or tha'll play for nobody,' the chairman told him. He has a dreamy look about him when he tells the story.

As it is, he looks back modestly on a wonderful career and a fulfilling retirement. He kept the best company, playing with the likes of Mannion ('my best partner'), Lawton, Matthews, Haynes, Peter Doherty. Di Stefano was the greatest footballer he ever saw. Of the players he watched after his retirement, Best was sublime, Dalglish would have shone in any company, Alan Hansen was as good a centre-back as Neil Franklin, and he could think of no higher praise. The best goal-scorer? 'Jimmy Greaves.'

When he left football, the apprenticeship he had served as a plumber made sense. It also made quite a bit of money. Today, Tom Finney Ltd employs 120 people specializing in plumbing, central heating and electrical work. He is president of the company and goes to work most days, despite the fact that, officially, he is retired.

He is still involved with Preston North End, is a Freeman of the town and was once chairman of the local health authority, responsible for a budget of £70 million. Tom Finney is a man you can trust, not just with money but with that more precious commodity – the awesome responsibility of being a hero.

4th December 1993

·5·

DICKIE BIRD

—

To SAY Dickie Bird loves cricket doesn't get anywhere near describing exactly what he feels for the game. It's a bit like saying that Romeo had a slight crush on Juliet or Abelard had a fancy for Héloïse.

The game consumes his life and defines its horizons. It shapes the very posture of the man.

Like a tree bent and moulded by the prevailing wind, so the curve in Bird's spine, the hunch of his shoulders, the crinkled eyes as he inspects the world, have been sculpted through a lifetime's dedication to cricket.

He is, nowadays, one of the landmarks of the game – an umpire as famous as any superstar, as much respected by cricketers as he is loved by the public.

In a few days' time, just before his 60th birthday, he flies to the West Indies to stand in three Tests against Pakistan. His presence has been requested by both sides. In any situation this would be a feather in his cap, but given that this is for the unofficial championship of the world, and taking into account the fierce arguments on the subject of neutral umpires, Dickie Bird could be forgiven for feeling that he has been given the ultimate accolade.

Mr Bird is pleased about the compliment, but worried. He spends most of his life in a tizz about something or other. It would, of course, be perfectly natural for anyone to worry about living up to a reputation of being the best in the world at a particular job. And if this was all he had to be concerned about, Mr Bird would be a happy man.

However, he is adept at inventing worry. He will, for instance, worry about getting to Heathrow to catch his flight to the West Indies on time. Having arrived at the airport, he will worry about the pilot being able to find the West Indies. When he is in the air he will worry about whether he left the gas on at home in Barnsley. You think I exaggerate?

This is the man who went to his doctor for an inoculation and ended up having a cystoscopy. Even he cannot fathom how a single jab against typhoid and yellow fever turned into an examination of his prostate. 'I worry about everything. I even worry about the odd time I'm not worried. I think something must be wrong. I'm one of nature's witterers,' he said.

I have known him for 40 years and he could have wittered for England when he was a teenager. He used to sit in the pavilion at Barnsley and chew his fingernails through his batting gloves while waiting for his turn at the wicket. On one occasion, and God knows how, he managed to fasten his batting pads together at the knees so that when it came to the moment he had to stride to the wickets he stood up and fell flat on his face.

Invited to lunch with the Queen at Buckingham Palace, he turned up at half-past eight in the morning. 'What's happening, Dickie?' the policeman asked. 'I've come for lunch with Her Majesty,' explained her most loyal subject. 'You are a bit early for that,' said the law. 'We can't let you in until after the Changing of the Guard.'

'What should I do?' said the world's greatest umpire, beginning to worry. 'Find a café and have a cup of coffee,' the policeman suggested. 'But tha' reckons I've got four hours to kill,' said the Queen's lunch guest. 'Have two cups of coffee,' said the bobby.

Having a private lunch with Her Majesty was a great moment in Mr Bird's life and when he describes what happens you have to imagine his manner of delivery. When he is telling a favourite anecdote Mr Bird stands up. When he does so he sometimes knocks over the furniture in his attempt to get at the story. He delivers in a loud, clear voice while looking over his shoulder, worrying in case someone might report him to the management.

'Somebody told me, "Dickie, when tha' dines with the Queen don't eat t'grapes. Tha' sees, they give you these great big scissors to cut them with and if tha's not used to 'em tha' could have a disaster on thi' hands." Well, I wished he hadn't told me because I wittered about them grapes all week. Anyway, when the time came I was in a terrible state and instead of refusing them I said I'd like some. Well, they gave me these long scissors and when I tried to cut t'grapes they shot all over t'room. They flew past t'Queen and went all over the floor.'

At this point Dickie Bird's face is suffused with worry as if spattering the monarch with grapes was a treasonable offence. 'What happened?' I asked. 'Well, the Queen just looked at me and said, "Don't worry, Dickie, the corgis will take care of things." And does tha' know t'corgis ran in t'room and ate t'lot!' He paused. 'Must happen all t'time,' he said. Hopefully.

I wondered if he was nervous before a game. 'Terrible,' he said. 'In and out of the toilet. Can't stop wittering. But once I'm on the field I change. I become calm and focused. I'm never thrown by what happens out there.' Ashley Harvey-Walker, the former Derbyshire player, once handed Dickie his false teeth on a pig of a wicket at

Buxton. Dickie enquired whom he should give them to in the event of Mr Harvey-Walker not surviving the over.

There have, however, been moments when he has been fazed. There was that time during a Test match when Allan Lamb walked in to bat and handed Dickie his portable phone. 'What's this?' said Dickie. 'A phone,' said Allan Lamb. 'And what does tha' expect me to do wi' it?' asked the umpire. 'Take calls,' said the player.

The prospect of a phone ringing in his pocket during a Test match triggered a few of Dickie's worry symptoms: the ruminative rub of the jaw, the shooting out of his arms in front of him in the manner of his great hero Tommy Cooper, 'Just like that, ahem.' The phone rang. 'Umpire Bird here,' said Dickie. 'Tell that bloody man Lamb to get a move on,' said Ian Botham.

Lamb has often been Bird's nemesis. At Old Trafford he removed all the wheels from the umpire's car and left it standing on bricks. On another occasion he locked the umpire's room from the outside and led his team on to the field, leaving Dickie Bird and his fellow official imprisoned. Play was held up while a steward found a sledgehammer big enough to knock the door down, by which time Dickie Bird was a gibbering wreck.

I dwell on these anecdotes because he loves telling them and they give an insight into his formidable sense of humour. The man you see on television, the twitchy, careworn, fraught individual with head bowed against the troubles of the world, is only a part of the whole being. There is a lot of laughter in him. His cap is homage to Albert Modley, an old-time northern music-hall comedian. He adores Tommy Cooper and Benny Hill. When he has a good laugh, like we did the other day, he sometimes cries with joy.

When Garfield Sobers appeared on Dickie's *This Is Your Life*, the umpire shed tears of happiness. 'Oh, master,' he said to Sobers. In all his years in the game, both as player and umpire, he has never lost his love for cricket's artistes.

Who have been the players to move him to tears? Well, Sobers apart, there's Lillee – 'the greatest. That's all you can say – the best'; Barry and Viv Richards; Boycott and Border – 'I'd have those two batting for my life any day'; Graeme Pollock, Greg Chappell, Michael Holding, Richard Hadlee. There are more.

'Fastest bowler I ever saw through the air was Frank Tyson. Lightning. Bowled against me at Scarborough and I went on the front foot and hit the first three balls through mid-wicket for four.

'As he bowled the fourth I was again on the front and all I remember was hearing him say, "Hit that bugger for four." Next thing I heard was the ambulance they sent to take me to hospital. I was trying to get up, saying, "Wheer's that Tyson? I'll reighten him if I get hold of him!"' He points to a dent in his jawline. 'Still feel it when it's cold,' he said.

He feels Wasim Akram, Waqar Younis, Curtly Ambrose and Malcolm Marshall are as good as any he has seen; Les Jackson comes close. 'Two Tests for England, it's a joke. If he played nowadays he'd be automatic choice. Played against him once and he kept hitting me in t'rib cage. I went down t'wicket and said, "I wish tha'd stop bowling like that," and he said, "Why?" And I said, "Because I'm not good enough to hit thi' that's why."'

He is not keen on a third umpire and electronic assistance. Reckons it takes something away from the craft of being an umpire. 'Also, it slows the game down. In any case, controversy is part of the game. I've always found players are understanding, provided you treat them right. They used to say Ian Chappell was a handful. Never had a problem. Lovely guy, marvellous cricketer. That Merv Hughes, he's a beauty,' he said. I asked him about sledging. 'Not a problem,' he said. I suspect they dare not try it on in his company. Neutral umpires? 'All right, providing they are the best 14 or so in the world and not selected on a quota basis.'

He will be 60 later this month and he lives alone. When he recently confessed to a television interviewer that he was sometimes lonely he received several offers of marriage, but he has already worked that one out. 'Nearly been married twice, but it wouldn't be fair with all the travelling I do. In any case, I'm married to cricket,' he said. If anyone else said that it would sound daft. Coming from Dickie Bird you accept it as a fair summation of his life.

But it's when he retires and cricket becomes a sometime mistress instead of 'her indoors' that you worry for Dickie Bird. Someone should stick a preservation order on him. He is, after all, a national treasure.

When I asked him what gave him most satisfaction in life he said he thought it was that his fellow professionals 'trusted' him. Interesting choice of word. Not 'loved him' or 'admired him' but gave him their 'trust'. When we parted I wished him well in the West Indies but I knew we would speak again before he left.

Sure enough I had been home five minutes when he called. He was worried in case I had misunderstood one or two of the things he had said. He told me he had been awake all night replaying our evening in his mind.

We checked the areas of his concern! Fifty-three Tests, 82 one-day internationals, four World Cups, not to mention meeting the Queen and Lady Thatcher and John Major. Not bad for a Barnsley lad.

'It was great the other night. It's been a long time since I laughed like that,' he said. He sounded worried.

3rd April 1993

·6·

ALLAN BORDER

—

FOR ALL his reputation as a stern captain and an implacable opponent, Allan Border is, like most Aussies, a friendly cove. The first thing you notice about him are his eyes, light and clear, giving a steely glint to an otherwise cherubic countenance. In the bar of the team hotel, his young players around him, there is no doubting his authority. A stranger breaks into a conversation Border is having, saying: 'Am I interrupting something?'

The players grin self-consciously at his unwitting rudeness. Border handles the intrusion with tact and diplomacy, making sure the visitor is not discomfited. I only mention these aspects of our meeting because if you had read the cuttings beforehand, as I did, this was not what you would expect. What you might have anticipated encountering was a surly individual with a liking for bollocking people who get in his way. In other words Captain Grumpy.

Merv Hughes came into the bar, blocking out the light, a huge presence in what looked like a blue romper suit. His captain inspected him. 'Two stone overweight, funny haircut, ridiculous moustache, big oaf and do you know what? A captain's dream. He'd shed a pint of blood for you. I love him. He's my kind of cricketer. Good bowler too. People are only just beginning to realize what a fine bowler he is.

'Statistics show that of all Australian quick bowlers his strike rate is second only to Lillee. He makes my point about Test cricketers. They are 40 per cent skill and 60 per cent character. You can have all the talent in the world and if you don't have the guts and determination to go with it you'll be nothing to me.

'I demand 100 per cent from all my players all the time. I'm tough on anyone who is goofing off or not performing. I'm a fierce competitor, always have been but it's not altogether about personal attitudes. We represent something important to the people of Australia. They want to be proud of us and we musn't fail them. "Only a game"? Don't give me that. After a Test match I go to the media conference and there's 40 cameras there and 50 journalists, and you say it's only a game.

'It's a lot more important than just a sporting event to a lot of people. The difference between winning and losing nowadays is enormous. It might well have been that once upon a time you could be looked on as being gallant in defeat. Not now. You're rubbish if you lose. You cop it. Look at what's happening to Goochie at present.

'They call me Captain Cranky or Grumpy and worse, but it doesn't bother me. I suppose I've given them the reason to call me names from time to time. I've had the odd flare-up with umpires which I shouldn't have done. I knocked my stumps down at Lord's this year and that was silly. Once or twice I've lost my temper with journalists and called them pricks. Little things like that. I've crossed the line a few times,' he said. What line might that be? 'Between being a hard-nosed competitor and a prat.'

For someone who professes to be shy of making speeches and who is happiest when surrounded by his players, he is an agreeable, pleasant and loquacious dinner companion. He has come a long way from being the gullible 12th man for New South Wales who was persuaded that his duties involved interrupting play in order to take orders for the players' lunch.

He started his Test career against England by getting what he thought was a bad lbw decision. He stormed back to the pavilion, threw his bat across the room, kicked his pads into the corner and cursed the cheating Poms before realizing that he was in the England dressing room receiving some strange looks from the touring officials and players.

He took over as captain of Australia after Kim Hughes's tearful farewell. He had a tough baptism and nearly gave the job up in New Zealand in the 1985–6 tour. He says now that it took him a while to commit himself totally to the idea of being captain. New Zealand was 'a cry for help'. His salvation was winning the World Cup in 1987, followed by some serious soul-searching about what to do in England in 1989. He decided he needed to be much tougher. One of his decisions was to dis-suade wives from travelling with their husbands.

'I took terrible flak for that. Towards the end of the tour some of the wives confronted me and told me what they thought. I said: "At this time on the last tour of England we were 3–1 down. This time we're winning three nil. End of story."' The rule still stands.

As he explains, he cannot stop wives travelling to where their husbands might be playing, but there is no question of them sharing the same hotel, or players attending to husbandly duties at the expense of team commitments. 'My wife is here now with the kids. She lives in Essex. Now and again she brings the kids to a game and we say "G'day" but that's it. The point is they're on holiday, we're working,' he said.

Border was even more tough with his players. While batting with Dean Jones in the tied Madras Test in 1986 when the Victorian scored a double century, he observed the player's distress. At one point Jones was so dehydrated he was throwing up.

'He had made about 180 at the time and I desperately wanted him to hang about a bit longer. He said he couldn't go on. So I said: "OK then, go off and send someone in with a big ticker." I knew that would anger him into staying because Jonesy prides himself on having a big heart. But I really didn't realize how crook he was.'

Jones stayed at the crease, completed his 200 and was taken from the field to hospital and put on a saline drip.

'I felt bad about it. I deliberately said what I did to goad him into staying but I really had no idea he was so ill. He's a tough competitor. He'd crawl over broken glass for you,' said Border. It says something for the strength of the Australian batting and the resolve of the selectors that Jones was not selected for this tour.

While on the subject of guts, I told Allan Border of Tom Graveney's assessment of him: 'A great player, particularly when it matters.' He liked that.

'Maybe being captain helped me with the batting. Maybe I was always aware of the added responsibility and that made me more determined to grit my teeth and play in a certain way. It would be lovely to play like David Gower, wouldn't it, or Mark Waugh? Make it look so easy, don't they?' They, no doubt, would wish to have scored as many as Border and equal his average of 51, which sets him apart as one of the great batsmen.

He might lack the grace and style of the likes of Gower and Waugh, he might not have the aura of a Richards or the personality of a Botham. What he is, *in excelsis*, is the good old Aussie battler. He's the tough little runt with the jutting chin and the unquenchable spirit. If you wanted a man to captain a team to play for your life, there would be only one choice.

'Captaining a side isn't all it's cracked up to be. Good captains are made by good teams. The best you can do is initiate a team structure, set a mood in the dressing room. But you can be the most brilliant tactician and if you don't have a team you're bloody useless.

'I've enjoyed being captain. I never imagined I would be, so I was delighted when I got it. I like having the respect of the players. I suppose I shall have to start thinking soon about giving the game up. We play South Africa after the Ashes tour and I'd like to skipper the side. After that I might retire. I don't want to linger too long. On the other hand, I don't want to go too soon. I know I won't like giving up the game. When I see these athletes who have just retired telling the media how happy they are I think they are talking absolute bullshit. You have to miss playing sport. It's such a wonderful life.

'I'd like to stay in the game. I don't want to be an administrator. I'm a player's person. I don't fancy the media. It seems to me that a lot of the old players who start commentating on the game become twice the players they really were. I'd feel uncomfortable with that. Meantime I don't have any goals. I'm a funny sort of person. I never set targets. Why set yourself 500 runs to get in a series. You might go out first knock and score 499. What do you do then? All my cricket ambitions centre around the team.'

What about the Ashes? 'I think we'll win. I'm not cocky enough or silly enough to predict the score but I do think we'll beat the Poms. I think we have the edge on bowling. McDermott and Hughes are as good an opening pair as you'll find. Our batters are in form. We're a happy team. We won the one-days, but you handed us two you should have won.

'England? Impressed by Caddick. Also liked the look of Salisbury. If England pick a 'keeper instead of Stewart I think Steven Rhodes is a good player. Got a big heart too. That's what you want. If I were picking the England team I'd pick some young players and perhaps be prepared to lose for a couple of seasons. Young players and Gatting. He'd be in my team.

'Whatever happens, this is special. I have never won a Test series against the West Indies and that's an ambition, but there is clear daylight between that and competing for the Ashes. There's nothing like it, nothing more important, nothing with the same edge to it.'

The captain of Australia is relishing the battle ahead. Whenever he appears we should go out of our way to say farewell because we shall not see him as a player again, and if we see his like in the near future we will count ourselves lucky. I asked him if there was an athlete he admired.

'Bjorn Borg. I liked the contrast between his confidence on court and his shyness off it. I like to think I've got something of that character. Quiet, but ruthless.'

29th May 1993

·7·

BRIAN CLOUGH

—

WHEN I told people I had been to see Brian Clough, the first thing they wanted to know was how he looked. They had heard the tales of him being found legless in charge of a football club, listened to the rumours that he had become an alcoholic recluse, looked at recent photographs and reached their own conclusions.

All I can tell you is that when I met him he didn't look like a pisspot to me, and I have met a few in a far from sheltered career. On the other hand, it would be misleading to pretend there had never been a problem and that he wasn't involved in a running battle to prevent booze dominating his life.

I asked him how bad it had been. 'I was in an environment where people drank. We drank after the match with the opposition. That was social drinking. Then we'd drink to celebrate if we won and drink to drown our sorrows if we lost. That way it becomes a habit. I am not making an excuse, merely stating a simple fact. Also, I was in an occupation where rumours abound. One day I was doing an interview with a journalist and his phone went. After taking the call he said: "That was my wife. She's just heard on the news that you are dead."

'Well, reports of my death were greatly exaggerated. Similarly so were reports of my drinking. Tom Jones once said to me that if he had knocked off all the birds he was rumoured to have had, he would never have had the time to sing a song, or the energy. Same with me and drink. If I had drunk every bottle of whisky I was awarded or seen off every bottle of champagne I was supposed to have supped, you and I wouldn't be here right now laughing about it,' he said.

In his autobiography he says: 'There have been times when I allowed my drinking to take a hold . . . Whatever steps are necessary to set my friends and

34

family at ease I will take them. No one is going to be able to brand Brian Clough as a drinker who lost control and could not conquer his habit. I will beat it.' When I met him he said he was off the booze.

He was gearing up for a nationwide tour to promote the book and had spent the morning signing copies in his publisher's warehouse. When he gives his press conference on Monday and then spends the next three weeks meeting the public, it will be a significant and intriguing return to public life and being under scrutiny.

What is more, given Brian Clough's penchant for making waves, it is unlikely to be without incident. Already he finds himself embroiled in controversy because of a chapter in the book in which he states he believes that the Liverpool fans who died at the Hillsborough tragedy were killed by Liverpool people.

I asked him why he felt it necessary to publish his opinion. 'Because I was there. [Nottingham Forest were to play Liverpool that day.] It would have been cowardly not to say what I saw and what I felt. Nonetheless it did cause me heartache and agony deciding what to say. I must admit that had they printed everything I said I think I might have been hung, drawn and quartered. My son plays for Liverpool. He is walking down the same street as people who went through that awful tragedy. So I have to be careful.

'But I was there and I can't forget what I saw. First of all, before two o'clock I saw the fans all looking smart and happy with their Liverpool rosettes, poking their noses through the fences. But before that I saw the other element spewing out of pubs. Not a shadow of doubt that many didn't have tickets. These were the ones that caused the trouble. I have no doubt that the police did make mistakes, but when a tragedy such as Hillsborough occurs several things are to blame,' he said.

I asked him if he had received any hostile reaction to his views. 'Not at all. The most reaction has been from people who said: "We all know what happened but we didn't say it."'

It is not in Clough's nature to be circumspect. He is impatient, dogmatic, arrogant and confrontational. His wife says that during his life he has lurched from crisis to crisis, that he didn't mature until late in life. He himself says that he was boastful and achieved 'pinnacles of rudeness'.

On the other hand, he has been married to Barbara for 35 years, his children are well brought up and loving and every Sunday there is a family get-together, so he is not all ogre. He must have done something right.

Professionally, there is little doubt that he was one of the greatest managers the game has produced, that he was the best manager England never had and that although those who played for him might tremble at his approach and live in fear of his wrath, few would deny that working with Clough was a unique and unmissable experience. Martin O'Neill, the manager of Wycombe Wanderers, who played under Clough at Nottingham, said: 'I've seen big men hide in corridors to avoid him.

'He was egocentric, sometimes a bully, often impossible. But I wouldn't have missed a moment of it because in the end, as a manager he was magical.' This was after O'Neill had read the book, in which Clough had written that he was a good player but 'a pain in the arse'. Some would use stronger language in their assessment of Clough. There are those who dismiss him as a loud-mouthed prat, while others place him as a manager alongside Shankly, Busby and Stein and as a human being regard him as a significant working-class hero. .

Both schools of thought will find comfort in the autobiography. In that sense the book is honest, because reading it is like meeting him: it is a rip-roaring adventure with Clough, broad-sword in hand, cleaving his way through life. It is as if Flashman had made football his career. What it doesn't give you is any real insight into or explanation of the man and his job.

Clough is not one for navel gazing. For someone whose greatest skill was in discovering gifts in players they didn't know they possessed, he is remarkably shy about putting his own hidden depths on display. 'I'm a bighead not a figurehead,' is the nearest he gets to self-analysis.

What is difficult to portray in print is Clough's warmth and sense of humour, at best displayed when he starts listening to himself then spontaneously erupts at what he has heard himself say. I will give you an example.

We were talking about the modern game and I asked what he thought about it. He said: 'The game has changed. Referees are in danger of becoming over-zealous in applying the letter of the law. They need to get the balance right. Mind you, some good has come of it. We are allowing players to play who were once too frightened to walk down the tunnel because they knew they were going to get a clattering. Today they come down like King Kong. They run all over the place thinking: "No bugger can kick me now." Not a bad thing.'

So far so good from a man who practised what he preached by producing teams more concerned with playing football than kicking opponents. But there was more, and this is where it went a bit off the rails. 'Mind you, I think it would be wrong to deny the physical part of our game. It is part of our culture to play hard. Like roast beef and Yorkshire pudding, fish and chips. Fish and chips are good for you. All right, let's take a chip. . .'

He held up an imaginary chip in his fingers and looked at it admiringly. 'Lot of vitamins in a chip; nothing wrong with a good old English chip. If you go on the bloody Continent they eat frogs' legs and all that. Nobody tells them to stop eating frogs' legs. You don't hear them cribbing about frogs' legs,' he said. By this time we were both looking at the imaginary frogs' leg that had replaced the chip in his fingers. Our eyes met and he started laughing at the lunacy of it all. 'Silly bugger,' he said to himself.

The most evocative part of the book is his account of growing up in Middlesbrough.

He was one of eight children. It was, he says, a blissfully happy childhood. He was useless at school and not much good when he sought an apprenticeship as a fitter and turner.

He settled for a motto: Ignorance is Bliss. Then he found football. 'Someone told me I was good at it. Then I found the confidence to believe I could play football. Next I was able to look at other kids and say: "I'm better than him." It gave me a yardstick in life,' he said.

Did he find football fulfilling? I asked because he was never a subscriber to Shankly's theory that it was more important than life or death. When he was a manager he insisted his young players go to college for an education, he went on holiday with his family in the middle of the football season, and he opened the turnstiles at Nottingham to striking miners as a declaration of his support. 'Yes, I've been fulfilled. Put it this way, I have had most of what the game has to offer,' he said.

When people talk of Brian Clough they often forget the fact that he was out of the ordinary as a player, never mind manager. Playing for Middlesbrough and Sunderland, he scored 267 goals in 296 appearances. He can safely claim his record will not be broken. He was only 26 and an England international when an injury to his knee forced him to retire. The rest, as they say, is history.

His first managerial job was at Hartlepool. He was joined by Peter Taylor, who was to become a major factor in his career. His book is dedicated to Taylor's memory. It says: 'Still miss you badly. You once said: "When you get shot of me there won't be much laughter in your life." You were right.'

Their first season together, Hartlepool won promotion. Next came Derby County. They were a Second Division side when Clough joined them. First Division champions when he left. Brighton and Leeds followed, both short stays and, in the case of Leeds, farcically brief.

Clough became manager of Nottingham Forest in 1975. Two years later they were promoted from the Second Division; the next season they won the First Division and the League Cup. They secured the League Cup three more times, won the European Cup twice and, in the 18 years he was in charge, were only out of the top 10 on two occasions, the last when Clough announced his retirement.

His mentors in management were Alan Brown and Harry Storer. Brown, who managed Sunderland when Clough played there, taught him discipline and the importance of good behaviour. 'He detested shabby appearance, unkempt hair. I always insisted that my players looked smart. He wouldn't stand any nonsense on the field, no arguing with the referee. Nor would I. He made an immense impression on me. Most of all, he taught me that a football club manager is the boss. You can have your chairman, chief executives and the rest. They are nothing, nobodies unless the manager gets it right.'

But what about the extra ingredient, that Svengali-like quality that enabled Clough to bring the best out of players who had hitherto been discarded by other good judges as being either troublesome, ordinary or over the top? John McGovern, John Robertson, Kenny Burns, Larry Lloyd, Dave Mackay, John O'Hare and Colin Hinton are just a few examples of footballers given a new life by the judgment of Clough and Peter Taylor.

Clough offers few clues. 'Coaching is for kids. If a player can't trap a ball and pass it by the time he's in the team he shouldn't be there in the first place. I told Roy McFarland to go and get his bloody hair cut – that's coaching at top level,' he said.

In the week before playing Hamburg in the final of the European Cup, with the German team planning tactics in a training camp, Clough took his players to Majorca. 'We did bugger-all for a week. The Germans were rehearsing corner-kicks and set pieces. We were busy doing nothing.' Nottingham Forest beat Hamburg 1–0 and won the European Cup for the second time.

Harry Storer, who managed Birmingham and Derby County, was another whose advice Clough sought and acted upon. Storer told him: 'When you become a manager and you are leaving for an away game, look around the team coach and count the number of hearts. If you are lucky there will be five. If there aren't turn the coach round and go back.' Clough said: 'I took his advice when appointing my captains – Mackay, McFarland, John McGovern, Stuart Pearce – all courageous men who led by example.'

In his last, unhappy season with Nottingham Forest he had cause to remember another Storer observation. Talking about directors of football clubs, Storer told him: 'Don't ever forget, directors never say thank you.' When Clough retired from Nottingham Forest after 18 seasons he received a silver rose bowl – 'very nice' – but not one of the directors wrote to him. 'One or two of their wives did but not the directors themselves. Strange, isn't it?' he said.

A sadness he has had to bear is that his judgment finally betrayed him when it came to deciding the moment of his leaving. He should have retired after Nottingham Forest lost to Spurs in the '91 Cup final. He didn't, and suffered the ignominy of leaving the club in the season it was relegated.

More than that, there had been allegations of shady dealings in Cup final tickets which, it seems likely, might be settled in court, and reports that his work at the club had been undermined by drinking, that he had sometimes been 'legless' before lunchtime. It would not have been typical had he gone quietly, but this was neither the closing ceremony he anticipated nor, more to the point, deserved.

When I ask him about it he is, for the first time, lost for words. He grimaces and shakes his head. 'It should have been different' is what he finally managed. But he is not complaining. He is too bold and positive by nature to be a whinger.

Looking back he has few regrets. He had an opportunity to stand for Parliament when Labour offered him the chance to oppose Winston Churchill in Moss Side. He was told they had visions of making him Minister for Sport. He decided to stay in football and wonders now what kind of a Member of Parliament he might have made. 'Not a good one,' according to Kenneth Clarke, the Chancellor of the Exchequer and a Nottingham Forest fan. 'He hasn't got the patience to be an MP. What's more, he doesn't debate, he argues.' I passed on the observation to Clough. 'He's quite right,' he said. 'If I went into the House I'd want to be the Speaker.'

He is still a member of the Labour Party, still gets involved in the odd cause. He was once heckled by a man who wanted to know how he could be a socialist and drive a big car. He thinks back to his childhood and mourns the lack of opportunity suffered by his parents and their generation.

'We were allowed to fulfil our ambitions, they were not. My mother was in her sixties before she flew. I sent her off in a helicopter one day to fly to the Channel Isles. When I saw her she said: "Is that flying?" I said it was and she said to me: "I don't want to travel any other way from now on." That's nice, isn't it?' he said.

And how is Clough taking to retirement? 'No bullshit, it is beautiful, should have done it long ago. The biggest question you have to ask yourself when you wake up is: "Is it Tuesday?" It's a lovely relaxing feeling. I hardly give soccer a thought. I have been to two matches to watch Nigel play at Liverpool but I haven't been to see Forest play. The last thing Frank Clark wants is to see me striding through the gates. He's doing well, Frank, and it might be that after Christmas I will see a bit more football. As it is, I work in the garden and teach my grandchildren how to cheat at dominoes. They might as well learn straightaway that life is not always bathed in sunshine.'

It will be interesting to see what happens to Brian Clough as he tours the country promoting his book. His patience might be stretched if the questioning concentrates on the state of his health as much as on his achievements as a manager. All he need remember is that, in the final analysis, he will be judged as a football man and that being the case, only a dolt would deny him a place in the pantheon.

One final question, Brian. In your book you say that you keep your mother's mangle in the front room at home. On top is the cask bearing the scroll declaring you a Freeman of the City of Nottingham. Why? 'Well, to remind me where I came from to where I arrived. When I was a kid I used to mangle the sheets for my mam. It's a symbol,' he said. I said I understood its significance, but wasn't a mangle a curious object to have in your front room?

He gave me the Brian Clough glare, chin tilted as if inviting a punch. 'Listen to me,' he said, forefinger jabbing the air. 'If Prince Charles can take a bloody teddy bear to bed, what's wrong with me having a mangle in my front room?' As another football fan with a sense of humour was fond of saying: 'There's no answer to that.'

5th November 1994

·8·

ANGUS FRASER

—

BOWLERS LIKE Angus Fraser are the foot soldiers of cricket, the beetle crushers, the poor bloody infantry. They might not be glamorous but, by God, they are useful for doing the hard work. They are the bowlers who run uphill and into the wind tying up an end, keeping it quiet while the quicks and the spinners come and go.

They are not exotic creatures. They tend to be large, phlegmatic men with the look of artisans rather than craftsmen, yet the best of them – and Gus Fraser belongs in that category – are as subtle as they are solid, as skilful as they are strong.

If Michael Atherton has a special prayer on his lips as he leads his team to the West Indies today it must be that Gus Fraser stays fit enough to bowl his heart out for five Tests. If he does then the odds of 14–1 against England winning the series might look a bit more contemptuous than they appear at present.

Staying fit is more of a problem for Gus Fraser than for any other member of the tour party. In 1991 he was told that he might not play cricket again. The most optimistic prognosis was that he might be able to turn his arm over at county level, but not for England. He knows what went wrong; he is not quite sure how it happened.

'My feet slipped from under me in Australia during the Perth Test and I went down heavily on my hip. Might have been then. Might just have been the wear and tear of bowling. I bowled a lot of overs. That's my job. People blamed Graham Gooch for overbowling me. Well so did Mike Gatting, and so did my captain in club cricket at Stanmore.

'But in the end it's down to me. I can always say I don't want to bowl. I'm too tired or whatever. The fact is I take it as a compliment if they think I'm the best bowler and give me the most work. In the final assessment my injury was down to me and no-one else,' he said.

We met in a London restaurant for lunch. He arrived carrying his England blazer and left it with an Italian lady in the cloakroom who looked with curiosity at the three lions on the badge. She probably thought he worked in a circus.

He is a tall, pleasant young man with the slight stoop and diffident manner you sometimes find in large men. When he sat at the table in the cocktail lounge his feet filled the gap between the base of his chair and the foot of the table. You wondered how, with supports like that to hold him up, he ever fell down.

He talks with quiet authority about cricket until you ask him about his own qualities and then he hunches his shoulders and sighs and looks uncomfortable. It is not that he is uncertain what to say. Quite the opposite. He knows exactly what it was that brought him to the top. He just doesn't want to sound big-headed about it.

'I've always been comfortable at whatever level of cricket I played in. I fitted into the Stanmore team without any fuss. I thought I might have played for Middlesex first team before they picked me. Same with England. I always wanted to play cricket so I've never been overawed by it. Each progression came when I expected it. I wasn't taken by surprise. It was never "Wow, I've arrived" or anything like that.'

His ambition was to take 150–200 or more Test wickets, be counted among the best of his kind. He was 47 wickets towards that ambition when he was injured.

'When they told me I might never play again I broke down and cried a couple of times. But then I became determined to prove the buggers wrong. I gained inspiration from people like Dennis Lillee who came back after awful injuries. I was prepared to do whatever it took to get back to the game: surgery, running up mountains, anything. I kept telling myself, "Sod the X-rays and the scans. They're wrong."

'They did an operation on my hip. Got rid of some floating bits and pieces, smoothed things down. I might require a similar operation every 18 months or so. I might need a hip replacement later on. At present I'm not too bothered about that,' he said.

After his operation he spent eight weeks on crutches. He came back to county cricket in 1992. Watching him for most of that season was a depressing experience for his admirers.

No one doubted his courage and determination, but he laboured so badly and seemed so miserable with himself there were not many who gave him a better than evens chance of continuing a career as a county trundler, never mind an England strike bowler.

What he lacked was the confidence to stretch his body to the limits required to fire the ball in like he used to, so that it hit the bat high on the blade causing the batsman to withdraw the bottom hand. The fizz, the zip wasn't there.

Towards the end of that season he started feeling more comfortable; by the next season he was bowling with something like his old zest. His return in the final Test match against Australia was a triumph and a new beginning.

'What I learned from my injury had made me harder than I was before, and I never was a soft touch. Sometimes, before my layoff, if I was bowling well and I did a batsman who was struggling with his form I'd feel a bit sorry for him. If I got him out I'd think "poor bugger", get a bit embarrassed by my success.

'What I found in '92 when I wasn't bowling like I can was that no one showed me any charity. They just said "thank you very much" and whacked me around. That taught me a lesson. The message now is if you aren't in very good nick I'm going to humiliate you if I can,' he said.

He's a doughty defender of Gooch. Likes the way he approaches his cricket. Holds him up as the exemplary pro. On the other hand he approves of Atherton's more relaxed style.

'It's comfortable with Mike. Everyone seems very happy. People are talking openly about the game. They're not inhibited about putting in their two penn'orth. We're looking forward to the tour. I enjoy bowling in the West Indies. The wickets aren't quick and bouncy like they say, more slow and low like we get in England.

'When you look how the sides line up you might think that they have the more experienced players such as Haynes, Richardson, Walsh and Ambrose, and that might be a crucial difference.

'But I like the look of our team. It's got one or two nasty little pieces of work in the batting. I don't mean they're terrible people, but players like Nasser and Ramps are hard characters, resilient. They aren't going to be overawed by the hostile environment or quick bowling.

'I'm a great admirer of Ramps. I think he has it in him to be an exceptional cricketer. Sometimes I bowl at him in the nets and he can do what he likes no matter how hard I try. Perhaps he has tried too hard for England, playing for a place instead of playing like he can.

'Flair players are always the most difficult to bowl at. The best bloke I played against was Azharuddin. On song he'd take you apart no matter how well you bowled. I'd rather bowl against a Geoffrey Boycott any day because you know that a good ball might get him out. With flair players like Azza, or Gower or Botham you know that if they are in the mood you can bowl your best but they're still going to get a hundred,' he said.

In terms of his original ambition Gus Fraser is realistic enough to know that he is only on the foothills of his mountain. He is going to need all his strength and resolve as well as a lot of luck before he takes his place alongside the likes of Alec Bedser, Maurice Tate, Ian Botham as men who have taken more than 150 wickets bowling fast medium for England.

'When I first came in the England side I thought it would be forever. Then came the injury. I'm not cured but I think if I look after myself, don't try and do too much in the lead-up matches, I'll get through it. My ambition remains the same as it always was. I want to play for England for another five or six years, get upwards of 150 wickets, be considered one of the best.

'I think I can play county cricket for longer. I'm in a good team at Middlesex. It's a hard school. People say what they think and you're not spared if you perform badly. But nothing's bottled up. You can have a shouting match with Gatts and argue with him but next day everything is back to normal.

'I don't want to sound as if I'm bragging but I rate myself. I think I'm a good bowler. That's been important to me in trying to overcome this injury. There's no great secret to it. I keep it simple. Just run up, hit the right part of the wicket and if it lands on the seam and moves then I don't know where it's going and neither does the batsman. It's not flashy. Boring really,' he said.

Foot soldiers don't wax lyrical about what they do. They let the damage they inflict upon the enemy do the talking for them. All the young men leaving for the West Indies today know they have a lot to prove, but none of them carries Gus Fraser's burden. 'I think we'll do well. I'm optimistic. It helps,' he said. So does being a battler.

15th January 1994

·9·

RORY UNDERWOOD

—

RORY UNDERWOOD does not give an awful lot away. Here are a couple of quotes to be going on with.

I asked him why he came back to rugby after giving the game up. 'Were you satisfied with the reasons I gave for retiring?' he asked. I said I hadn't really thought about it. Truth to tell, I was wrong-footed. I had assumed I was asking the questions.

Try again. Would rugby union ever become a truly professional sport? 'Don't know. Speaking for myself, I wouldn't want paying to play the game.'

'Why?' I asked.

'Because when they pay you, people can tell you what to do,' he said.

He is an interesting mixture – Oriental inscrutability mixed with canny Yorkshire. Malaysia meets Middlesbrough. Certain words keep cropping up when you research him: honest, reliable, quiet and modest. Makes him sound like a magistrate. What you are hoping for is something more – what's the word? – raffish.

We are talking real heroes here. To start with, he's a pilot, not someone who trundles around the world in jumbo jets, but someone who is training to fly fighters. He plays rugby for England. No player has played more games, no player has scored more tries for his country. He is a great winger, one of an élite group . . . glamorous.

Then there is the name itself. Not Kevin Underwood, or Ralph or John or something equally safe, but Rory. Know why? Well, his dad was a film fan and round about the time young Underwood was born 29 years ago there was a film star called Rory Calhoun doing the rounds. *Halliwell's Film Guide* says he was 'an

44

American leading man with an easy manner who didn't quite reach the top rank'.

I must have been one of the few people on this planet to have interviewed both Rory Underwood and Rory Calhoun. I mentioned this fact in the hope he might leap in the air with excitement or say 'gosh!' or something. Instead, I was rewarded with a pleasant smile.

'Undemonstrative' is another word which often crops up when you start reading about Rory Underwood.

Then there is the business of his fitness. Apart from being one of our greatest rugby players he is also one of our fittest athletes. Tom McNab, the national fitness coach, devised a set of tests for the England rugby team and concluded that Underwood's results would be equalled only be Daley Thompson at his best. Thompson is awesome. (He is so fit he hums with energy. When he enters a room it crackles.)

Not so Rory Underwood. He slips into your presence quietly and politely. In repose he is not as solid-looking as you had expected. He's graceful, feline even, relaxed like a big cat. If he had a Coat of Arms it would feature a man asleep in a deckchair with two panthers couchant. The motto would read: 'Actions Speak Louder than Words.'

He reminds me very much of David Gower. He has the same languid grace, the same polite disdain for exaggeration in either movement or thought. Like Gower, it makes him an easy target when things are not going well. 'Laid back' becomes 'lackadaisical', 'relaxed' becomes 'careless', 'an equable temperament' becomes 'a lack of fighting spirit'.

Against Wales he appeared to be contemplating the meaning of life when Ieuan Evans went past him like a runaway train and scored. Underwood took the rap. It didn't matter that the England team played well below par. The media put it down to a lack of concentration, a careless lapse. Sport can be cruel to its heroes.

What does Underwood say? 'I looked over my shoulder to see what was happening and he went past me on the other side. I didn't see him, didn't hear him. If I had known he was there the ball would have been out of the park.

'I wasn't daydreaming. I didn't suffer a slip of concentration. I thought I had taken all the precautions and then he zips past me, hacks the ball on and it stops three yards over the line. Why is it when I try that move the ball ends up in the stand? Nothing I could do about that.

'Nonetheless, I didn't read the press all the following week. I knew what they'd be saying about me. I try to keep level-headed. I don't leap about if things go right and I'm not suicidal when things go wrong. I try to keep calm.

'I am fatalistic in the sense that there are things you can do nothing about. What annoys me is when people misinterpret this and accuse me of being sloppy and not caring.

'What nonsense. Do you know any international player who doesn't try his hardest? I don't. So I didn't read the press, but there was no escape. A week after the game I was out shopping in town when a stranger said, "Look out, Rory, Ieuan Evans is behind you."

'That's all right. That's funny. What is not acceptable is the criticism that you are casual and don't care. It's stupid. Have I put my flying career on hold for two or three years to go out and *not* try my hardest? Have I decided to go through all that training and travelling once more just because I like coming for a few days to this hotel?'

Now I want you to know that Rory Underwood wasn't het up at this point. It might read as if steam was coming out of his ears, but it was all stated in a gentle, almost resigned manner.

I ventured the thought that he might be eager to shove the words down his critics' throat at Twickenham this afternoon. He said he thought the team might be as keen as ever to do well.

'When I first started playing for England I'd come off the park after a good game and think, "That's all right, then, I played well." We all did. We were all content with just our personal performance. Not now. That's why this is such a good team.

'We judge our performance on how well we play as a unit. We've not been at our best this season. The new turnover rules have made it difficult, particularly for wingers. I've not enjoyed the games so far.'

Is he regretting the come-back? 'Not at all. When I retired I did so for all the right reasons at that time. It had been a hectic few years.

'There is a lot of sacrifice of time and family involved in playing top-class rugby. I came to the point when I'd had enough. I retired. Then I spent a summer at home and I started thinking that you are a long time retired. I would hate to end up wishing I had played longer. That would be very sad. So I decided to come back.'

I made the point that obviously big-time rugby was addictive. Mr Underwood treated the possibility that he might be hooked on something with a fine contempt.

'I don't think so. I enjoyed the summer off without suffering withdrawal symptoms. It just gave me time to consider the possibility that I might have two or three more years at the top level.'

But what about the thrill of playing at Twickenham in front of a full house? Doesn't that get to him? 'I don't get nervous. Not now, not just before a game, even. I never worry about what my opposite number is thinking, either. I leave him to wonder about what I might do.'

The joy of rugby is that we all have to wonder what the winger might do. What we hope is that he will give us something to remember the rest of our lives, something to tell the grandchildren. Rory Underwood has provided his fair share of magical moments, so how does he account for his own great gifts?

'What do you mean?'

'Well, how does the winger function? What are his strengths, his secrets?'

Nothing.

'What I mean is how do you keep prepared in a game where you might not get the ball for 79 minutes, your hands are cold, your feet are frozen and then suddenly you are in a situation where you can win the match? How do you do it?'

Mr Underwood considered my thesis for a minute. 'There's a lot more to it than that,' he said with a smile.

The trouble with sports writers is we require great players to define what they do. We expect too much. Maybe what we hope to analyse is more a matter of intuition than intellect, and it could be that athletes don't like pondering where their great gifts come from in case they end up worrying where they might disappear to.

In any event, their responsibility is not to some hack who daydreams about scoring the winning try at Twickers, or playing in the Ryder Cup or turning out against the Aussies at Lord's. Their job is to deliver the goods. Actions speak louder than words.

What observers should be content with is that we still produce great athletes like Rory Underwood who, no matter how coarse and vulgar the times might be, remind us of old-fashioned virtues, like good manners, unpretentiousness, sportsmanship. To accuse them of nonchalance is to miss the point. All great athletes, even the weavers of dreams, like an Underwood or a Gower, have spines of steel!

A final thought, Rory. . . How will we do against Scotland? 'We are good enough. I have no thought of losing,' he said. With a smile and not a snarl.

6th March 1993

DEREK RANDALL

—

FOR SOME time now they have been putting it around that Derek Randall is barmy. It is the first thing he mentions when we meet. 'They say I'm an idiot, a bit of a dope,' he said. Well, not quite that, I said, being polite. Scatterbrained, perhaps. A bit eccentric, certainly. But let's find out if he really is daft.

For instance, there is the famous story, enshrined in the folklore of cricket, that a reporter visiting the Randall household in mid-winter was greeted at the door by the owner wearing a brand new set of cricket pads. 'Just breaking them in. Come in and meet the wife,' said Derek, whereupon the reporter was confronted by Mrs Randall sitting by the fireside wearing another set of pads.

'Not true, nay, never, never,' said Derek when I checked the story with him. 'Not even a little bit?' I said. 'Well, maybe I was wearing pads but not the missus. I mean she wouldn't wear pads, would she?' he said. 'Why not?' I asked. 'Because she's Italian,' he said, triumphantly, as if that explained everything.

Sometimes you look at him, the guileless face, his indefatigable and utterly charming desire to please and wonder if he isn't really pulling your leg. On the front of his benefit brochure there is a picture of Randall on that marvellous day of the Centenary Test at Melbourne where he scored 174 and played one of the most famous Test innings of all time.

It shows Randall on bended knee doffing his cap at Dennis Lillee. It should be explained that he arrived in that position after evading a bouncer from the great man by turning a somersault. In the picture Rodney Marsh is shown standing behind Randall, his mouth open in disbelief that anyone could be so foolhardy as to taunt Dennis Lillee.

It is reported that Mr Marsh was moved to remind Randall: 'This is not a garden party.' Lillee's response was more brutal. He hit Randall on the head with another bouncer. 'There's no point hitting me there, there's nothing in it,' Randall told him. Two years later, playing what many consider his greatest innings at Sydney, Randall so riled Rodney Hogg that the bowler tried four consecutive bouncers, all of which the batsman smashed to the boundary. Randall and Hogg had a confrontation in mid-wicket. 'I'm going to knock your effing head off, Randall,' said Hogg. 'You're not quick enough, Hogg,' said Randall. 'I wasn't thinking of using a ball,' said Hogg.

This is Derek Randall's 22nd season playing for Nottinghamshire. It is also his last. When he departs the scene he will leave a gap as large and impossible to fill as that created by the other colourful son – albeit adopted – of the county, Brian Clough.

Wherever he plays this year all true lovers of cricket should turn up to wish him farewell and a happy retirement. It is not a melancholy sight. This is no disenchanted, rheumaticky hack being granted the favour of a farewell tour. This is 'Arkle' Randall as we have always known him, quick and darting in the covers, still challenging batsmen to beat his throw. There are few takers. His willow still makes sweet sounds and he bats as he ever did, making music and not statistics.

In the first game of the season he played beautifully and made 98 before – as his team manager Mike Hendrick puts it with a shake of the head – 'He contrived to get himself out.' In the field he chirrups all day long, humming, whistling, singing and chatting to anyone within earshot.

Fielding in the covers at Grace Road on a lovely and gentle day with the sun high, he still came in with that jaunty jog, followed by a hop and a skip and the swooping run towards the batsman. At one point Nigel Briers, the Leicestershire captain, broke his stance to have a word with Randall. 'What was all that about?' I asked him, later.

'Nigel complained he couldn't concentrate because I was whistling,' said Randall. 'I told him it wasn't me but a happy bird he could hear.' What are Randall's favourite tunes? 'On a good day in the field I'll get through most of the Simon and Garfunkel song book,' he said.

His decision to be the happiest cricketer on the circuit was a conscious one taken as a teenager when he went to a county game and couldn't help noticing that the fielder at cover point grew grumpier and more hangdog as the day progressed.

'I was determined never to be like that. I love fielding and I love talking to people. I talk to opponents, team-mates, umpires, spectators, anyone who'll listen. I am just so happy to be on a cricket field. What is there to be unhappy and miserable about if every day of your life you have a game of cricket?' he said.

'I stood out there at Grace Road today with trees round the ground and the sunshine and the lovely turf under my feet and thought what a lucky man I am. My only sadness is that this is the last time I'll run around on those grounds, so this season's a farewell to that as much as anything else.'

As a cover fielder Randall must rank with the greatest of all time. As an entertainer he was surely incomparable. Geoffrey Boycott said of him: 'His strength is his ability to anticipate where the batsman will seek a single. He challenges you to match your pace with the speed of his reactions. I always tried to memorize field placings before every ball but with Randall there is never any certainty he will be where you expect him. His great asset is that he can clown yet concentrate. That is a marvellous gift.'

Boycott's perceptive observation about Randall's ability to remain focused while pulling funny faces is, perhaps, the key to the man. It is a theme he warms to. 'Like I say, they reckon I'm dozy and whatever, yet I've been a first-class player for more than 20 years. That's because I am serious about my job. I work hard at keeping fit. I don't smoke or drink. I go to bed early and next day, after we've got the kids off to school, I start thinking about my work that day on the cricket field.

'I am frightened of failure. Always have been. It's not been easy trying to gain security for me and my family. And if you play like I do it's doubly difficult because people won't take you seriously. When I finish I'd like to stay on with the club in some capacity, but that doesn't seem likely,' he said.

'Would you like to coach?' I asked. 'Not bothered about coaching,' he said. Then what might he do at the club? 'Just hang around making myself useful, I suppose,' he said. He has bought a small shop near Trent Bridge where he sells dried flowers. 'I'll be able to pop in from time to time to look at the cricket,' he said.

You might think there ought to be a continuing place in the game for someone of Derek Randall's stature. He is, when all is said and done, one of the greatest players ever produced by his county. He has the most caps, only five players – George and J R Gunn, Wally Keeton, Joe Hardstaff Jnr and Reg Simpson – have scored more than his 21,330 runs in county championship games.

In Sunday League his record of more than 7,000 runs at 33.91 is bettered only by Graham Gooch. His Test average is 33.37, which, he admits, is disappointing. It could have something to do with the fact that during his England career he batted in every position from one to seven.

His singular achievement as a cricketer is that long after he is dead people will still talk about the innings he played in the Centenary Test. *Wisden* described him as 'That perky, immortal figure'. Dennis Lillee called him 'a bloody pain in the arse'.

As part of his benefit year the teams of '77 will be reunited at Trent Bridge on June 13th. When you look at the players who made up the two teams and realize that Randall is the only one still playing first-class cricket you get some idea of his durability. England: Brearley, Woolmer, Underwood, Randall, Amiss, Fletcher, Greig, Knott, Old, Lever and Willis. Australia: Davis, McCosker, Cosier, Greg Chappell, Hookes, Walters, Marsh, Gilmour, O'Keefe, Lillee and Walker.

'I sometimes feel an old bugger when I look round our dressing room,' said Randall. 'But you know I've never got fed up with this game. It's changed, of course. A lot more tactics around nowadays and not enough banter. Cricket managers have moved in. It's not the same.

'Mind you, in a sense, I've always been a bit of an outsider because of my attitude. I once let a young cricketer get a run for his century. Didn't affect the game but meant a lot to him. I was criticized because they said it wasn't the pro thing to do. Like my batting. I've always thought: "What's the point of scoring 150 if you are the only person in the ground who enjoyed it?"'

The other thing that puzzles Derek Randall as he reflects on his career is the meaning of the word 'loyalty'. He demonstrably understands it, having played for the county of his birth with never a thought of moving and, moreover, having turned down both the South African krugerrand and Packer dollar. He remains genuinely baffled by the conduct of those, like Gooch, who took the money.

'I turned them all down because I couldn't bear the thought that by doing so I might miss the chance of playing for England. All the money they could offer just wasn't worth the price of one England cap. Not to me, anyway. Some felt differently. Look at Goochie. He's got 100 England caps but it could have been 130, couldn't it? I wonder if he ever thinks about that?' he mused.

He is, in the twilight of his career, a curiously old-fashioned figure with his belief that cricket is fun, that playing for one's country is better than turning out for a brewery team and that the duty of every cricketer is to entertain the spectators.

When you ask him how he would like to be remembered, he says: 'As a fair, honest and entertaining cricketer. And as a good sport. That's all there is to it.' It's the sort of thing other cricketers might think but would be wary of stating lest they be thought soppy and unworldly.

Watching him at Leicester the other day, his shadow lengthening across the ground, I had melancholy thoughts until I suddenly realized that of all the athletes I have known none has enjoyed himself more than Derek Randall. He has had more than twenty seasons in the sun and it is still only May.

When he went in to bat at Grace Road he was caught first ball off bat and pad. He walked back to the pavilion with a knowing smile on his face.

What Derek Randall has always understood is that you don't have to be crackers to play cricket for a living but it does help to have a sense of humour.

15th May 1993

·11·

GREG NORMAN

—

FIRST OF all he doesn't look like a Great White Shark. Anthropomorphically speaking, the world's No. 1 golfer is more a bird of prey than a fish, his features aquiline, his pale eyes slightly hooded. In a straight comparison with the rest of the human race, Greg Norman would come in that special category manufactured by the Lord on one of his better days.

He is perfectly equipped to be a modern sporting hero. He looks the part: broad-shouldered, slim-hipped, good legs. He has the appearance of a contender for the light heavyweight title. In a game sometimes dulled by a grim pursuit of perfection, he is a glorious individual, striking the ball a country mile in an exciting charge for the spoils. He is an idol pursued by doting fans; a bankable commodity sought by advertisers and sponsors who want to stuff his pockets full of dollars; a superstar lionized by captains of industry, showbiz glitterati, prime ministers, presidents and kings.

He owns a jet worth £6 million, has a company building 19 golf courses in Asia. He is a major shareholder in a firm manufacturing gold clubs with sales of £15 million a year. He owns a boat, seven Ferraris and a Rolls Royce. Without exerting himself unduly, or overtaxing the imagination of those employed to extend his fortune, he can reckon on a basic income of £7 million each year. He has just been paid more than £300,000 for playing five rounds of golf in Australia. It is estimated his net income is £30–35 million.

Gregory John Norman is 39 years old and on top of the world, yet driven by the notion that it might all end tomorrow. He is still pursued by demons. In the past two years he has changed his swing, his coach, his caddie and his management team. Everything except his wife.

Observing him in Australia these past two weeks has been a fascinating and sometimes confusing study of a man coming face to face with the advisability of treading softly on native turf. In the public estimation a convincing case could be made for Norman being the most respected and adored Australian sportsman since Don Bradman. The Australian media has always taken a more sceptical view.

Its caution seemed justified when Norman made a series of criticisms in Melbourne about the Australian Masters event he was playing in. In particular his critics made much of his complaint that the prize money of $750,000 compared unfavourably with purses in America. It was pointed out that in a country in recession with high unemployment some might regard three-quarters of a million dollars as a lot of money for a game of golf. An even more hurtful observation was that the prize-money would be substantially more if Australia didn't have to cough up appearance money to players, like the $150,000 paid to Greg Norman.

The predicament his critics face is they know that in the absurd, not to say obscene, financial wheeler-dealing of golf, Norman is worth every penny, and that without his presence any major golf tournament in Australia would be struggling.

It is a dependency weighing heavily on both Greg Norman and his beloved Australia, and it is part of the turmoil within a man who, perhaps for the first time, has begun to feel confident enough to stand alone and say what he really feels.

His break with IMG may be the most significant manifestation of his state of mind. Together he and Mark McCormack's organization were a formidable proposition in the world of golf. But when you are the best golfer in the world, do you need to be part of a stable? Moreover, approaching the age of 40, does a man need a nanny? Greg Norman is about to find out. It will be a fascinating journey.

We talked in Laguna Quays, Queensland, near where he grew up. He occupied the Presidential Suite (what else?) of the hotel. From his window the Whitsunday Islands were hazy in the morning sun.

The day before he had buzzed the hotel in his jet. 'My wake-up call,' he explained.

'Did I ever think I'd own an aeroplane? Jesus, I never thought I'd even own a house. I was an assistant pro earning £14 a week. They told me I'd never make it. I earned my fare to fly to Europe by gambling on a game of golf. It was a tough school. If you had a bad round on Friday you could be qualifying again on Monday. Taught you tenacious golf. Made you like a bull terrier. Nowadays young players are stroked like poodles, wined and dined.

'Mine was a tough school but I have to say I was lucky because I was put on earth at the right time in the right place with the right skills.

'I came into golf with the big money, not just from tournaments but the golf course design boom, people wanting to spend $800 million on a monument to themselves. Even my setbacks have proved positive. At the lowest point of my career, in 1991, my wife said she thought I ought to give the game up for 12 months.

'I talked to myself in the mirror. It's something I do when I need to find out the truth, what I really feel. I said: "Do you want to give up golf?" And the mirror replied: "No, because I'll miss the competition." I said: "Do you really want it again? Are you prepared for all the hard work and the sacrifice?" And the answer was "yes", so I said, "Let's go out and get it."

'I was in my car driving to practice and I pulled into the side of the road and watched the clouds. They were so peaceful. And I thought: "God, I want peace in my mind again." I decided then and there to get all the bullshit out of my brain. It worked, I just stared at the clouds and let all the good things come back into my mind. Within 90 days I had stopped worrying about what to do on a golf course and was concentrating on what I love to do which is play golf. I didn't seek out a sports psychologist, I think it's better to go through your problems alone.

'When I was a child I was frightened of going into a darkened room. I used to reach my hand in first to switch on the lights. But I taught myself to enter the dark without putting the lights on. I conquered my fear. It's the same with playing golf.

'Larry Bird, the great basketball player, told me that with five seconds to go and his team losing by a point he *wanted* the ball. I thought that was interesting. Not hiding, no fear of failure. In the British Open at Sandwich on the last day I hit a nine-iron at the ninth to within two inches to go into a one-shot lead. And all the way in I kept reminding myself of what Larry had said. I *wanted* that one-shot lead.

'It is this mental approach to golf I've only just started learning about. I have a book called *Zen and the Martial Arts* which I read all the time and I try to incorporate ways of relaxing and breathing into my golf game. I am going to see the champion kick-boxers in America because the way they relax their big muscles until the point of impact is very much what should happen when you are playing golf. None of this might work but I like a challenge.

'I am a long way from my peak. Mentally I am only just learning about myself. What is important is to look at a 240-yard shot to the green over a lake, take the three-wood and be in the right frame of mind to succeed. Then you can say: "Boy that was great because I *wanted* it!"

'I have written down at home a statement by President Roosevelt that he would rather experience the ecstasy of victory and the pain of defeat than spend any time in the grey twilight of life. That's what I feel. That's the way I want to play my golf,' he said.

His critics will tell you that Greg Norman is in danger of forgetting he is a golfer, that he is concentrating more on creating a business dynasty than winning Opens.

It could be he proves them wrong. If the thrilling impetus to his play last year is maintained this season and beyond, he might well be proved right in his prediction that we ain't seen nothing yet.

26th February 1994

·12·

DENIS

COMPTON

—

IT WAS clearly season's end at Lord's. The staff were busy wrapping up the ground for winter and even though the sun shone there was a nip in the air. A few spectators sat quietly as Middlesex and Gloucestershire performed the closing ritual to another season.

On a balcony, high in the Mound Stand, sat an old man with white hair and carrying a stick. Drink in hand, he looked down on the scene. At the age of 76, Denis Compton was surveying his kingdom. In his pomp he did not simply play at Lord's, he possessed it. When he walked to the middle he was not a cricketer coming out to bat on his home turf, he was an impresario performing a one-man show in an auditorium he owned.

There are bits of Denis Compton all over Lord's, reminders – if ever we needed them – of his glory days. There is, most spectacularly, the stand bearing his name at the Nursery End. In the Middlesex shop are souvenirs celebrating his reputation and in the Mound Stand, at the party held in his honour, copies of a new biography of the man written by Tim Heald and called, simply, *Denis: The Authorized Biography of the Incomparable Compton.*

Interestingly, the book reveals another part of Lord's that is forever Compton. In the MCC archive there is an old biscuit tin containing the knee cap that Denis Compton had removed in 1955. I was unaware this treasure existed and so, I suspect, are the majority of cricket lovers. It prompted the thought, however, that when they start preserving bits a player has had surgically removed and storing them in vaults like saints' bones, then we were clearly talking about someone of unusual significance.

Nearly 40 years ago Compton's knee was big news, a matter for national concern. So much so that the orthopaedic surgeon who performed the operation, Osmond Clarke, kept Compton's patella as a souvenir and would show it to visitors to his consulting rooms. Before he died, Clarke sent the knee cap to Gubby Allen, who placed it in the MCC archive.

There it resides to this day in an old biscuit tin bearing the legend 'Contents – One Knee Cap'. Tim Heald describes it as 'one of the most crucial pieces of human anatomy in the history of cricket; a macabre memento of physical frailty which played havoc with the career of one of the few sporting geniuses of the twentieth century'.

When you mention his knee cap, Denis Compton shakes his head and smiles ruefully. He remembers that the problem started in 1938 when he collided with the Charlton goalkeeper, one Sid Hobbins. Many years later, when Compton's knee was newsworthy, Hobbins wrote to Compton. 'Dear Mr Compton, I am terribly sorry for the trouble I have caused you over the years. I am very sorry indeed. Sincerely, Sid Hobbins.'

'It wasn't his fault,' says Compton. 'But it obviously nagged him all those years.' In fact there can be little mystery to Hobbins's remorse. What happened was that in 1938 he collided with a fellow pro. But at the end of the 1940s, after Compton's golden summer of '47, he was aware he had lamed a hero.

Compton's reputation is, of course, founded on a much broader base than his achievements in one season, yet there is little doubt that the very special place he occupies in the mythology of the game has to do with the glamour and excitement he brought to the dreary and plain immediate post-war years.

Neville Cardus wrote: 'Never have I been so deeply touched on a cricket ground as I was in this heavenly summer when I went to Lord's to see a pale-faced crowd, existing on rations, the rocket bomb still in the ears of most folk – see this worn, dowdy crowd watching Compton. The strain of long years of anxiety and affliction passed from all hearts at the sight of Compton in full sail. . . There were no rations in an innings by Compton.'

Compton remembers Cardus with affection. 'He used to seek me out. He would say to me: "You make me feel young." ' It was a prescient remark. Even today, white hair, limp, stick and all, Compton has a mischievous, almost raffish air. He is one of those people who, when he arrives somewhere, never seems likely to stay very long.

Sometimes he doesn't arrive at all. At the publishing party an old friend shook his hand and said: 'On the way here I made a bet with myself that you might forget to turn up for your own party.' He once arrived for lunch at a cricket match at close of play. 'Sorry I'm a trifle late old boy,' he explained to the host.

He said the same thing when he arrived for net practice at Old Trafford as the England team were finishing dinner. Compton had been instructed to turn up for practice in Manchester at 3 pm. An hour before the appointed time he was in Sussex on holiday with his children. He persuaded a friend, who owned a light aircraft, to fly him to Manchester. The plane set off but had to make an emergency landing at Derby and he eventually arrived in time for coffee and liqueurs at the eve-of-Test dinner.

Peter May, his skipper, was not amused. What Compton dared not tell him or Gubby Allen, the chairman of selectors, was that he didn't have any kit. The plane was a small one and he had been forced to leave his cricket bag at the airport. The next day he borrowed a bat from Fred Titmus and scored 158 against the South Africans. In the second innings he made 71.

It was this daredevil quality about Compton that made him attractive and irresistible. In a film about his younger days he would have been played by someone as dangerous and dashing as Errol Flynn. The Compton we saw at Lord's the other day, full of mellow charm and gentle twinkle, would need to be played by Maurice Chevalier at his most agreeable.

The majority of those who turned up for his party had seen him play, but there were some, brought by their fathers or attracted by the legend, who were born long after he had retired. I observed one or two of them watching him, wondering no doubt what it was about this old man that made him such a significant hero. I wanted to help them but it would have taken too long, involving an explanation of long-forgotten days when men of exceptional talent could play for their country at both cricket and soccer – and all that the rest of us needed to be as successful and sexy was a dab of Brylcreem.

Compton wasn't quite the last of the double internationals but he was the greatest. There is no more compelling image of the all-round athlete *in excelsis* than Compton returning from the South African tour of 1948–9, having scored a triple-century and averaging 84.80 for the series, and stepping into the Arsenal team that won the Cup in 1950.

He did not just make up the numbers at Highbury. He was, as Heald points out in his book, a star, if not *the* star. Brylcreem devised a campaign around the 1950 Cup Final using Compton. 'When Up For The Cup Make Smartness Your Goal – Brylcreem Your Hair.' When Arsenal reached the final, the caption on Compton's photograph on the hoardings was 'The Final Touch'. He was the first commercial superstar of British sport.

He remembers that at half-time Alex James, the great inside forward who had partnered Denis at Arsenal, sought him out and told him he was not playing well. The answer, said James, was a tot of brandy, whereupon he produced a hip flask and gave Denis a shot.

'It did the trick. I played better in the second half. It was the only time I could be accused of using drugs on the field of play.'

James was Compton's hero. 'I was lucky to come across him at the start of my career. He was a wonderful footballer. When we first played together I was overawed by playing alongside my idol. We travelled together on the bus. I called him "Mr James" or "Sir". I asked him if he had any instructions to give me on the way I should play. He just said: "All you have to do is watch me and when you see I have the ball just run. I'll do the rest." And he did. It was as simple as that. Made me look a good player.'

He doesn't care much for soccer nowadays. The romance has gone. He liked watching George Best but that was a while ago. In cricket he admires the energy and aggression of young Darren Gough and thinks that Shane Warne might rank alongside O'Reilly. He can think of no higher praise. He would have left Graham Gooch out of the team to tour Australia but would have included Neil Fairbrother.

'I saw him make a most marvellous century and I said to Ted Dexter, who was then the chairman of selectors, that we had just seen the player who would bat at No. 5 for England for many years to come. And Dexter said: "Oh no, I don't agree. I think Fairbrother is simply a one-day player." I couldn't believe it,' he recalls, shaking his head.

I wonder if nowadays the same judgment might not be made about Denis Compton. In these times of theory and analysis, when coaches are gurus and the commentators become oracles of the game, what judgment would they pass on a man who delighted in sweeping the ball off his middle stump, could not resist hooking the bouncer, and who once fell over in the middle of a shot and while flat on his back late-cut the ball, one-handed, for four? Might they not come to the conclusion that he lacked the application to be a Test match cricketer and that he was ideally suited to carnival cricket?

But back to Compton at Lord's the other day. It was good to see him, drinking champagne, surrounded by admirers, enjoying himself. He rolled back the years. That is his knack. There is a lovely story in the book about Denis receiving his CBE from the Queen after his retirement from the game. 'Oh, Mr Compton, how is your poor head?' she said. Denis thought for a moment she was enquiring about his hangover and wondered how she came by the information.

Then he realized she was talking about an incident that had happened more than 10 years earlier when, in 1948, he was struck on the head by a ball from Ray Lindwall. The point of the anecdote is that the genius of real heroes is to convince all of us, even monarchs, that it was only yesterday we saw them play.

10th September 1994

·13·

PETER
THOMSON

—

STANDING ON the first tee at Sunningdale Tommy Horton acknowledged the polite applause with a touch of his white hat and said: 'I brought the wife along to clap just in case no one turned up.' This was the first day of the Forte PGA Seniors' Championship. The three-ball teeing-off at 9.30 am had sunk a few putts in their time.

There was Horton, a rookie senior, clearly enjoying his new lease of life; Neil Coles, inscrutable of countenance, elegant of swing; and Peter Thomson, a man who won the Open five times and therefore carries with him that special aura of a sporting legend.

I had come to interview Mr Thompson who was making one of his rare appearances on an English golf course. When was he last at Sunningdale? 'Well, it's so long ago that this was a heathland course,' he said. What is it now, I enquired? 'A forest,' he said. I should explain that Mr Thomson had just shot 76 and was not best pleased.

But let's go back to the beginning of the day. We assembled in the morning sun. A love of golf apart, both competitors and spectators had one other common denominator: we were all aged 50-plus. Even one or two of the caddies were using battery-operated trolleys. It was like a convention of wrinklies or a golf trip organized by Saga Holidays.

The genius of golf is that it thumbs its nose at age. It allows men like Horton, Thomson and Coles to compete with real skill and purpose, far beyond the time when participants in every other sport are past their sell-by date. Moreover it encourages those not blessed with their skill to pursue a dream of breaking 80 before they die. In any other sport the purchase of a new set of equipment after the age of 50 would be classified as a vainglorious gesture; in the case of golf it represents a sensible investment in the future.

So for those of us who believe that the back nine of life might have more to offer than we had at first been led to believe, Sunningdale was a good place to be. The Old Course at Sunningdale is my idea of perfection. Every hole poses a different problem and reveals another breathtaking vista. A mature setting suited to our mellow entourage.

It was the first course Peter Thomson played when he arrived in England from Australia in 1951. It has remained a favourite ever since. Thomson was one of the players who provided the foundations of the modern multi-million dollar industry called golf. He won a hat-trick of Opens in '54, '55 and '56. The following year he finished runner-up to Bobby Locke. In 1958 he won it again.

The critics said these victories didn't count for much because the great Americans were not competing at the time. In 1963 he answered them by winning at Royal Birkdale in a field containing all the top Americans including Tony Lema, the holder, Arnold Palmer and Jack Nicklaus. When he joined the American Senior tour as he turned 50, he won 11 tournaments in 13 months. He was a pioneer of the Asian tour, a pithy commentator, a journalist and erstwhile politician. He is one of those nuggety Australians who only speak when they have something useful to say and who observe the world through crinkled and shrewd eyes. Nowadays he builds golf courses, with 20 projects on the go including a new course at St Andrews. 'A great honour,' he says.

He was and is a maverick, a man set apart by his ruthless ambition to succeed. It made him successful but it didn't win him many charm contests. Gary Player wrote of him: '. . . he was aloof and could be very sarcastic at times. It always seemed to me that he wanted to reveal his superiority and knowledge to people.'

One incident particularly narked Player. The South African took 29 hours of air travel to get from France to Melbourne but in spite of the delays got off the plane, went on the course and won what he thought was the most amazing triumph of his career. Thomson remarked: 'What's so amazing about that? You were sitting down and resting all the time in the plane, weren't you?'

Judging by our talk I wouldn't say that Peter Thomson has allowed old age to soften him. Physically he is much the same. Broad shoulders, narrow hips, slight fold at the belly but not too much to worry about. He's 63 and looks 10 years younger. He has started writing his life story. He didn't bother during the years when he was a superstar golfer, the time when he might have cashed in on his life story. Why didn't he write it then? 'I've not grown up until recently,' he said. Similarly when, after winning his third Open title, he was asked to write a golf instruction book he declined. Why? 'Because I didn't think I knew enough. Still don't.'

Starting his autobiography has meant asking questions about himself and what happened. Cricket was his first love. He wanted to be a leg-spin bowler like Shane Warne. His mother went to an aunt who read the tea leaves. She saw the young Thomson standing triumphant in a green field. She said he would be famous throughout the world. Mrs Thomson took this to mean that her son would captain the Australian cricket team. She didn't tell him in case it turned his head. She finally told him about his aunt's prediction when he was 50.

He came to golf by chance. 'I had bandy legs. My mother was told by doctors to put my legs in irons. She thought this was pretty radical. She took me to a physiotherapist. In those days they were treated like witch doctors. He told her that what I needed was long walks. I used to go with my uncle and his dogs and walk the golf course. It started from that. I didn't have any heroes. The men were at war, there was no one to learn from. I just picked the game up myself. I've never had a lesson, no one taught me how. I have a suspicion about the coaching that goes on nowadays. I think it ruins young players. You have to be self-reliant to play golf well. That's the key to it, you have to do things for yourself.

'I went to America when I was 21 and saw Sam Snead and Ben Hogan play. I wanted to be like Hogan. He played like a machine. He would go a whole round without hitting one bad shot. The rest were slapdash by comparison. I set my sights up there.

'When I came to England the difference between myself and people like Dai Rees and others was that they were club pros and relied on what they made at the clubs for a living. I had nothing. I had to win tournaments to pay the rent. It instils in you a powerful need to win.'

For winning an average tournament he was paid £300. Winning the Open earned him £750. When he totted up at the end of a successful season he would have made about £3,000. Nonetheless, he doesn't moan about the money in modern golf.

'Let the golfers have it. Otherwise who takes it? The agents, those people on the edge of the game. They're not important. I don't think I was born too soon. I won enough to live comfortably, I've made enough to spend what I want and know there's more where that came from. Money isn't everything. When someone says that you can be sure they have plenty,' he said with a rare smile.

The changes in the game? 'Golf courses. Some designers have a terrible ego problem. They design courses for Open championships, courses that would be tough for the likes of Faldo and Norman. They think of themselves as being wimpish if someone goes round their course in 64 or so. The great art of designing is to make the course suitable to all kinds of golfer.

'Coaching has become big business. I count myself lucky that I received no coaching. Children should be left to their own devices. In Australia we have the Institute for Sport. There are 500 coaches, it costs A$36 million a year. That money should go into grassroots sport providing facilities at schools. I'm against spending money to create a sporting élite.

'I think the biggest difference in golf in my time has been the change in the golf ball. The larger ball has made it much easier to play and taken some of the subtlety out of the game. It's bigger and heavier and it doesn't move in the wind like the small ball used to. My suggestion would be to make the ball a couple of penny-weights lighter and then we'll see a difference,' he said.

Gary Player called Peter Thomson 'the best I have ever seen with the small ball on a links course'. His record gives him an unchallenged place in the pantheon.

He remains unconvinced about something as fanciful as his own legendary status. He is keen to get back to his book, finding the voyage of discovery 'very therapeutic'. What would he call it? 'Oh, I haven't really thought about that,' he said. 'Nothing fancy,' he added. What a good title.

7th August 1993

·14·

JOHN
EMBUREY

—

JOHN EMBUREY was in Monaco watching the Grand Prix when they phoned telling him he wasn't in the squad for the one-day internationals against New Zealand. It wasn't Raymond Illingworth who called, but one of Emburey's mates who had been instructed to stay glued to the radio for the selection news.

Now, when you consider that Mr Emburey is at present recovering from an operation on a detached retina, that he has barely turned his arm over in anger this season, that with the bat he has been dismissed twice first ball, once third ball and was dropped from the first ball he received in the only game he scored any runs in, and still reckoned he might be picked for England, you will have the clearest possible indication that we are dealing with a supreme optimist.

John Emburey is approaching his 25th year in the service of Middlesex County Cricket Club. He is keenly anticipating the season, as he has always done. His continuing ambition to play for England is fuelled as much by a desire to be part of the new set-up as it is by natural ambition. He approves of the new chairman of selectors, respects his knowledge of the game, welcomes his resolve, admires him as one thinker about cricket to another.

The feeling is mutual. At the start of the season Illingworth sought out Emburey and asked his advice about various players. Emburey was impressed: 'Didn't happen before. Illy's a marvellous choice. He was an important figure in my career. In my first season in county cricket I played at Leicester when Illy was captain of the opposition. I was batting and Garth McKenzie and Ken Higgs were bowling. They were getting tired and we were playing them comfortably. All of a sudden I saw Illy having a go at them. He said: "Come on you bastards, put your backs into it." The next ball I received was a yard quicker. The pressure was back on.

I've never forgotten that moment. It showed his determination and concentration on winning. I think he is a great choice. We've had it easy in the past. When players did badly they did not get a kick up the backside. Under Raymond Illingworth all that will change.'

In spite of Emburey's unquenchable optimism and Illingworth's high regard for his qualities, it appears unlikely that the two will work together in the England side. Udal seems to have taken his chance, bowlers of the quality of Such and Croft wait in the wings. However we should be careful before writing off Emburey's international career. Any study of his form so far would show that he makes a habit of emerging from the shadows and into the sun.

It is also true that, as well as being the architect of his revival, he has also more often than not been the cause of his original downfall. In other words, there have been times when his judgment let him down.

He has twice been banned from playing for his country because he went on rebel tours to South Africa. Whatever money he earned must be balanced against a five-year period when he was unable to win an England cap.

Moreover, there is little doubt that the first tour to South Africa in the early Eighties also cost him the chance of captaining Middlesex. When he went on the tour he was vice-captain to Mike Brearley and groomed to be his successor. When he returned, the job of vice-captain, and the succession, was handed to Mike Gatting.

That rankled. It still does. Across the intervening years, Emburey has carried a conviction that he was unfairly treated. What he has not done (and it speaks volumes for the man) is nurse a grievance. Instead he has dedicated himself to helping Mike Gatting forge a fine Middlesex team, setting formidable standards on the field of play.

He says: 'Mike has done a fantastic job. For the past six or seven years he has been the best captain in the game. We work well together. Gatt's much more aggressive than I am. Some of the younger players might get scared of him. My job is to talk to them to find out what's bothering them and then have a word with Gatt.

'It's a volatile dressing room. We argue a lot, get things off our chests. We don't allow things to fester in a corner. If there's a dispute we have it out and then forget about it. It's a tough school that we've created at Middlesex and we don't spare anyone. There are times when Gatt and I have a go at each other in the dressing room. I always tell him beforehand that it's going to happen so he is prepared. But we have it out in front of the others and I think it does the younger players good to know that they are not the only ones who get a bollocking, that the senior players are not spared either.

'I have to say that it was difficult working with Mike at first. He must have thought he got the job by default. I was peeved. I wasn't as helpful as I might have been. I also remember getting the hump because it seemed to me that whenever I gave Gatt advice he would ignore it.

'I was standing at slip one day with Roland Butcher and I complained to him that Gatt wouldn't do anything I suggested. Butch said to me: "If it sounded like a suggestion rather than an instruction he might take notice of you." That struck home. I was bossing him about. I stopped and from that moment we had a partnership.'

Ironically, it was Gatting's dismissal from the England captaincy in 1988 that gave the job to John Emburey. It was not a happy experience. 'I always felt I was filling in for someone else. I wasn't ready for it, wasn't tough enough. I hadn't suffered the hardships of skippering at county level. I tended to sit back and let things happen.

'Also, I wasn't happy with my bowling. I had become a containing bowler. I had lost the loop, forgotten how to give the ball air. I was embarrassed by the way I bowled in that period. Strangely enough my batting improved. There was a point where my batting and bowling averages crossed, but going the wrong way,' he said.

Nowadays Emburey's batting is good enough for him to be considered as an all-rounder. Last season he had a splendid time with both bat and ball. He played Shane Warne as well as anyone, got up Merv's nose. 'He said something about me prancing about like a big fairy and a lot more you couldn't possibly tell your readers,' he said.

He does tend to upset fast bowlers who sometimes try to knock his block off. Why? 'Don't know why I aggravate them so. Perhaps it's because of my style,' he said. How would he describe the way he bats? 'I fiddle and fart about,' he said.

He was always going to be a cricketer. He decided that was what he wanted to be when he was nine years old. His heroes lived at the Oval. He started life as a medium-pace bowler with ambitions to bowl fast. One day, in a school game, he ran up, turned the wrist over and the ball turned and bounced. The teacher who was umpiring raised an eyebrow. 'Can you do that again?' he asked. Emburey bowled another off-break. 'That's what you bowl from now on,' he said.

At Surrey, Arthur McIntyre took a shine. When the club decided to off-load Emburey as surplus to requirements it was McIntyre who directed him to Lord's, where he served an apprenticeship under one of the game's great off-spinners, Fred Titmus.

That was 25 years ago and when you ask John Emburey to look back over those years, the word he uses most to describe his career is 'under-achiever'. He 'under-achieved' on the last tour of India when he bowled badly on wickets that turned. He 'under-achieved' when he went to South Africa for the second time instead of concentrating on getting his bowling right and forcing his way back into the Test team. 'The biggest mistake of my career,' he says.

There is a sense in which he employs his ability to be self-critical as a spur to his ambitions. When you ask him why, going on 42, he wants to commit himself to another season on the county treadmill, he says it is to do with this feeling that he hasn't yet fulfilled his potential.

'I know it's unlikely now, but I want to play at the highest level. I really want to get back into it. The point is, I still want to play and I still enjoy it. Every time I go out there I want to score runs, take wickets, make catches. I still set myself targets. I see Fred Titmus's record of 2,600 first-class wickets.

'Now I'll never get to that. I'm about 1,300 short, but I can get my overall average down from 24 to 22 and get my batting up to 26 or 27. I want to set a standard like the greats. I'm not saying I'm in that class but I'd like to compare my Test figures with Illy. You should always try to put yourself on a level with your idols,' he said.

John Emburey reckons he has another couple of seasons in him. Then what? 'Team coach, manager maybe. I think it would be a shame if people with the experience of Gooch, Gatting and myself were not given a role to play in the future of cricket. But I'm not thinking too much about that. I'm looking forward to this season and trying to get my eye right. I've had an operation for a detached retina. Still have a bit of distorted vision. It gives me a problem judging the pace of the ball. I can't field at slip and in bright sunlight I get double vision. A lens would solve the problem, but we want it to heal itself. Hopefully it should be better in about six weeks' time. Then, if I'm still bowling well enough and have scored a few runs, I would hope to catch the chairman's eye.'

He was smiling when he said it, but he wasn't slapping his thigh.

21st May 1994

·15·

STEVEN RHODES

—

THE URGE to keep wicket, like madness, runs in families. The comparison is not made lightly. It is not obligatory for a wicket-keeper to have a slate loose, but it sure helps. Theirs is the taxing job in cricket, the most dangerous and the least glamorous, because it is an established fact that the best of them make the job look easy and only when they make a mistake are they noticed.

Sensible parents do not encourage their children to be wicket-keepers. If they have done the job themselves they tend to nurse their secret and hide the equipment away. Steven Rhodes was 10 before he found his father's wicket-keeping gloves. He came across them while rummaging through a cupboard.

Until that point, he had not thought about playing cricket. He played rounders at middle school. When he found the gauntlets he asked his dad to show him how to use them. He could hardly have had a better teacher.

His father, Bill, had kept wicket for Nottinghamshire for six seasons before buying a newsagents shop in Bradford. Father and son converted a cellar into a practice area. Dad bounced the ball against the wall and tutored his son in the mysteries of his art.

From that moment on Steven Rhodes wanted to keep wicket for a living. He joined Saltaire in the Bradford League as a junior but was frustrated at his secondary school, where there wasn't a master willing to take a cricket team.

Young Steven organized four other pupils who were also playing in the league into picking a team. They then 'bullied' the French master into giving their team the imprimatur. They won the Bradford Schools competition at the first attempt.

Today, at the age of 30, Steven Rhodes keeps wicket for Worcestershire and England. In his first season as a full England player he has established a presence of such significance that the captain declared Rhodes his player of the summer.

Michael Atherton first came across Rhodes's potential on an A tour. Atherton made the full team and became captain, while Rhodes was designated an A team regular. There were many good judges who thought that when he finally got the call it was justified but late. He doesn't see it that way.

'All the claims that were made about me when I was playing in the A team concentrated on my "potential". When they finally picked me they had to because of my talent. I had arrived.

'People have remarked that I took quickly to Test cricket. Two reasons why. The first is I served a long apprenticeship, I was ready. The second, Mike Atherton. He said: "I want you to play for England like you play for Worcestershire." Marvellous, because if I have to change then that's a problem. But if I can be myself then the pressure of being a Test cricketer that gets to some is taken away.'

I mentioned that he had become the unofficial senior pro of the England team. He said: 'Again I was lucky. Alec Stewart is vice-captain and I didn't want him to feel that I was invading his territory. But he has been marvellous because as a 'keeper he knows the value of the view of a game we get behind the stumps. I'm always on the look-out for ways of winning a game. My job is not to fall asleep for a second and to make sure that no one dozes off.

'Ray Illingworth said when he took over that Test cricket is about concentration. And he is certainly right. He said that unless we were absolutely tired out when we came off the field, wiped out physically and mentally, we hadn't been giving it our all. Every Test match I've been totally knackered, so I must be doing something right.'

We met at the county ground in Worcestershire, looking across the empty pitch to the cathedral. It is one of cricket's loveliest settings, even on a day when melancholy drizzle dulls the view. He came here 10 years ago having finally decided that he didn't have a future at Yorkshire. David Bairstow was Yorkshire's 'keeper and the county captain.

The club, not for the first time, was in a dilemma. The cricket committee's decision to release Rhodes was particularly upsetting to the county coach, Doug Padgett. Early on he took a shine to Rhodes. He knew the boy was going to be a first-class cricketer. Rhodes remembers him fondly: 'He was a strange man: dour and hard. But he was a lovely man when you got to know him and a wonderful coach.'

He was also, in those days, a formidable smoker with a dislike of draughts. Rhodes remembers being driven to matches in Padgett's car while the coach went through a pack and refused to have the window open. 'I would arrive at the ground feeling I had eaten 20 Benson and Hedges,' he said. Some good came of the ordeal: it put Rhodes off smoking for life.

It was while he was under Padgett's tutelage that Duncan Fearnley and Basil

D'Oliveira came to watch him play and offered him a contract should he ever leave the county. When Yorkshire made their decision, Rhodes's move was a foregone conclusion.

'I love it here,' he said, nodding across the ground to the town. 'We've had a lot of success and it's a well-run club. I don't regret not having played for Yorkshire. I'm a Yorky through and through, but they made their decision and I don't blame them for it.

'Being a successful wicket-keeper is a matter of luck. There is only room for one in a team so if the guy has a 20-year career, you can bet that in that time the three reserve 'keepers fall by the wayside in the second team waiting for a chance. I was lucky. Yorkshire let me go and they took me here. Now I'm in the England team. That is what I have always wanted,' he said.

You get the feeling that, all things being equal, he will take some shifting from the England team. It is not in his nature to give up. He looks a battler.

He is 5ft 8in tall and weighs just over 12 stone. He is broad of beam and solid-thighed. His chin juts and the eyes are clear, the stare unflinching. I imagine he would be a handy man in a ruckus. His hands show little sign of damage. He has broken both thumbs but the fingers are straight, the nails intact and unblemished. He inspects them critically. 'A bit splattered but they'll do,' he says. Even relaxing he exudes energy.

It is going to be interesting to see what Australia makes of Rhodes. I have little doubt that had he been Australian he would have been playing Test cricket for a long time now.

He welcomes the fight ahead. 'They are tough, but so are we nowadays. Raymond Illingworth is a very positive bloke and he has encouraged us to think that way. We have picked a very positive and aggressive side. There's a bit of feeling, bubble, character about the team. I think we can match them,' he said.

He sees what he is explaining epitomized in Darren Gough. 'I'm a massive big fan of Darren Gough. Took to Test cricket like he was born to it. I like the way he thinks he has to be kingpin. You can never fault the size of his heart. A diamond. He is genuinely quick, too.

'At Old Trafford I was standing 25 yards back to him. That is as far back as I have ever stood. It was a yard further back than I stood for Devon at the Oval. Mind you, I was 25 back for Craig White. He's quick, too. With Devon, Darren and Craig, we've got three of the fastest bowlers we've ever had. McCague's not exactly medium-paced either, so it means that even in State games we'll always have pace to call on.

'What I like most about Darren Gough is the way he meets a problem head on. He doesn't let a tense situation nag him or gnaw away at his confidence, he simply goes out and attacks it. I call it "reversing pressure". It's about not letting yourself be dominated by the opposition, about fighting back so you overturn the tables and put them on the receiving end, make them worry.

'The last day of the Leeds Test against South Africa was a nothing day, but Daffy bowled a couple of off-cutters that turned, so he said he was going to bowl "Basils" [Basils are medium-paced off-breaks, named after the Glamorgan bowler Steve "Basil" Barwick]. Mike Atherton agreed and Goughie said he would bowl the same way.

'After a while, Cronje started squirting Darren around. Now, as I said, there was nothing in the game, we were just playing out time. But Darren got the hump. "I've had enough, I'm going to bowl quick at the bastard," he said. And, by God, did he bowl quick. It was one of the most lethal spells I've kept to. That's what I like. Showing the opposition who is the boss.'

In just over two weeks' time, Michael Atherton and his England team face the ultimate test of nerve and skill, a Test series against Australia Down Under. It would be a foolish fellow who made predictions, but there is no doubt that the manager and his captain have the team in the right frame of mind.

'It's the tour to go on, the series to play in,' said Rhodes. 'I'm confident we'll do well. I'm a bit like Darren Gough: when it comes to winning, I've got tunnel vision.'

8th October 1994

·16·

LAURA DAVIES

—

I N THE sometimes neurotic and obsessive world of professional golf, where beta-blockers calm the palpitating heart, where God and Sigmund Freud are called upon to soothe the mental turmoil and coaches are witch doctors casting spells to ward off the yips, it is refreshing to come across a golfer with a healthy disregard for such taradiddle.

We may draw what conclusions we like from the fact that we are reporting on a woman. There will be those who will see it as a significant statement in the battle of the sexes, and others – I have in mind several male golfers of my acquaintance – who will use it as yet futher proof that there are two different games, golf and the version played by the members of the ladies' section.

Laura Davies takes no part in such conjecture. What she knows is that, as the newly crowned No. 1 woman golfer in the world, all she has to do to face life at the top is keep reminding herself that playing golf sure beats working in a supermarket.

As she says: 'Playing golf for a living isn't a real job is it? It's a privilege. It's also well paid.' At the same time as she went to No. 1 in the ratings she passed the million dollar mark in earnings.

I am grateful to Miss Davies. An hour in her company was music to my ears. It is reassuring in the often loony world of professional sport, where half-formed youths are transformed into half-baked adults – and worse – to find someone like Laura Davies, who is both a genuine star and seemingly untrammelled by success.

For instance, she arrived a little late for the interview at the Berkshire Golf Club, not because this was her due but because she had been lurking in the car park not daring to enter the building until she was sure that someone she knew was inside.

After the interview she began her preparation for rejoining the American tour not by consulting her coach – she doesn't have one – or hitting a thousand balls on a practice range, but by playing a friendly four-ball; a fiver front and back nine and a tenner on the game.

As she teed up, our photographer asked her if she would mind the noise of a camera clicking at the top of her backswing. Certain male golfers of my acquaintance would swoon at the very thought. What Laura Davies said was: 'Go for it.'

What I am trying to convey is that Laura Davies is a pleasant and uncomplicated individual. It shows in her face, her frank and clear eyes and is sustained by her conversation, which is straightforward, unpretentious, nothing fancy.

She is 5ft 10in tall, broad-shouldered, with big feet. I don't know what she weighs but, as my dear departed grandfather would say, she'd crush some grass.

She hits the ball a country mile. In fact, this year, she has already recorded one drive of more than 350 yards and one just short of that target. Both were wind-assisted, but anyone who has seen her play knows that she is capable of starting most tournaments 16 under par because she can reach the majority of par fives in two.

She has brought excitement to women's professional golf. Wherever she appears people turn up to see her play.

When she stood on the first tee at the Berkshire there was an audience of club staff and golfers standing around wondering just how far she would smite it on the par five opening hole. Can she really hit it as far as the men pros?

'I'm no Greg Norman,' she says. 'But one day I'd love to play him off the back tees just to see how my power game stood up under the kind of pressure the men play under.

'When I practise, I play off the back tees all the time. Length isn't a problem. On a 465-yard par four I can take a driver from the tee and then a three-iron to the green.

'That's what I do when I practise. What I'd like to see is if I could do it under the pressure of playing a men's tournament. Probably miss the cut, but I'd love the chance.'

She started playing golf when she was 14 because her brother, Tony, took it up. Whatever Tony did, his sister imitated. She played football and cricket. Last year, just before an event in America, she hurt her wrist playing cricket in a car park. She missed the cut.

As a child she envisaged a career as a sports teacher. As soon as she picked up a golf club she knew what she really wanted to do for the rest of her life. Her headmaster rebuked her ambition.

'You'll never earn a living playing golf,' he said. At 16 she was playing for Surrey and already creating a stir with her big hitting. Playing at Sunningdale, she reduced the opening par five to a drive and a nine-iron.

She was ready-made for an American sport scholarship. She declined. Why? 'Dunno really. Just wanted to stay at home.

'I played the amateur circuit for five years. Worked six months, played six months. I got a job at a supermarket, a garage and a bookmakers before turning pro.

'My mum and step-dad were marvellous. Made a lot of sacrifices. When I turned pro I borrowed £1,000 from my parents. I missed the cut in the first tournament I played. Then I won £4,000 in the second. Since then I've never looked back.

'If any younger player asks me what they should do to become a professional golfer, I tell them to first of all get a job so that when they come to play golf they'll understand it's a darned sight better than working. That's my philosophy.

'I had a couple of not so hot years in '91 and '92 and I started moaning and getting miserable. Then I just took stock and remembered what I was doing before I played golf every day.

'Since that time if I have a bad week I don't worry. It's an absolute privilege to be travelling the world playing golf. I think we have the best of the sporting world.

'Look at all the other champions in other sports, like Nigel Mansell, who say they'd really rather be champion golfers. Ours is the best life. Look at how the men can go on earning money on the seniors tour,' she said.

I asked her if she thought there would be a seniors competition for women. 'Don't think so. Maybe the men will let us join theirs. That would be a way of playing with them. But most of the girls on the tour play until they're about 40 and then retire to have a family. Me? Another 10 years I suppose. More if I'm still winning. Then I might think about packing up,' she said.

She is 30 years old, has won 27 tournaments and sets herself the target of 50. There are good judges who claim that Laura Davies could dominate women's golf in the next 10 years like the young Jack Nicklaus once ruled the men's tournaments.

The question is: Will the kind of success and fame we are talking about spoil Laura Davies? Will she be afflicted by the doubts and fears suffered by many of her male counterparts? Might she be tempted to employ a guru?

'I think that too much can be made of coaching. Look at Seve. I'm sure if he got back to being Seve, when it was just him and his brother and there weren't all those people telling him what to do, things would be better.

'I'm lucky. I've never had a golf lesson in my life. I learned by mimicking others I saw play on the telly. I pick up more just watching the great players and copying them than I would from any teacher.

'You can't take your coach with you to Thailand, can you? At least I can't. So if things go wrong I go to a range and start mucking about, getting the feel back. I'm more about feel than technique,' she said.

What's 'feel'? I asked.

'Shaping the ball, drawing and fading it,' she said. Now this *is* highly technical. People have been trying to make the golf ball obey their command for hundreds of years.

Books have been written on the subject, videos have been made, coaches have become rich by telling us how it's done.

What is more, a multi-million dollar industry with space-age technology exists to design golf clubs to master the game.

So come on, Laura Davies, what's this old baloney about feel? 'Well, if I stand over a shot and I think I've got to hit a draw, something happens to my swing and the ball goes right to left.

'If I want to hit a slice then I feel myself cut across the ball as I hit it. If I want to hit a draw or a slice or make the ball go low or high, I know what to do simply by having watched the great players on telly. I learned a lot watching Seve play, and Langer.

'What I learned from Bernhard was his rhythm with the irons. Woosie gave me a couple of tips for chipping, which came in useful. But the rest is what I've picked up just watching people. With me it's all about confidence. At present I'm confident and playing well. I feel I can't hit a bad shot,' she said.

The other good question to ask Laura Davies as she faces her glittering future is: What about all that money waiting to be won? What will she do with it?

'Spend it,' she said. 'I love spending it. I've got three or four cars, bought a couple of cottages I've knocked into one next door to my mum. I don't worry too much about pensions.'

She loves a gamble. Indeed she confessed that as she passed Ascot racecourse on the way to our meeting she was tempted to pay a call. As it was she settled for a bet.

Not only bookmakers have been on the receiving end of her generosity. She didn't mention it, but others told me that when Laura Davies won her first tournament she gave part of her winnings to the amateur organization that had nurtured her.

She has helped out fellow pros who were struggling and has supported the European Tour without regard for the larger rewards that would come her way if she devoted all her time to playing in America.

When I asked her to name her greatest triumph, she said being part of the team who won the Solheim Cup from the Americans.

When I asked her what she was most looking forward to in the future, she said defending the cup in America.

Why? I asked. 'Because it'll be great fun,' she said.

Interesting word, 'fun'. I think the reason I liked her so is because she can use the word and still convey the will to win that all great champions possess.

9th April 1994

·17·

MICHAEL HOLDING

—

THE SIGHT of Michael Holding gliding in to bowl was one of the great aesthetic spectacles in all of sport, unless you happened to be the batsman he was running towards, in which case you were more concerned with survival than any appreciation of a great athlete in action. He ran with such style and balance that he seemed to float over the turf.

Dickie Bird said he was disconcerting to work with because you couldn't hear him approaching the wicket. 'You can hear most bowlers pounding up, grunting and snorting. But often I'd stand there when Michael was bowling my end and wonder where he had got to. And then he'd flow past me like a ghost. "Whispering Death" I called him,' said Dickie.

Today, Michael Holding looks as lean, trim and stylish as ever he did when he was part of what must rate as the deadliest quartet of fast bowlers ever assembled in one team: Roberts, Holding, Garner and Croft. There have been other combinations – mainly West Indian – but none containing four bowlers of such class and ruthlessness, nor four practitioners of the same craft offering so many different ways to test the technique and nerve of their opponents.

Nowadays Michael Holding observes the game he adorned from the commentary box, his comments made in a voice so deep and rich it sounds as if his vocal cords have been soaked in molasses. When you first meet him you are struck by the thought that he doesn't seem brutal enough to be a frightener. His manner is affable and languid and he has the most beautiful hands with long tapering fingers, like his great hero Muhammad Ali.

He told me he loved the fight game until he sat ringside for the first time. What he hadn't counted on was the noise made by leather hitting flesh. He has never been to a boxing match since. This sensitivity to human suffering will come as news to one or two of his opponents, most notably Brian Close and our new selector, John Edrich, who received a terrifying mugging from Holding, Wayne Daniel and Andy Roberts at Old Trafford in 1976.

Holding was warned by umpire Bill Alley for intimidatory bowling and Clive Lloyd, the West Indian captain and inventor of the ordeal by fast bowling, was forced to admit that his men did get 'carried away a bit'. When Close bared his chest for the cameras you couldn't quite see the ball-maker's name on his flesh, but the seam marks were very noticeable. It was a severe test of Brian's theory that there is no such thing as pain.

I asked Michael Holding if he had ever deliberately set out to hurt an opponent. 'There were two names in my book of players I didn't like and I gave them both a bit of trouble,' he said. Who were they? He wouldn't say, although I have a shrewd idea that one of them might have been Tony Greig whose boast that he would make the West Indians 'grovel' must rate along with General Custer's statement that he couldn't see any Indians as one of the most unfortunate observations of all time.

It was during that 1976 tour when the West Indies beat England 3–0 that Michael Holding produced one of the greatest Test-match bowling performances of all time. At the Oval, in the final Test on a lifeless wicket, he took eight for 92 in England's first innings of 433 and won the match by taking six for 57 and bowling England out for 203 in the second innings. Holding's bowling was a classic demonstration of how great fast bowlers win matches on pitches offering nothing but heartache to less gifted practitioners. In that series Michael Holding took 28 wickets at just over 12 apiece.

It tells you much about this remarkable athlete that the performance at the Oval is not the one most people talk about when they discuss Holding's place in the all-time list of great fast bowlers. If he did nothing else, he will be remembered for one over he bowled at Geoffrey Boycott in Barbados on the England tour of 1980–1. In the folklore of cricket, those six balls have acquired the reputation of the most lethal over ever delivered. It is not something you can prove except to say that anyone who witnessed what happened, as I did, is bound to say they never saw anything quite like it.

Boycott admits he still has nightmares about that over. Holding smiles at the memory and says: 'If you believe Geoffrey, England would have been six wickets down without scoring had he not been batting.' The man who had the best view was Graham Gooch, Boycott's partner. Gooch recalls that the first five balls were virtually unplayable, throat balls which followed Boycott as he swayed out of line. The sixth ball was pitched up and sent Boycott's off stump flying. 'It was one of the most lethal, enthralling overs I have ever seen. Classic fast bowling from a very great bowler,' said Gooch.

He remembered with a smile dear old Ken Barrington's advice as he and Boycott prepared to go out and bat in that match. He told them: 'You have just got to go steadily through them swing doors, walk calmly up to the reception desk and book yourselves in for bed and breakfast.'

I asked Michael Holding who was the fastest bowler he faced. 'Without doubt Jeff Thomson. When we toured Australia in 1975–6 he was awesome. He was the only bowler I saw who could make Lawrence Rowe play a hurried shot. How quick? Well, let's say he could have hit me any time he wanted. I just couldn't see him.' Holding was never in any danger of being injured by Thomson because in those days the Fast Bowlers' Club operated, which guaranteed that the quick men did not do damage to each other.

When Fred Trueman was in his pomp (now there was an action) it was unthinkable that when he batted he would receive a short-pitched delivery. Indeed, Fred's first move at the wicket was a firm step forward. Nowadays that would guarantee him a bed in the nearest casualty ward.

There is a famous story about Fred going out to face a young quick bowler who was making his debut and who had been wound up by his captain to bounce him just for fun. The young bowler, having more testosterone than sense, took up the challenge and whistled three balls past Fred's head. The great man was mortified. At the end of the over he approached the fast bowler. 'Tell me, young man,' said Fred, 'does tha' want to die young?'

29th May 1995

·18·

MARTYN MOXON
—

THOSE WHO know nothing of Yorkshire assume it is a largely untamed chunk of England inhabited by a loud and aggressive warrior race at war with the rest of the world.

In fact the county is an uneasy alliance of hostile tribes who sometimes meet to beat each other up. These get-togethers are known as meetings of the Yorkshire Cricket Committee. Amid the sound of battle, Yorkshire County Cricket Club went to pot. For the past 25 years they have won nothing worth a mention, not because of the strength of the opposition but, more often than not, because someone born in Bradford couldn't bear sitting next to a man from Leeds, who hated the man from Barnsley who couldn't stand the man from Harrogate who thought the bloke from Rotherham was a complete prat.

This turbulent civil strife found common cause in Geoffrey Boycott, who became a figurehead of dispute. While there can be little doubt that there is, shall we say, a quirky side to Mr Boycott's personality, there were others in opposition much more devious and Machiavellian than he. And much less talented. There are signs, and they are no bigger than a speck on the horizon, that things are changing for the better. The committee is reduced to 12 and presided over by Sir Laurence Byford who, as a long-serving copper, gained a useful insight into how to prevent people getting at each other's throats. Chris Hassell is an energetic and imaginative chief executive.

What is more, since Mr Illingworth took charge of the England team there have been regular sightings of selectors in the county. Once more there are Yorkshire players in the England squad, creating an interest and enthusiasm for cricket in the county not experienced since Closely was a lad.

If there is to be a revival of fortune it will be proper reward for Martyn Douglas Moxon, who has borne the disappointment and hardship of captaining an unsuccessful Yorkshire team with exemplary patience and no little style. As a child of the Sixties he grew up with the great Yorkshire side of that era. His team won the County Championship seven times from 1959 to 1968. Every year since then the county slid deeper into despair, the committee riven by internal disputes, the players confused by regular changes of captaincy, disheartened by a dressing room that was, at times, as jolly as an abattoir.

Martyn Moxon made his debut in 1981 and in the coming years, as he sat quietly in his corner breathing in the discontent around him, must have pondered if it wouldn't have been wiser to have opted for the career of professional footballer which presented itself when he was a teenager. But he wanted to go in first for Yorkshire like Sutcliffe, Hutton and Boycott. Here he was opening the innings with Boycott. It should have been heaven, but it wasn't.

'What I could never work out was why we had such a good team in those days and never won anything. There was Boycs, John Hampshire, Chris Old, Phil Carrick, Ray Illingworth, Bill Athey, Richard Lumb, David Bairstow. It was almost a full international side and yet it performed so badly.

'There was a terrible atmosphere, petty jealousies in every corner. It was a dressing room of factions and cliques. People turned up for the game, played and then left as soon as they could. Illy and Boycs were at odds with each other and I used to sit there and imagine what it would be like if only they got together and worked for the good of the club.

'In fact, what I have never been able to come to terms with is that in Fred Trueman, Brian Close, Raymond Illingworth and Geoffrey Boycott we have four men with unequalled knowledge of the game, and yet they have not been able to work together to help Yorkshire in the years of struggle. Over the years when we've been criticized for not winning anything I've often thought why people didn't blame them as well. 'Wouldn't it be marvellous if Fred told Darren Gough what it requires to be a great Test bowler? Imagine the effect on young Michael Vaughan if Geoff Boycott took an interest in him. To be fair to Geoff, when he was on the committee he did get involved. But in those days it was difficult to ask him for help because if I did I would have been criticized by the anti-Boycott element on the committee. It wasn't easy.'

His four seasons opening the innings with Boycott gave him an insight into one of Mother Nature's most intriguing creations. He says: 'Unfortunately I found out too late how Geoffrey Boycott worked. His philosophy was that he should be asked for advice. I thought he might offer it. He never came down the wicket and said "that was a crap shot" or offered information about how I should be playing against a certain kind of bowling.

'After he finished playing I mentioned this to him and he said: "You should have asked." But I did learn a lot watching him. I've not seen anyone with a better technique against all kinds of bowling. A very fine player, and he had all the shots when he wanted to play them. I enjoyed batting with him because I always felt he took pressure off me in the sense that every bowler wanted to get him out, so perhaps they eased up a bit when I got down to their end.

'He had this great desire to score hundreds and he was never satisfied. I remember batting with him all day against Worcester. We put on more than 350 together. I was out for 160 and Geoff was out in the last over of the day for 180. He came in the dressing room, put his head in a towel and sat there for a full 45 minutes, miserable as sin.

'Two days later they arranged a picture of the two of us in front of the scoreboard showing how many we had put on together. As we were standing there he said: "Why did you get out?" I mumbled something about being tired. He said: "Well, if you were tired why didn't you tell me and I would have taken strike." What he wanted was not the fourth-best opening partnership in Yorkshire's history, which we had achieved, but the best, beating the 555 made by Sutcliffe and Holmes.

'I believe that in a sport like tennis or golf, Geoff would have been a Borg or a Faldo. I think that he was both misunderstood and, at times, his own worst enemy. I have a sneaking feeling that as he gets older he might regret he wasn't a bit more flexible, that he might do one or two things a little differently. Question is would he have been the same player had he been easier to get on with?'

There are those who believe that, had there been a coherent and sensible selection policy for England throughout the Eighties, Martyn Moxon might have established himself in that great tradition of opening for Yorkshire and England. As it was, he played 10 times for his country and today the ambition that once burned now flickers hopefully. He says he is batting better than he has ever done, that he is a more complete player than when he played for England.

Where some have found the captaincy of Yorkshire a fretful chore, Martyn Moxon has matured in office both as a man and as a player. In his own quiet and undemonstrative manner he brought a sense of pride and purpose as well as fun to the Yorkshire dressing room. He didn't need telling by Raymond Illingworth that he had one or two England players in his side. He has known for some time.

Similarly, when Keith Fletcher said England's selectors concentrated on players in the south because there wasn't much worth looking at up north, Martyn Moxon knew he was talking through his hat long before recent events proved the stupidity of the observation.

'We've got a handy team now. All the players have the right attitude. They are people who want to do well. It's premature to say we're going to win things, but I'm encouraged. We've got some England players and there's a buzz about the place.

The club is better run than at any time since I've been here. Our cricket academy is turning out good players. Our problem is keeping them. They are being seen at 16 and being offered contracts by other clubs, so we're having to make judgments at an earlier age.

'There have been times during my career when I have looked around and thought, "Is it worth bothering about?" But now I feel genuine optimism. Richie Richardson has been a great help. He is a tremendous bloke, unassuming, knowledgeable. It was Richie who encouraged Darren Gough to bowl quick. It has transformed Goughie from a talented but wayward cricketer to a Test bowler of genuine pace.

'It means something when the captain of the West Indies says he thinks you can bowl quick. The biggest compliment I can pay Richie is that he has fitted into our side like a Yorkshireman,' Moxon said.

At 34, and proud of his brood, Martyn Moxon has time yet in which to fulfil one or two ambitions, complete some unfinished business. On a personal level he would like to score the 7,000 runs he needs to be included in the top 10 Yorkshire batsmen of all time. He would then be in the company of Sutcliffe and Hutton, Boycott and Hampshire, Hirst and Rhodes. That would be something. Then he wants to captain Yorkshire to the County Championship. That would be something else again.

18th June 1994

·19·

ELLERY

HANLEY

—

WHEN I told people I was going to interview Ellery Hanley, they looked at me as if I had a screw loose. They wanted to know how much we had paid him. Not a cent, I said, and they shook their heads in disbelief. When I called acquaintances of Hanley for quotes about this Garboesque sportsman, I was met by an *omerta*, which any Mafia godfather would have envied. People tread warily around Ellery Hanley. The road to his door is strewn with eggshells.

What they will say — and all agree — is that Hanley is almost certainly the most complete rugby league player the game has seen. Maurice Lindsay, the chief executive of the Rugby League and Hanley's old boss during the halcyon years at Wigan, has no doubt. 'At his peak he was the greatest player I ever saw in 40 years of watching rugby. At the age of 33, he's still not far short of that standard,' he said.

Steve 'Blocker' Roach, the Australian forward who would rather die under torture than be complimentary about a Pom, is on record as saying that Hanley is the best. Cliff Morgan, who is as shrewd a judge of rugby as ever drew breath, says that Hanley is the rugby player *in excelcis*.

Up until now, Hanley's contribution to his own reputation has not been forthcoming. He has kept silent. He has become the most famous name in his sport; he has acquired legendary status without once bothering to give the time of day to journalists.

He took an early jolt when newspapers appeared more interested in the fact that he had been in trouble with the law as a teenager than in his potential as a rugby player. He took the view that he had paid his dues. End of story. The tabloid press in particular had him in their sights and, in a running battle that has lasted all of his long career, he claims there have been many times when the line he draws between his public and private life has been breached.

He became determined early on to maintain a polite but icy attitude towards reporters, no matter what the subject might be. One journalist told me that, when he called Hanley to ask him how he felt after he had been to the Palace to collect his OBE, Hanley said: 'No comment.'

On the other hand, it is to his eternal credit that he has not followed the example of other public figures who criticized the media and then sold their stories to the very organizations they had condemned. He might be stubborn, but he is not a hypocrite. Nor, in spite of regular temptation from talk of large advances, has he yet written his life story. After 16 years in the game, a superstar like Hanley would reckon on having at least three autobiographies behind him.

Little wonder, then, that as you set out to interview Hanley, people give you the sort of look that Captain Oates encountered when he announced he was going for a walk. It is my experience that people with a reputation for being either impossible or difficult to interview do little to deny that reputation once you meet them.

I was told all I had to do to interview Frank Sinatra was meet him at his hotel and have a drink or two. Mr Sinatra knew all about me and just wanted to say 'hi'. Our mutual friend introduced us. 'This is Mike,' he said. 'Hi Steve,' said Frank. As we were leaving, our friend said: 'Frank, Mike's leaving.' 'Goodbye Dave,' said Frank without turning round. Goodbye Frank and farewell.

John Lennon said he would only answer questions about the Beatles if I climbed into the sack. I did. Anything for a quote. Peter Sellers said he would do a television interview with me if I spent a week having lunch with him. He called the day before the interview and said he couldn't do it. I asked why. 'Because I can't walk on the set looking like myself,' he said. 'Then walk on in disguise,' I said in desperation. He did the interview dressed as a German stormtrooper.

I digress only to demonstrate that when I approached Mr Hanley, I was prepared for the worst. I imagined the interview taking place at dead of night away from the prying eyes of the tabloids. I thought Mr Hanley might follow the example of Sellers and turn up disguised as a U-boat commander. Instead, he suggested that we meet in the lounge of a Manchester hotel. He arrived early. When we met, he offered me an aniseed ball.

He was dressed in a high-collared Nehru jacket and white sweatshirt. He ordered a lemonade and orange juice. He doesn't drink or smoke. He looks as fit as a proverbial butcher's dog, but in that lithe and unconcerned way that separates the natural athlete from the muscle-bound steroid-designed imposter. What you are not prepared for face to face – having only seen him on the field of play where he is as awesome as a fighting bull – is the soft, polite voice, the fine-boned features, the absence of battle scars. As far as I could tell, he owns a complete set of his own teeth, his ears are small and perfectly formed and the instruments of his famed hand-off appear too manicured for their reputation as the most jolting rebuff in the game.

You would have a hard time convincing a Martian that this was one of the most rugged practitioners of the toughest team game yet invented on Planet Earth (please, no letters from fans of American football – if the players removed their helmets and the body armour, they might warrant comparison, but not until).

Today Hanley will take Leeds out at Wembley to play Wigan in the final for the Silk Cut Challenge Cup. The rumours about him being unfit to play are likely to be found to be greatly exaggerated. He is not renowned for letting injury interfere with his ambition never to finish on the losing side in a Wembley final. He has been four times before with Wigan and on each occasion enhanced his reputation as the greatest player in the best club side in the world. He started the interview by announcing that today's game might be his last: 'I'm thinking of retiring. I don't want to play for anyone else; I've achieved all my ambitions in the game. It's getting harder. Players are fitter, stronger. I'm not saying I'm slowing down but perhaps the reflexes aren't the same. That's when you get the injuries. Even now, at the end of the season, I can feel injuries I picked up a year ago. What might it be like in five years' time? Wake up on a morning and find you've got arthritis or whatever. So it's time to call it a day. It could be that, in a year's time, I wish I'd given it one more season but I have got the rest of my life to think about now,' he said.

There are those of a cynical disposition who see Hanley's statement as being no more than a tactical threat during on-going contractual negotiations with his club. Maurice Lindsay, however, believes Hanley is serious, and rightly so. 'It would be a good time for him to go. He's still at the top. Athletes like Hanley are rare. They are more than great players. He was born with a rare spirit, a will. He's been as important to rugby league as Bradman to cricket or Ali to boxing. He was surrounded by great players when he was at Wigan in the Eighties, but he was special. He was the indispensable player,' he said.

When asked how he felt about being described as the world's best rugby player, Hanley thought for a minute and, without the slightest affectation, said: 'I wouldn't go as far as that. It's flattering, but I don't believe there are "greatest players". I think there are great teams and they're about a collection of good players blending together.

'Wigan was the launching pad of my career. I owe everything to the club and Maurice Lindsay. It was a privilege to play in that team. People talked about "the Wigan factor". That's significant. Not "the Hanley factor" or "the Gregory factor". It was about the team. You could feel the power in the crowd. When we walked out, we were six points ahead before we kicked off. If we scored, you could look in the eyes of the opposition and see they were resigned to defeat. They were saying to themselves: "This is what's supposed to happen. We're not expected to win, not here we're not." That is what a great team is about.'

So, how will the youngsters of Leeds cope with the psychological pressure of playing Wigan? 'I don't like talking about games that are in the future. Who knows what might happen? All you can say is that it will be special. What you have to understand as a player is that it's not sufficient just to have reached Wembley. The job finishes when you've won. I'm not superstitious, I don't have any special ritual. I just aim to be ready to go 10 minutes before kick-off. I aim to be as prepared as I always am, whether it be a Cup final or a nothing game against a Second Division side.

'I approach every game in the same way. I've never been nervous. I've always had this confidence in myself from being an amateur. I want to be best, to win, whether it be badminton, chess or rugby. I've always been prepared to put in that extra bit to win, that extra session of training, running that extra yard, playing through pain. If I'm injured during a game, I never let my opponents know; I don't even tell my team-mates. I've always been like that.'

He was brought up in a tough area of Leeds. His parents were from St Kitts and have since returned to the Caribbean. His mother will be at Wembley today. He was, he says, 'enveloped in sport' from the earliest days. He learned it on the streets. He didn't have heroes, just a certain knowledge that one day he would be the best at one sport or another. His reputation as a combative soccer player led to offers from League clubs. He became a rugby league player because Bradford Northern proposed the better deal. When he joined the club, he had never seen a game of rugby league, had little knowledge of the history of the game, knew no heroes. Even today, when you ask him about other sportsmen he might put on a pedestal, he ponders a while and shakes his head. Then he says: 'Do you know who I really admire?' Go on, you say, awaiting the revelation. 'Doctors,' he says, without elaborating.

In five years at Wigan the team won three championships, four Challenge Cups, four Regal Trophies, one Premiership and the World Challenge Trophy. This was Hanley at his most glorious. Put most simply, he was unstoppable, a unique combination of tireless skill and unremitting concentration. But, most of all, there was what Lindsay characterized as Hanley's 'will'. It was the outer casing on all his formidable gifts, the metal with which he could pierce the toughest armour. Does he have any idea what it is, where it comes from?

He shrugs. 'I don't know. I never liked losing. The only time I was stressed as a child was if I lost at a game,' he said. It was later, when I asked him about racism in the game, that he offered another clue. 'There was tons of racism about when I first came into the game. I used to get abused by players and spectators. It's still there but not like it used to be. I never get racial abuse from a player nowadays. Take it as a bit of a compliment really. Looking back, I think the abuse stood me in good stead. It made me stronger, even more determined to be a winner. It might seem a strange thing to say but I've no doubt it made me a better player.

'There are still isolated pockets of abuse on the terraces. I just feel sorry for them, for the way they've been brought up. I don't hate them. If I was in the street and someone abused me I would simply walk away.' He thought for a moment and smiled: 'It doesn't happen very often.'

So if this is to be his swansong, what next for Ellery Hanley? 'I fancy coaching. I've learned a lot from people like Doug Laughton, John Monie, Graham Lowe and other great coaches I've worked with. I think we still have a lot to learn from Australia, where they've been more advanced in coaching techniques and preparation,' he said. Lindsay has little doubt he would be a fine coach. 'He's the model pro. No one better to teach others. All they have to do is follow his example,' he said.

It might be that the only obstacle to Hanley's ambitions as a coach will be his attitude towards the media. Up until now, any journalist wanting to know what goes on inside his head would have been better off trying to interview the goalposts. He says that when he was a young player he tried co-operating with the press but found they always let him down. How? 'By writing about private things that had nothing to do with rugby. I have found photographers creeping around my garden. I'm a private person. Whoever we are in life, ordinary working man or royalty, there have to be some protected areas. I've got every nasty article ever written about me. One day soon I'm going to write the book, then people will understand the difficulties I've had. Then they'll be able to make up their own minds about Ellery Hanley.

'In the end, there's not that much of a mystery. All I ever wanted to do was play rugby, enjoy it and hope the spectators enjoyed watching me. Then, one day, they might remember. That way you are part of history, aren't you?'

Anyone who ever saw Hanley play will be quick to reassure him that he achieved his ambition long ago, that what he brought to the game will be remembered wherever and whenever people gather to talk about or watch rugby. As a teacher of the game it could be that he has yet more to offer. As a communicator with the media, he may find that the book will put paid to one or two rumours, settle some old scores and give both estranged parties the chance to start afresh.

It might be, of course, that Hanley keeps his guard up for some time yet. There are those who believe he has earned the right to be accepted on his own terms. Denis Betts, who played alongside him at Wigan, said. 'He's a great professional and he speaks for all professionals on the pitch. He doesn't need to say another word to anybody.' Hanley might well regard that as being the ultimate accolade.

30th April 1994

·20·

BERNARD GALLACHER

—

BERNARD GALLACHER reminds me of a Physical Training Instructor I met in the Army. This man made you feel scruffy just looking at him. Everything about him shone, from his burnished cap badge to his shiny black pumps. You could see your face in his pumps and I often did when he gave me 20 press-ups.

Bernard Gallacher is, I suspect, the sort of man who polishes the soles of his golf shoes, the soldier who looks forward to kit inspections. He is one of those fortunate and blessed individuals who never looks crumpled.

Last Monday, as captain of the European Ryder Cup team, he stood before the scrutiny of journalists and cameras and announced the names of the golfers who would face America. The only twitch in his composure came when he announced Haeggman as one of his wild card choices. As he did so he twiddled the papers in his hand. He didn't know what to expect. What he got was a round of applause and from that moment on he was never again in danger of breaking sweat.

Ninety minutes later he was still answering questions with patience and humour. An exemplary figurehead. That done he moved into the next room to present prizes to the members of Wentworth Golf Club who know him as their professional. It was a reminder to Bernard Gallacher that on the same day as the world's press hung on his every word he could still be given the golf shoes of a Wentworth member and asked to re-stud them. It would bring anyone down to earth, not that Bernard Gallacher is ever likely to lose touch with reality.

He was born 44 years ago in the mining community of Bathgate. The course where he learned to play golf near Edinburgh was situated between a railway line and a factory. His father and uncles were keen golfers and he was never in danger of becoming anything other than a golf pro. He turned professional at the age of 19 and immediately became Rookie of the Year. The next year he was the leading money-winner and from then until 1984 never fell below 30th on the money-list, seven times being placed ninth or better. He played his first Ryder Cup in 1969 and thereafter was a member of eight consecutive teams. In that time he played 31 games, won 13, lost 13 and halved five. In 1976 he became the club professional at Wentworth. He is about to sign another five-year contract. We talked in the garden of his home near Wentworth. I asked him if there was ever a problem re-adjusting from being captain of the Ryder Cup team to club professional.

'But what I am is a club professional. That's what I started out to be. I'm proud of the fact. Even when I was playing the circuit full-time I always regarded myself as the pro at Wentworth. I never had a sponsor, just the club behind me. It's a good relationship. They can cope with me being Ryder Cup captain. One member rang Lesley, my wife, and said: "Tell Bernard he ought to pick Canizares, he's playing really well."

'Whatever success I had on the tour was due to the great support I've always had from the club and the members. The tour was much different in the Seventies from now. In those days they simply told you there was a game in Germany or France and you made your own way there.

'My education was travelling around Europe with a suitcase and a golf bag when sometimes even the local taxi driver didn't know where the golf course was. It made you self-sufficient, durable.

'Nowadays the players have travel agents, sleep at first-class hotels, one or two have private planes and helicopters. They travel the world but see nothing. Very different. Another difference is you can get rich very quickly. You can also get finished very quickly, too. As I see it, the people at the top in golf are going to have much shorter careers and there are going to be many more casualties at the bottom,' he said.

He points out that there is possibly only Sam Torrance of the current players on the European Tour who shares his memory of what it was like before the gravy train arrived. It gives Gallacher a clear view of the way modern golf is going and the threat to its treasured traditions.

In his book about the last Ryder Cup at Kiawah Island, Gallacher contrasts the start of the competition with what it has become. When Samuel Ryder and Walter Hagen took tea at Wentworth in 1926 to discuss the possibility of British and American professionals playing against each other on a two-yearly basis they could never have imagined that their idea of a friendly get-together would grow into the multi-million dollar monster it is today.

Nor would they have approved of the shenanigans at Kiawah, when in the aftermath of the Gulf War the American team wore military-style forage caps much favoured by Stormin' Norman, and one message of encouragement to the Americans exhorted them to 'kick butt'. It was a strange baptism for a purist like Gallacher.

He knew something was fundamentally amiss when, at the official dinner welcoming the two teams, the chief executive of the American PGA said grace and took the opportunity at the same time to pray aloud for an American win.

Gallacher said: 'Dave Stockton [the American captain] upped the temperature. He did so because he thought our supporters were more supportive and vociferous than theirs. I found the military forage caps distasteful, as I did Azinger's statement that they had beaten the Iraqis and were about to do the same to the Europeans.

'When I met Dan Quayle, the Vice President, I told him this had nothing to do with golf and it was an insult to the Europeans who had fought and died in the Gulf. It affected their spectators. I've never heard golfers being chanted on to the greens before.

'Then I got a phone call from a local disc jockey in the early hours of the morning. He said it was a "wake up the enemy" call. Nick got one, so did one or two of the other players.

'I was proud of our team, they didn't respond. I was proud of myself, I said nothing. But I don't think there will be a repeat this time. Tom Watson stood on the sidelines at Kiawah and saw what was going on and I don't think he approved of what he saw.

'What I want our spectators to do is behave exactly as they do at a British Open. I don't want barracking on the greens or people making a noise on a player's backswing.

'So far golf has been free from the kind of crowd behaviour we get at soccer – and sometimes cricket – matches. I hope it continues to set the example because if it doesn't that will be the end of the Ryder Cup and that would be a great pity,' said Gallacher.

Is he confident in his team? 'Very, I never had any doubt about picking Seve. I'm afraid he's going to be under added pressure now to play well but he carries that sort of pressure with him. He's never let alone and maybe that's a reason why he's finding it difficult to regain form,' he said.

Might it be that Ballesteros will never be the same player again? Put most cruelly, is he past it? 'I don't think so. After all, he's only 36. He turned pro when he was 16.

'I suppose something has got to give, even in a genius like Seve, but I think that under certain circumstances he will still win majors. He has got to work things out for himself. The trouble is he's offered advice from all quarters. There's such an overwhelming desire for him to come good.

'But in all the speculation about Seve let me tell you that he's still the one the Americans fear, the one they most want to beat. He was the first European to start winning in the States. He would play in Europe, nip over to America and win a big one, come back home, play some more then nip off again to America and win again. They didn't like it. But he broke the mould, showed the others it could be done. If Nick, Langer, Woosie and Sandy owe anybody anything, they owe something to Seve. He was the one who showed them the way in America.

'Although we lost in Kiawah I was very heartened by what happened there. The last hour of play revealed a lot about the quality of my team. When Langer missed that putt it didn't really matter because we had done our best and that was the important thing.

'What I said at the time was that I didn't think that in future any player, either European or American, should have the awful responsibility of a putt on the last green to decide the match. It should be settled before that.

'It was fortunate, in a sense, that it was Bernhard who had the putt. He's the strongest, most resilient of players. It could have destroyed a younger, less purposeful man, ruined his career. As it was, Bernhard went out at the very next tournament and won it. What a man. But I still wouldn't want anyone to face what he did again.'

But it could happen, so what would he suggest? He thought for a moment and said: 'If at The Belfry the Americans have a two-foot putt to tie on the last hole I hope I'd have the guts to walk on the green and give it to them.'

4th September 1993

RAY WILKINS

—

THERE IS a serene quality about Butch Wilkins. It's about being comfortable with yourself, not finding reasons to show off. Watching his play nowadays there is a mellow quality to his style. It is mature, well-tuned, relaxed, untroubled. If football needed an ideal image with which to promote the game it would have to invent something like Butch Wilkins.

He is stylish both on and off the field, knowledgeable about the game without being assertive, self-effacing; a star without the bulldust. He is the kind of modern professional the Football Association should be employing to promote the many virtues of the game while, at the same time, helping to disprove the growing theory that football is being run by a gang of halfwits.

Raymond Colin Wilkins cannot remember a time when he wanted to be anything other than a footballer. His dad had played for Nottingham Forest, Leeds and Brentford. The son joined Chelsea as a schoolboy in 1970, made his League debut in 1973 and since then has played with Manchester United, AC Milan, Paris St Germain, Glasgow Rangers and, now, Queens Park Rangers. Along the way he has won 84 England caps and a deserved reputation as one of the finest players English football has produced in the post-war years.

Today, as he steps out at Loftus Road against Sheffield Wednesday, he will be starting his twenty-first year as a top-class professional footballer. As he says, in his quiet way: 'Things have worked out very nicely.'

The remarkable part of the longevity of Butch Wilkins is that the older he plays, the better he gets. There are those who would claim that at the age of 37 he is playing the best football of his career. He would agree with them.

'I find that playing football gets better as I get older. When you are young you bomb around for 90 minutes at 100 mph hoping things are right. At my age you take it easier, dictate the pace, use technique and experience as well as blood and guts.

'I'm old enough to be the father of some of the kids in our team. They give me stick about being old, about the hairline [he is follicly disadvantaged], but it keeps me young. So does playing at the top level. I never allow myself to take for granted the fact I'm still playing football. I never want to be picked just on reputation alone.

'When I joined Glasgow Rangers from Paris St Germain I couldn't believe the pace of Scottish football. We think the English game is quick but it's nothing compared to the way they play in Scotland. My first game they were whizzing past me. I also discovered they love a shoulder charge and a tough tackle. I thought, "I'm going to be a bit too flimsy for this lot." But I went in the gym, worked with the weights, got stronger and fitter and after a month I was ready to take my place. It took some doing but what drove me was I wanted to show that I was still a top-class professional footballer.

'I think a lot of what's wrong with modern football could be changed for the better if players took more responsibility for their own careers. Nowadays a player gets dropped and he wants a transfer. Don't understand it. It's as if they have a divine right to play. Just walk away from the problem. It's too easy.

'Generally speaking, players don't analyse themselves and their game enough. That's why we lack the technique of foreign players. It's a matter of pride. An individual knows what's wrong with his game, knows what's required to put it right. He shouldn't need telling to go and improve his weak foot or make his first touch better. To be the best you have to work at it.

'When I was at Chelsea I'd go out with John Hollins after training and we'd hit 50 balls at each other using both feet, outside of the foot, curving, chipping, lobbing them. When I was at AC Milan we spent 20 minutes every day juggling with the ball as part of our exercise. We had to keep it in the air all that time. It gave you a wonderful feel for the ball and marvellous close control.

'When people say: "It's all very well talking about the Italians, but they have a lot more time in Italy," they miss the point. The fact is the Italians make more time because their first touch is so good. There are signs things are improving in our soccer but there's still a long way to go.'

He loved Italy. He had three years at Milan and cried when he left. He knew he had arrived where he wanted to be, when, after his first game of Italian soccer Nils Liedholm, the coach of AC Milan, told him he was doing too much running around. 'That is not the way we play football,' he was told.

'This was a total change in philosophy. I'd been told in England that I didn't put myself about enough. At Milan they were telling me to slow down and think about it.

'They savour their football in Italy. Every game is an event. We had Easter off, a Christmas and New Year break. Here we had a schedule of four games in seven days. Players take the field with injuries, they're tired. It costs a lot of money to watch football nowadays. I sometimes wonder if we are delivering the goods. The whole life in Italy was magnificent. You were put on a pedestal and they kept you there.

'I went to a teacher to learn the language. I was learning all the tourist phrases like: "Can you tell me where the bus station is?" I wanted a more conversational style so I asked my team-mates to teach me. One day I was in a restaurant, eager to show off my skills, and I asked our goal-keeper what the Italian for a toothpick was. He gave me a word and I shouted across to the waitress. She looked stunned and the place shook with laughter. What I had said was: "Waitress, I require a prick." '

He was happy at Milan. So much so that he couldn't bear the thought of playing with another Italian club so he went to France and Paris St Germain. Then he moved to Glasgow for an enjoyable time under Graeme Souness before moving back to where it had all started, in London. He says: 'Playing with me is like a bug, an illness. I don't know when I'll be cured. It's all about how long I can keep playing in the Premiership. I still get the same buzz about playing. I'm not jaded or cynical. I still think that being a professional footballer is a magnificent life. I'm frightened of going too soon, scared that it might eat away inside me.

'For me the saddest happening of sport was the retirement of David Gower. Jesus wept, why? He is still a great player, a unique entertainer. I compare him to George Best. That same extraordinary talent. And he wants to pack it in. I don't understand it.'

His contract with QPR lasts until the end of the season. Then what? 'Don't really know. When I do eventually stop playing I would love the chance of managing a club. I'd jump at it, but I wouldn't let it kill me. Sadly, part of the problem in finding the new England manager is that some of the candidates are saying it's not worth the price you pay in terms of your private and family life.

'I haven't been approached for the job but I'm flattered that I've been mentioned in the media as someone being considered. My choice would be Terry Venables. He fits the bill. His teams play the right way. Gerry Francis would do a good job. Personally, I hope he stays at QPR. I'd love to win something with him and the rest of the lads.'

Butch Wilkins excused himself in order to get a couple of hours' kip before playing a floodlit game that evening. I asked him if he had difficulty getting to sleep with a game imminent.

'Strange thing is, if I'm not playing a game I can't sleep at all in the afternoon. Too restless. If I am playing I sleep like a baby.' Why? I asked. 'Because if I'm going to be playing football later on then I know I'll wake up happy.'

1st January 1994

·22·

TONY GREIG

—

TONY GREIG is a purposeful man. When he strides across a room for an appointment you half expect him to break into a run and bowl a bouncer. The thatch of blond hair has been harvested by time – in other words he is a bit thin on top – but the rest is as it was. He has not shrunk any, he is still 6ft 7in, broad-shouldered and athletic. A big man, and I would guess that not many have volunteered to throw a punch at him. I only mention this because many people would dearly love to take a swing at Tony Greig. When I told a friend of mine who I was going to interview, he said: 'Talking to traitors now.'

When, as captain of England, he threw his hand in with Kerry Packer and World Series cricket, he was denounced and reviled. The fans forgive and forget and nowadays he is given a cordial reception whenever he visits England. The establishment take longer to heal their wounds.

There are some at Lord's who cold-shoulder him; he is still waiting for news that he has been given honorary membership of the MCC like every other captain of England before and after him. He is not holding his breath.

Attempting to explain what he saw as Greig's disloyalty by signing with Packer, the cricket correspondent of *The Times* wrote in 1977: 'What has to be remembered, of course, is that he is an Englishman not by birth or upbringing, but only by adoption. It is not the same thing as being English through and through.'

What, I wonder, would the writer say about the English 'through and through' cricketers who went on rebel tours to South Africa and included in their numbers one or two captains of England? When put to the test, their loyalty depended not upon birthright but the lure of the krugerrand. Similarly, Greig, and others, were bought by the Aussie dollar.

What was never in doubt was Greig's determination on the field of play to make England the best cricket team in the world. He did not succeed but what he did do was hand over to Michael Brearley a much better team than the one he inherited from Mike Denness.

In 1977 Brearley's team won the Ashes. *The Times* wrote a leader in celebration of the event and gave Greig the credit. It said: 'He took over a side being compared with the very worst in England's cricketing history, made its members believe in their individual and collective abilities, and by his own flamboyant, perhaps over-aggressive example, instilled confidence into a team that had become accustomed to losing.'

In other words, just the kind of chap we want right now to rejuvenate our cricket team. In any shortlist of candidates approved by the TCCB, Greig's application to be our next chairman of selectors would be slightly ahead of Pol Pot and only just behind Geoffrey Boycott. Not that he is inclined to apply.

At present he works for Kerry Packer's 9 Television Network as the sales director for satellite television. Packer looks after his own. He also fronts up the Channel 9 television presentation of cricket and very good he is at it too, being knowledgeable, provocative and outspoken.

Nor does he allow his audience in Australia to forget that he was once captain of England and on our side in any Ashes encounter. Such loyalty has left him a forlorn figure during this season's débâcle.

'A nightmare' is how he describes it. 'For the first time this year I gave up. I never threw the towel in when I was playing but watching England over the past few months has left me speechless. Worst of all, my fellow commentators are feeling sorry for me. They've stopped having a go at me for supporting England because they've seen how hopeless the situation is. Fifteen years of creating a commentating style undermined by a single series.'

He shakes his head in sorrow. 'When I took over the captaincy we were struggling, Lillee and Thomson were knocking us over. I wanted someone to stick there, someone with guts and a good technique. I spoke to the old pros on the county circuit, people like Bob Cottam, and asked them who was the person they found most difficult to get out. They all said David Steele.

'I went to the selectors and said I wanted Steele in my side. They thought I'd gone bloody mad. But we picked him and he did the job for us,' he said.

Steele, for 12 seasons an ordinary county pro, found himself nominated as one of *Wisden*'s five cricketers of the year. He became a national hero. The next season Tony Greig made his famous prediction that his team would make the visiting West Indians 'grovel'. Roberts, Holding and Daniel took up the challenge in such a manner as to question the resolve of all but the stoutest hearts.

'We were playing on a road at Old Trafford and I wanted a couple of tough old bastards to go out there and face up to the quicks,' said Greig. He persuaded the selectors to recall Close and Edrich. In England's second innings they were battered by a sustained assault of fast, short-pitched bowling which Close, in typical fashion, chose to play with his chest.

It was glorious but it was futile. England lost. Close and Edrich were dropped for the next Test. 'The point I'm making is that Alec Bedser, who was then the chairman of selectors, would accommodate me if I felt strongly about picking a player. But more than that I was the person who talked to the press. Not the chairman of selectors, but the team manager. So in that respect I was accountable.

'The first thing Michael Atherton should do is insist on being the only person in the England set-up to speak to the press. The captain should give a press conference every night after play no matter what the situation. If he feels uncomfortable with it then find someone to appear who isn't. You have to establish a proper relationship with the media.

'I once kicked out a senior England player who came to one press conference in his new career as a journalist. He was drunk. I told him: "I'm sober and am here to talk sensibly to you. You're drunk. I suggest you leave and come back when you're capable of doing your job." He left and wrote me an apology.

'Alec Bedser wrote a piece the other day pointing out that he was the only chairman of selectors for the past 38 years who didn't go to Cambridge University. It was a fair point.

'Who are these people running England's cricket? At least when Gubby Allen was at Lord's you knew where you were, but who's in charge now, who's pulling the strings: A C Smith, Wheatley, Doug Insole? What the chairmen of the counties should demand is that people are made accountable for their actions. Who, for instance, was in favour of giving Fletcher a five-year contract?

'If M J K Smith gets Dexter's job, who are the people promoting him? So often it seems that the counties are merely rubber-stamping decisions taken by some TCCB committee.

'I'm worried about the idea of a supremo. If we went that way Boycott would be the ideal man. He knows so much about the game and he's developed into a first-class communicator.'

Greig favours three or four selectors: 'Boycott, Brearley, Illingworth, Fletcher even. Then I'd appoint a coach, but this would be the captain's choice. If Atherton wanted Boycott then Geoff would have the job so long as Atherton was captain.

'But in the end we have to look at what's wrong, at the foundations of English cricket. What World Series cricket did for Australian cricket was to show how strong commercial influences could work to the benefit of the game and the players. The best players, the Test cricketers, have benefited the most.

'The message to the rest of the players is clear: either graduate to Test cricket standard or make way for someone else who might. English cricketers ought to be put to the same examination.

'You've got to make the game more exciting, more glamorous. In Australia we did this through the one-day, day-night games. To the purists who denounce it as being tacky I would only say it's like eating hamburgers and then graduating to dining in French restaurants. In other words, the one-day leads a new audience to Test cricket.

'I'd get rid of all the present one-day competitions in England. If the Sunday League survived I would like to see the TCCB issue a directive saying that each county side must contain four or five players chosen from local clubs.

'This would give the chance to the good club player to test himself at a higher level. I'd also have a 15-match one-day triangular tournament, like we have in Australia,' he said.

'I think there is a real crisis in English cricket. Things won't change until we target and eliminate the people responsible for the current state of affairs. They have created a bloody almighty mess. The trouble is the real villains don't show their heads. Until they are identified and made accountable for their actions things won't change for the better.'

What are the chances of radical change, I asked?

'About the same chance we have of flying to the moon,' said Tony Greig.

21st August 1993

·23·

DAVID LEADBETTER

—

DAVID LEADBETTER has a demanding kind of fame. When people recognize him, they request something more than an autograph. They ask him to spend a moment or two watching their golf swing so they might become better players.

'It happens all the time,' he says. 'Airports are particular traps. I'm running for a plane and someone says: "Hey, Dave, good to see ya. Spare a minute to check over my swing?" And, right there and then, they take an imaginary club and hit a drive down the departure hall.'

This happens to David Leadbetter wherever he goes in the world. He is the most famous golf coach on the planet, the only one as famous as his clients. He may not earn their money but who does? In any event, he isn't grumbling. His videos are best-sellers, so are his books. He has David Leadbetter golf academies in America, Malaysia and Europe and he has just opened a new one at Chart Hills, in Biddenden, Kent. He employs 30 teachers throughout the world. He works with 20 professional golfers on the American circuit and 12 in Europe. The most famous clients are Nick Price and Nick Faldo.

His promotional material refers to him as 'The King of Swing', which is a bit of a cheek if you happen to be a fan of Benny Goodman. Anyone old enough to understand the last observation will also know what I mean when I say that David Leadbetter looks like Cardew 'The Cad' Robinson. He is a tall, angular man; everything about him is lean and knobbly. When he talks, he is forever exercising his fingers. They look as if they might be double-jointed.

He says 'Hey' a lot, as in: 'I thought about playing in Europe but, hey, America is where the action is', or: 'Something inside of me said, hey, that's the wrong choice.' He is friendly and approachable, which is why people stop him in the street and ask him to make them better golfers.

'People think you're a miracle worker. Touch them, lay on the hands and behold, they have a golf swing. You give them a quick fix, they go out on the course and hit one good shot and think they've cracked it. The fact is, the average amateur doesn't realize how hard the pro works,' he says.

In his book *The Golf Swing*, which, if you were so inclined, you could read in eight languages, Leadbetter explains why the seemingly simple proposition of hitting a stationary ball is so complicated.

'With a hitting surface on the clubface of 2.5 inches, you have to strike a ball only 1.68 inches in diameter. The 14.25-ounce club, which builds up a dynamic pulling weight of approximately 100lbs during your 1.5-second motion, has to be swung at a speed of approaching 90 mph through an arc of approximately 18 feet.

'The ball is on the surface for just 0.00035 of a second and, to be hit the desired distance in the right direction, has to be launched at an angle of 42 degrees.' This does not take into account wind, rain or the fact that your ball is lying in a divot and you are suffering from a hangover.

The men whose job it is to unravel the mysteries of hitting a golf ball in the direction you desire are the gurus of sport. There is no other game where so many rely on so few, where – in extreme cases – the golf teacher takes on the mystical qualities of a witch-doctor or a faith-healer.

There is no other game where an industry as sophisticated as that which put men on the moon has been created to put pimples on golf balls, grooves on club heads, broom handles on putters and much else besides to allow the amateur golfer his vain pursuit of perfection.

But technology is not enough. 'It's amazing that, given the improved equipment people play with and the better conditions of golf courses, the general standard of play remains what it was, say 25 years ago,' said Leadbetter.

Why? 'The reason there are a lot of duffers out there is that most people don't understand the golf swing. Most people swing as if they are digging for worms. They don't bother to learn the rudiments of the game. Most people think if they play once a week and have a lesson now and again that will make them into a good player. It won't,' he said.

In Florida, where he lives, he advertised in his local paper for golfers to take part in an experiment. They ranged from single-figure players to one or two with 36 handicaps. He put them through routines of fitness training, coaching and sessions with a sports psychologist. All improved but the high handicappers the most dramatically. One man whose best score had been 105 was breaking 90 on a regular basis. I asked him what this proved.

'That everyone can get better with the proper coaching,' he said. But perhaps not everyone has the ambition to improve? Perhaps most of us enjoy being duffers?

Mr Leadbetter gave me an old-fashioned look: 'I think that nowadays golf is much more than a game. It's a lifestyle. It means so much to people, so why not play it as well as you can? If you learn the rudiments of the game then you're going to enjoy it more and if you enjoy your golf then perhaps you might enjoy everything more. A happy golfer is a happy person,' he said.

He grew up in Rhodesia with Mark McNulty and Nick Price. He played the pro circuit for a while but Price recalls that he was always to be found with his nose in a golf instruction book, learning about the game. When Leadbetter turned to full-time teaching, Price was his first star client. Faldo followed and his reputation was consolidated. Price says Leadbetter's greatest gift as a teacher is in spotting quickly what is wrong and then making the player understand why he has a problem.

I watched him working with Peter Baker. He picked up the fault immediately and gave him one thought to work on. Instantly, the player began to hit the ball differently. 'When I first started teaching, I gave too much information. It was like giving a prescription and telling them to take all the pills at once. Nowadays, when I coach I feed the knowledge intravenously, a little at a time,' he said.

He is imaginative in his use of teaching aids. According to Faldo, when Leadbetter was remodelling his swing, they used rubber bands, medicine balls, water wings, towels and fishing rods to achieve what Leadbetter calls 'feeling'. 'If anyone saw what we got up to, they would say we were off our rockers,' said Faldo.

David Leadbetter's critics – and they are plentiful, as you might imagine with someone as successful as he is – claim that not only are his methods crazy, but they have created a generation of golfers who are thoroughly confused by an over-application of perplexing technique.

I once composed a humorous article about Leadbetter's teaching methods and four or five teaching professionals wrote serious letters to me making the point that his teaching was more confusing than funny. One said he was delighted that Leadbetter's disciples taught the way they did because it meant more work for him sorting out deranged golfers.

'I have never said there's only one way to teach. All I know about teaching is that individual people have their own particular needs. Critics don't bother me. I didn't set out to be high profile but, because of my association with the two Nicks, I started getting publicity. I think it has enabled people to see golf teachers in a better light. It has been good for teachers as a whole. I think people say, hey, if Nick Price and Nick Faldo can work at the game, then so can I,' he said.

I asked him if he had ever looked at a golfer and given up. If he said 'No' I was thinking of showing him my swing. He said that some golfers could suffer such a lack of confidence that they were beyond teaching. Not never, but the process could not start until they sorted themselves out.

He thought Ian Baker-Finch was going through such a crisis. 'All you can do is feel sorry and hope it doesn't last too long,' he said.

I asked him who were the best people to work with, apart from the pros. He said that Geoffrey Boycott was a model pupil. Now this was interesting. Only a few days before I interviewed Leadbetter, I had watched Mr Boycott win a two-day tournament on the West Course at Wentworth. Playing off a handicap of 11, Boycott dropped eight shots in two rounds of golf. His caddie said he had seen pros play worse.

Mr Kenny Lynch, one of his playing partners on the last day, while admiring Boycott's play, was not happy with his meticulous and painstaking progress around the golf course. When interviewed at the end of his round, Mr Lynch said that he imagined it would have been more fun playing with the National Front.

However, Mr Leadbetter has nothing but praise for his pupil. 'Boycott's mental attitude is exemplary. He understands the fundamentals of the swing, he loves practising. He's a joy to teach. Had he taken up golf instead of cricket, there is little doubt he would have made a very fine professional player,' said David Leadbetter.

I thanked him for the information because I have a game of golf against Mr Boycott coming up and, if he thinks he is playing off 11 after what I have heard, then he can find another sucker.

When I first arrived to interview David Leadbetter, I came across Ken Schofield, chief executive of the European Tour. He asked me what I was doing and I said I was looking for David Leadbetter. Ken said: 'I hope you find him because, if you don't, about 40 per cent of our players will have nervous breakdowns.'

David Leadbetter is an important figure in the history of golf because he symbolizes the mystery that is at the heart of the game as well as representing the means by which we attempt to find a solution. His critics would argue that what he typifies is the period in the game when man learned how to play like a robot and flair and enjoyment were taken from golf.

Whatever the truth, David Leadbetter has the prospect of future fame and riches without a foreseeable horizon. I mean, if you can go on earning millions playing golf as long as Arnold Palmer, how much longer might you last teaching it? Hey.

24th September 1994

·24·

MARTIN
CROWE

—

MARTIN CROWE is the ad-man's idea of what a cricketer should look like. He is tall, broad-shouldered and handsome. He's intelligent with an easy smile. He has curly hair, blue eyes but I searched in vain for a dimple. Off the field he wears jeans and a faded blue shirt and manages to make the suits in the restaurant seem scruffy. On the field of play he has formidable presence. He looks like what he is, a great cricketer and a star. Yet there is a wistful quality about him, a slight sadness.

Why so? After all, this is the finest batsman his country has produced. He has scored nearly 5,000 runs in 67 Tests at an average of 47. If you asked the *cognoscenti* to pick a World XI to play Mars from the current crop of Test cricketers there is little doubt that Martin Crowe would be in the line-up. If the coming Test series between the sixth-worst international team in the world (New Zealand) against the seventh (England) is short on superstars it is not his fault.

In effect, of course, the fact that the teams languish in the doldrums makes for an inportant series with both having a lot to prove. Sir Richard Hadlee has said that New Zealand cricket will be fighting for its credibility on the international stage. England need a convincing performance against both the Kiwis and the South Africans to, as Brian Bolus put it, stop the bleeding.

It is obvious that New Zealand will rely greatly on their best and most experienced player, not simply for the runs he might score but also for his tactical knowledge and experience. That being the case, why did he give up the captaincy? A rueful smile: 'Good question. First of all I was injured. I damaged my right knee when I was a kid. I injured it last year on the tour of Australia and had to return to New Zealand. Really it needs reconstructing by surgery but that must be a last resort. I can't bowl on it, I'm all right standing at gully, but it doesn't affect my batting except when I'm running.

'We needed a captain who was certain to take part. I couldn't guarantee that so I didn't have a choice really. Then there were other things,' he said. Like what? 'Well, since Richard Hadlee's retirement I've dominated the cricket scene in terms of having a high-profile presence, endorsements, publicity and all that. Critics have tried to undermine my position.

'It's a difficult problem being famous in New Zealand. Only three million people. Everyone knows you. Everyone knows what the media says about you. I took a lot of stick. There was too much about what I was about and not what the team was doing. So I stood aside from the captaincy to give the team a breather from all that. I mean, if people start getting hung up about . . .' The words trailed away and he shook his head, sadly.

About what exactly? I asked. 'When I was 21 I had a manager. He was a homosexual. I was in the public eye, so I became a target. Rumours began about homosexuality. Nothing direct, just gossip and innuendo. It was crap so I just ignored it. Wasn't worth bothering about. Then in 1988 I had a back problem and became quite ill. I took homoeopathic medicines for eight months. One of the consequences was I lost weight and the medicines changed the colour and tone of my skin. That's when the rumours started about me having Aids.

'The tabloids would ring me up. I'd deny that I had Aids. They would accuse me of hiding the truth. Again nothing direct in what they wrote. But it was implied. "Mystery virus" and all that. Then the rumours started that my marriage was in trouble. In situations like that your whole persona is opened up for scrutiny. It caused problems for my wife and family. Fortunately we are close and solid but it was a time of huge stress. As I said, New Zealand is a small place. You can't hide. On the other hand, it is impossible for them not to be influenced by the rumours and the gossip. The tabloids are a dark element in that situation.

'I went to the South Island and walked for four days to get away from it. I just wanted to breathe. Then last year I went to the convenor of selectors and said I'd had enough. I said that what was happening to me was not good for the team. I asked him to sack me. He persuaded me to stay on. He said: "Ride it out." The next thing it's in the papers that I don't want the job and it all starts again. "Is he the right man for captain?" and all the rumours were revived to suggest that I was unfit for the job and should be sacked in any case. Just what I needed.

'So I was fed up. I called a press conference and I confronted the three journalists who I thought were most responsible for the rumours. I said to them, straight out: "Do you think I am homosexual?" They said they didn't. So then I asked them why they kept implying that I had Aids. I didn't get an answer but at least from that point the crap stopped. I did choose to be high-profile I suppose. But I don't want it any more,' he said.

That was the most poignant thing he said. In a situation where he and those around him should be revelling in his celebrity and the media and populace celebrating his excellence he shouldn't be made to feel defensive and cornered. The argument that you choose to be famous and are therefore fair game to have your dustbin searched or your life viewed through a telephoto lens is as spiteful as it is banal.

In Martin Crowe's case there was little he could do about being a first-class cricketer. His father was one, so was his older brother. As a child he grew up reading *Wisden*, compiling statistics of great players, immersing himself in the history and traditions of the game. He was scoring centuries at the age of 12. He had an instinct for cricket, a hunger for it that was vocational and had nothing to do with the need to be famous.

He made his first-class debut at 17 and played his first Test match two years later. At the age of 21 he joined Somerset and scored 2,600 runs, 1,870 of them first class. In 1987 he scored another six championship centuries for the county and made more than 4,000 runs in that calendar year. Then came the illness. He says that before becoming ill he wanted to be known as the best batsman in the world. Now he says his ambition is to be the best he can be after the illness.

'I've always been statistically motivated. I am a goal setter. I'd like to be regarded among the best players like Hammond, Boycott, Sobers, Richards, the blokes who have scored more than 20 Test centuries. I think that's the mark to aim for. I've scored 15 so far. Perhaps if I play another 15 Test matches, last for two or three years more, then I might get there.

'My favourite batsmen? I thought David Gower and Greg Chappell were perfect to watch. Viv was fearless, wasn't he? He would intimidate you with his presence, keep you waiting on the field before he made his entrance. Richard Hadlee was a very special cricketer. I've never had a bad thought about him. One of the things I am proudest of as a cricketer is that he never got me out in a first-class match and I had to survive a couple of green tops when he was playing for Notts. He still bowls at us in the nets. Perfect practice for a Test match because he bowls where great Test bowlers put it, probing away at your technique, demanding that you play properly in the V.

'Shane Warne is, without doubt, the best leg-spinner I have ever played against. I played a lot against Qadir but Warne is better if only for the fact that he bowls a better leg-break than Qadir. Never mind about variations. We are talking leg-spin here so let's pick the man who bowls the best ball of that variety. Of the quicks Michael Holding used to make my heart jump. An intelligent, lovely bowler and I had great satisfaction facing Derek Underwood with Alan Knott keeping wicket behind me. They were a class act,' he said.

From other sports he is a great admirer of Nick Faldo. 'I like the way he works at his game. He's a technical player. So am I. When he's not winning the critics suggest his head is too full of theory, that he should go back to being what he used to be. They forget that he only started winning the majors when he worked on his game, changed his technique. Same with me. I came to England in 1990 and decided I'd go back to basic instincts in batting. Longest innings I played lasted 90 minutes. I scored a great 59 at Trent Bridge. Useless. I had to sit down and admit that I am what I am, a technical player, someone who plays better if he thinks about and works on his game.

'It is a problem if you are constantly seeking to be better. It tends to cut you off, make you misunderstood. It can create a funny relationship with your team. Rather than sit in a bar and have a drink I would prefer to retire quietly and visualize my next performance. You are seen as a cheese and wine man rather than someone who has a pint and a pie with the lads. All I am trying to do is maximize my talent. If I perform well then my team will do better and perhaps it might help me back in New Zealand. All I want is to be respected as a professional cricketer,' he said.

You wouldn't think that Martin Crowe had anything to prove to the people of New Zealand. His reputation as a player is established world-wide, his personality and demeanour both on and off the field of play are a credit to himself and the country he represents. Yet the fact is he feels debased by gossip, defiled by innuendo. His story is a parable of our times, an indication of the price sometimes paid for daring to be talented, an example of what can happen when a public figure confronts the unacceptable face of tabloid journalism.

Martin Crowe isn't bitter about what happened to him. More bemused. He is also determined to fight back in the only way he knows how by performing like a sporting hero. It's a tough one. He is not 100 per cent fit, his team is young and inexperienced. He says: 'This tour is going to tell me one or two things.' Let us hope it is good news.

7th May 1994

·25·

GEORGE BEST

—

THERE IS still a buzz when he enters a restaurant, a frisson as he makes his way to his table. There will be those whose interest is largely to see if he can cross the room without falling down, but in the main there is a warmth of feeling for a man whose life has been an almost unparalleled mixture of triumph and disaster.

In the 30 years since he made his debut as a footballer George Best has played for glory in the European Cup final and for a few quid in a scruffy paddock to buy a drink or two. He has known what it is like to live like a millionaire and slop out in prison. He went to bed with a thousand beautiful girls and ended up so lonely he tried to kill himself. He was hailed as the first pop superstar of football, the Fifth Beatle, and became a pathetic drunk.

Whatever we make of George Best's life we have to admit that it certainly wasn't predictable and that while defending him as a soak was sometimes difficult, loving him as a friend never was.

The two most extraordinary aspects of George Best are that he came through his misadventures more or less intact and survived the assault on his personality caused by an excess of fame and booze to remain, essentially, the same modest, loveable rascal he ever was. He still drinks. Sometimes too much. But nowadays there seems a new purpose to his life, a desire to put his matters in order, an urge to go to work. He is planning a new tour with Rodney Marsh and Denis Law of a show where the three of them sit on stage and chat about life and times. Last year a similar show with Rodney Marsh played to 2,000 people at the Palladium.

As a speaker he is in demand all over the world and on Sky Television he is a knowledgeable commentator, his enthusiasm for the game undimmed, the antithesis of the jaded old pro. He has cleared his bankruptcy and says he is so busy he is turning down work.

A business associate told him the other day: 'Since you stopped drinking you've become a pain in the arse.' Best took this as a huge compliment while admitting that it wasn't altogether true since he still drinks. The difference, he reckons, is that the booze is not ruling his life and ruining it like it once did.

'A doctor friend once said to me that one day I'd wake up and either switch on life or switch it off. I think that's what I did. I was falling off the edge, getting deeper and deeper in the shit. If I'd gone on I'd have ended up without a penny, not working, back in prison,' he said.

The spell he had in Pentonville and Ford open prison – he served two months of a three-month sentence – was a severe jolt to the system. 'It gave me time to look at myself and see just how much I was screwing life up. I came out a much wiser man. It sounds silly to say it, but it might have been the best thing that happened to me,' he said.

Two other stabilizing elements in his life are his long-time girlfriend Mary Shatila, who has taken on the job of organizing his often chaotic business affairs, and the strengthening of a friendship with Denis Law and his family. Law the family man, Law the joker, Law, a man of great commonsense, has become an important factor in the rehabilitation of George Best.

'When we played together at United I admired Denis Law but I wasn't really friendly with him. I wasn't really friendly with any of the team. They were all a bit older than me. Nowadays we spend a lot of time with Denis. He cheers me up, he has this lovely infectious sense of humour,' he said.

He recently had the chance to trace the roots of their friendship when he returned to Manchester to make a video with Ryan Giggs. The result is a charming film which provokes comparisons not so much between Giggs and Best but between the United team of the 1960s and today.

George Best says: 'I saw that Bobby Charlton was asked to make a comparison between the two teams and he thought this present side just a bit better than ours. I disagree. Mr Ferguson's side is a good one and it's great coming back to Old Trafford now because there's a real buzz about the place. But I think we had the better side. I watched a recording of the European Cup final the other day and I had forgotten how well we knocked it about, how everyone got a kick, how little we just belted the ball down the middle.

'I think that week in, week out we played against great teams both here and in Europe and beat them. In 1967 when we won the League there were some special sides around like Arsenal, Spurs, Liverpool, Leeds. West Ham had three World Cup members in their team, the Everton midfield was Kendall, Harvey and Ball.

'I think the quality of defenders in the 1960s was better. They were certainly harder. They don't tackle nowadays. There was no one harder than Tommy Smith, Chopper Harris, Norman Hunter, Paul Reaney. Forwards could tackle too. What about Johnny Giles and Mike Summerbee? Best compliment the Boss ever paid me was when he said I was the best tackler in the United side. That's what I like about

Giggs. Doesn't like it when he loses the ball. Takes it as an insult. Wants it back.

'I think it's silly to make comparisons between Ryan and myself. It's unfair to call him the next George Best. He's the first Ryan Giggs. He is a marvellous player. I love watching him. There's room for improvement. He is very left-footed. If he works on the other peg I reckon he'll score another dozen goals a season. Sometimes the final ball lets him down. But he's a terrific player and a level-headed lad and he's not frightened of working hard to improve.

'It annoys me when people say to Ryan or myself, "Oh, it's all right for you very talented players, you don't have to work hard at the game." The fact is the best players work harder. That's why we are the best players. I went back every afternoon and trained by myself. I was naturally right-footed; I practised until I was a better player with my left foot. I was small and couldn't head the ball so I used to hang a ball from the roof on a piece of string and head it until my forehead was bruised.

'It's fascinating comparing the two teams. Schmeichel and Stepney. Nothing in them. Peter is probably the best keeper in the League, Alex kept for England when we had three or four of the best keepers in the world. Dunne and Brennan, Parker and Irwin? Again not much in it. Tony Dunne, a terrific full-back. Didn't score as many goals as Irwin, didn't pass the ball like he can. Brennan, of course, never gave the ball away. Mind you, he couldn't defend. Didn't know what a winger looked like. Parker? Good defender, not the greatest passer of the ball.

'Paul Ince is a fabulous player. Keeps them ticking over. We had Paddy Crerand who could get stuck in and was a marvellous passer of the ball. Like Ince, he was the man you didn't want missing from the team. Then there are the three great forwards: Giggs, Hughes and Cantona. We had me, Denis and Bobby. I don't want to sound big-headed but I think we just shaded it.

'I'm a great admirer of Cantona. When he came to United I was worried by his attitude. I thought he lacked commitment and that he was a lazy, great player. Not now I don't. He's got them all playing at United. I think if he had joined the club three seasons ago and been lifted then to the heights he's at now he would be recognized as the best player in the world.

'Apart from all else I love the way he won't go down in the box, the way he rides tackles and stays up when they're trying to kick his legs from under him. Shows his great balance. All the best players have wonderful balance. Eric has, so has Ryan.

'I hope Cantona decides to stay at United. He couldn't get the same buzz anywhere else. Going to Old Trafford nowadays is to be reminded what it was like in the 1960s when you just walked in the ground and knew you were with one of the great clubs of the world,' he said.

Those of us who were lucky enough to be there in the 1960s and who have followed United to the present day can only agree. I don't know who is right in the argument about which was the better team, although if pressed I would make the point that the deciding factor might have been George Best. Similarly, any comparison between Giggs and Best must take into account that while the young forward is magnificently gifted there are weaknesses in his game. Best, at his age, was the finished article.

Going back to Manchester, stirring ghosts, watching them materialize in old haunts was a strange and nostalgic journey for George Best. He would love to be part of the present-day set-up. 'I dream of Alex Ferguson picking me in his team, running out on to the pitch like I used to. Probably have to play sweeper nowadays. I look at the way Mr Ferguson has looked after Ryan, protected him against too much publicity and I wonder if it might have made a difference to me.

'I'm not criticizing Sir Matt. The problem was no one knew what was happening to me. It was the first time a soccer player had become a pop star. None of us knew what to do. Nowadays there's a lot of protection for people like Giggs if they want it. Ryan's a level-headed lad, more so than me. It's probably true that if they'd told me how to behave I would have done just the opposite,' he said.

While they were filming the video, Best took Giggs around the Manchester of his youth, the venues where he was the centre of the action.

There's a poignant sequence in the Brown Bull, a pub so vibrant 30 years ago that the only way to have a conversation was to stand in the street.

I remember once entering the establishment with George just as a trouble-maker was ejected by being thrown like a javelin, head first through the swing door. He landed in the middle of the road and caused a traffic jam. It was like the last days of Dodge City.

Nowadays it has quietened down a bit, so much so that George and Ryan sat in a corner with only the barman as company: a middle-aged man showing a tenderfoot the ways of his youth.

The young man seemed generally bemused by the experience. There is little danger that Ryan Giggs will ever jeopardize his career by developing the same affection for drinking establishments that George Best did. It is also highly likely that he will have the satisfaction of prolonging his career to the point where he will know how good he was.

The ultimate tragedy of George Best is that he left first-class football before all his great gifts came to their most spectacular bloom. Nonetheless it is doubtful if Giggs will blaze a trail across life like George did, if he will engage the same concern from admirers or stimulate their curiosity like the lad from Belfast.

Doing a question-and-answer session during a recent personal appearance George pointed to a middle-aged woman in the audience and said: 'What's your question, love?' She asked: 'I've often wondered, and perhaps you'll tell me, George, exactly how big is your willy?'

29th January 1994

·26·

KEITH MILLER

—

FATHER TIME has no heroes. If he had then Keith Miller wouldn't now be so bad on his pins. He uses a frame to perambulate around his house and a stick when he takes the odd walk. In recent years he has fought cancer, arthritis and a stroke. 'Bloody wreck really,' he says. Not him. There is strength in the handshake, laughter in the voice, and the tilt of the chin and the challenge in the blue eyes belong to a man who has reached 75 without ever taking a backward step. I first saw him in 1945 with the Australian Services team. He was tall, long-legged, broad-shouldered and incredibly handsome. When he batted he hit the ball with great power and classical style. He bowled like the wind and caught swallows in the field.

I was smitten. He was my hero. Fifty years on and nothing has changed. I still think he was the most glorious cricketer I ever saw. John Arlott summed it up when he said: 'If I had my choice of a player to win a match off the last ball, whether it required a catch, a six or a wicket, I would pick only one player: Keith Ross Miller.'

When I called him to arrange the visit, England had just lost in Brisbane. Shane Warne was the new hero of Australian cricket. 'We will talk about Mr Warne,' he said on the phone. When I arrived at his mellow and quiet house above Newport Beach in Nullaburra Road on Sydney's North Shore, he led me to his study which contains the only memorabilia he considers worthy of display. There is a photograph of the Australian Services team taking the field at Bramall Lane, Sheffield, just after the war. Miller, Hassett, Pepper, Carmody and Sismey, all young and smiling in the Yorkshire sunlight. Underneath is pinned the cover of a magazine showing the war hero Guy Gibson, VC, DSO, DFC, sitting in a field of red poppies.

Keith Miller was deeply affected by the Second World War. It changed him. It gave him an insight into human nature and a set of values that have lasted until the present time. The way he played his cricket in the immediate post-war years was as much a celebration of surviving the war as it was the product of an impulsive nature and a lifelong desire never to be bored either by a person or a game. Keith Miller embraced life passionately because he had seen the alternative.

As much as he loved cricket, he never believed it was anything more than a game. This philosophy made him the darling of the fans but also brought him into conflict with those for whom cricket was more a business than a pleasure.

Donald Bradman was one such. Miller remembers that his first Test match was at Brisbane against Hammond's side. Australia made a massive score and then it rained and, in those days of uncovered pitches, England were caught on a sticky wicket. Miller said: 'It was unplayable. I took seven wickets but Blind Joe could have taken 10. My old mate Bill Edrich was playing. He had a serious war and he survived and I thought: "He's my old Services mate. The last thing he wants after five years in the war is to be flattened by a cricket ball," so I eased up. Bradman came up to me and said: "Don't slow down, Keith. Bowl quicker." Do you know, that remark put me off Test cricket? Never felt the same way about it after that.'

He didn't do badly for someone not very interested in playing Tests. His record shows that in 55 matches he scored 2,958 runs at an average of about 37, and 170 wickets at 22.97. Like so many others, the war robbed him of his ripening years and there is no knowing what he might have achieved. On the other hand, to judge Miller, the cricketer, by looking at statistics is a bit like judging a writer by the number of books he has written. It misses the point. When the Centenary Tests between Australia and England took place an English newspaper conducted a poll asking people to nominate the cricketers they would most like to see in their dream team. Keith Miller came top by a long way. Bradman was second.

If there is anyone in modern cricket with Miller's star quality and commercial potential it is Shane Warne. They represent vastly different eras – Miller the Brylcreem Boy, Warne the Nike Kid – but they share a glamour and a talent to entertain which is both rare and priceless. Keith Miller was keen to talk about Warne. He had made little notes on yellow paper so he wouldn't forget what he had to tell me.

First up, he thought that Warne was the biggest spinner of a cricket ball he had ever seen. A great bowler. On the other hand he thought the Poms played him with too much reverence. He said: 'I was over in England last year having my portrait painted for Lord's and I was guest of honour at a dinner. I told them then that they had better start sending their batsmen to the Fred Astaire School of Dancing if they wanted to play Shane Warne. In other words, use their bloody feet. You could see what I meant at Brisbane. The Englishmen played him from the crease, he dominated them and will continue to do so unless they attack him.

'When I first saw Warne bowl he took one for 160 against the West Indies. But I was impressed by his accuracy and the fact that he tried to spin the ball. I called Tiger O'Reilly and asked him what he thought. He agreed. Tiger had been praying for years for a greater spin bowler to emerge. I imagine that today he is looking down on us and saying "halleluja".'

Miller said it was absurd for any side to become as dominated by a bowler as

England appeared to be by Warne. He would love to see the present Australian batsmen, the likes of Slater and Mark Waugh, playing Warne. 'We have the best crop of young batsmen in Australia I can ever remember. In my time there was Bradman, McCabe, Archie Jackson. At present we have about 10 young players of enormous talent. They are quick-footed, aggressive, a delight to watch.'

Miller said that when Allan Border retired he would have appointed Dean Jones as the next Australian captain. He thought it a pity that Jones's career had been cut short because of his inability to bite his tongue. He no doubt sees parallels in his own life. In the opinion of many good judges, Richie Benaud included, Miller was the best captain Australia never had, but the playboy who delighted the audience terrified the establishment. After all, this is the captain of the New South Wales team who led his men on to the field and ordered them to scatter. He smiles at the memory. 'Perfectly true, but you have to remember that my team knew their places in the field,' he said. All right then, but what about the time 12 came on to the field and when told of his mistake Miller said: 'One of you bugger off, the rest scatter.' Alan Davidson, the great Australian all-rounder who played in that game, recalls that when Miller arrived in the middle after issuing his famous instruction he turned around to find he was the only player on the field.

Then there was the occasion that Miller got so drunk the night before the big game, celebrating the birth of a son, that he arrived late at the ground, ran on the field with a colossal hangover with his bootlaces slapping and took seven for 12 to win the match. And what about that day in England when he was asked to present the cup at the Greyhound Derby and arrived at the track from a wedding wearing morning coat and top hat. He backed the winner and made his way to the podium where he picked up the successful dog and kissed it on the nose.

There are a thousand stories like that making up the legend of Keith Miller, but I'll tell you just two more to sum him up and illustrate precisely why he never captained his country. At Manchester, on the tour dominated by Jim Laker, Australia faced a deficit of 375 runs in the first innings. With Laker rampant it was a lost cause. Ian Johnson, the Australian captain, tried a pep talk. He told his team: 'We can fight back. We need guts and determination. We can still save this match.' Keith Miller was studying a racing guide at the time. He looked up: 'Bet you 6–4 we can't,' he said.

On Bradman's tour in 1948 Australia made 721 runs in a day against Essex. All the Aussies filled their boots except Miller, who walked to the wicket, didn't take guard, lifted his bat and let the ball hit the stumps. He said to the wicket-keeper: 'Thank God that's over,' and walked off. Raiding sweet shops wasn't his style. A noble sentiment, but it cost him dear.

Nonetheless it has been a 'helluva good life' he says. He has been married for 48 years to Peg, his intelligent and charming American wife. They live within reach of their sons, seven grandchildren and one great-grandchild. Speaking personally, I would have ennobled him long ago for his services to cricket, his dedicated support of the brewing and bloodstock industries, and his significant contribution to the gaiety of life. He is delighted with the portrait commissioned by the MCC, not so much by the likeness – 'I look an old bugger' – but by the fact that it hangs in the Long Room over the entrance to the bar. A copy is furled in a tube in the corner of his study. I doubt if it will make it on to the wall with Bramall Lane and Guy Gibson.

He starts ticking off the faces on the Bramall Lane photograph. Most of them are dead. He points to Graham Williams, a spindly figure. 'Tall fella, no flesh on him because he'd just been released from a prisoner of war camp where he'd been for four years. He'd only been back two weeks and here he was playing cricket at Lord's. When he walked out to bat the whole ground rose to him and applauded him all the way to the middle. It was the most touching moment of my life. I often wonder what must have been going through Graham's mind. Here he was, being cheered all the way to the middle, playing cricket at Lord's when he must have been thinking: "Am I really alive? Is this really happening? Am I dreaming?" I think of it often and it always brings tears to my eyes.'

There are two more photographs in the room. They show Miller and another pilot standing in front of the Mosquito and Beaufighter aircraft they flew during the war. He keeps them to remind him that he was one of the lucky ones who made it back. I asked him if it was true that after one raid over Germany he flew his Mosquito in a detour over the town where Beethoven was born in an act of homage to his favourite composer. 'Perfectly true and why not?' he said, which is probably what he said when reprimanded by his commanding officer back in England.

Miller's love affair with England has deepened over the years. He says he only met one Englishman he didn't like. It will be difficult to think of even one Englishman who didn't like Keith Miller. Of all the Australians to visit our shores he is the best loved, the most welcome. On the morning of his birthday he was on the phone for nearly four hours, many of the calls coming from England. There are many reasons for his popularity, not least his outlook on life, summed up by a favourite saying: Remember only the happy hours.

While we are looking at the picture taken at Sheffield all those years ago and he is naming the players for me, he comes to his own image and says: 'That's a bloke called Miller. I wish to God I looked like that now.' In the picture Miller is carefree and laughing, every inch of him proclaiming a formidable athlete.

I wanted to tell him that when people thought of him that was what they remembered, that no one who ever saw him play the game of cricket would forget the image of Miller in his pomp. But I didn't, lest he damn me as a silly old sod. Or, more likely, regard me quizzically and say: 'Lay you 6–4 they don't.'

3rd December 1994

GRAHAM THORPE

—

THERE IS something reassuring about Graham Thorpe, something instantly comforting about his presence. The cut of his jib is sturdy and dependable. When he walks to the wicket he reminds me of John Edrich. You feel you might have to shell him for three days before trying to bowl him out.

It will be interesting to observe the relationship that develops between Thorpe and the new England batting guru, but it is difficult to think of any other player in the England squad who stands to benefit more from what Edrich has to offer. After all, left-handed batsmen are an oppressed minority. Generally they have a more difficult life than their more conventional colleagues, and when they seek inspiration they do so from fellow members of the Cack-Handed Club.

Thus Thorpe says he has learned most watching Mark Taylor, Jimmy Adams, Brian Lara and David Gower. 'What I look for are technical things like head position and footwork. Mind you, when you watch Gower and Lara all you can do is marvel.'

It was Gower who gave Thorpe his first memorable moment in professional cricket. On his debut for Surrey as a bustling medium pacer he bowled to Gower. His third ball to the great man nipped back and Gower nicked it on to his pad. Thorpe remembers: 'I was so overjoyed that he hadn't hit it for six that I gave a yelp of triumph. The umpire mistook it for an appeal and gave him out lbw.'

How did he change from medium-pace trundler to the man who will hopefully prop up the England middle order for the next decade? 'I woke up,' he says. 'I was batting at eight and Monte Lynch broke an ankle so they sent me in and I battled against Malcolm Marshall at Basingstoke. You could say it was an interesting encounter. Anyway, he hit me on the head a few times but I batted all day for 115.'

Thorpe's sudden appearance as a batsman of great promise was followed by a dreadful season when he could barely hit the ball off the square. 'That season was a thump in the guts. It taught me not to get carried away. For the first time I had doubts about my ability. Then I got picked for an A team tour of Sri Lanka. I was playing for Surrey seconds at the time. That gave me confidence.'

Since then Thorpe has steadily built his career to the point where, on the recent tour of Australia, he looked something like the finished article, a batsman with the talent and nerve to make runs at the highest level.

At Perth, where Gooch and Gatting played their last games for England, Thorpe and Ramprakash took up the challenge with a partnership of 158 which gave an indication that the future of English cricket might be in good hands.

The Australian tour taught him a lot. 'The Australians have set new standards of athleticism and fitness. Nowadays it's not enough just to bowl or bat, you've got to be a specialist fielder, too. Then there's the mental toughness. The Aussies have dominated us for the last four or five series. We need to find a new frame of mind. We have to learn to stand up for ourselves and not give in.

'Then there's the question of how much cricket we play. I'm not whingeing, but I have to say that we do play too much in this country. We have the longest season in all of cricket. It's particularly hard on bowlers. Take Darren Gough. He can't relax with his county, can't be half-hearted. But you do wonder how long his career will last unless a way is found not to overburden him. In Australia, Craig McDermott's career has been deliberately prolonged by the selectors. David Boon has played once in three years for Tasmania,' he said.

Unlike most professional athletes, Graham Thorpe had no burning ambition to play sport for a living. He didn't know what he wanted to be, except he felt that one day he might 'make something happen'.

There were early indications of a real all-round talent. As a 15-year-old making his debut with the Farnham first team he scored 93. He won three caps playing for England schools at football. For a while it seemed as if he might become a football professional. He played in mid-field. 'I used to ruffle the opposition' is how he describes his style.

He was offered a trial by Brentford. 'The rest of the squad were all signed up with pro clubs. I remember our coach asking me which club I belonged to. I said: "Old Farnhamians".' Surrey approached him at the same time as Brentford. 'I chose Surrey. I always imagined that if things didn't work out I'd go back to soccer,' he said.

He scored a century in his first Test match at Trent Bridge in 1993, his second 15 Tests later at Perth in 1995. 'It was about time I got another. With Goochie and Gatts going there will be a lot more responsibility on me to deliver the goods. Can I do it? I think so. Let's say I don't like being beaten,' he said.

He still agonizes over the humiliation of England being bowled out for 46 in

Trinidad. 'I was getting dressed by the fall of wickets. One down, I thought I'd better put my batting trousers on. Two down, I put the boots on. And so it continued,' he said.

When it came to Thorpe's turn, he batted for 90 minutes and was praised for his courage and tenacity. He only remembers being part of the humiliation. 'It was the worst experience of my life. But it toughened me because it made me more determined never to let that happen again.'

The other experience he could have done without occurred at Melbourne last year when he was fielding in front of the notorious Bay 13. He remained good-tempered as he was pelted with eggs, tennis balls and tomatoes. He did, however, become severely tested when he was hit by a condom filled with water. 'Let's give them the benefit of the doubt and say it was water,' he said. He turned to his tormentors and indicated it was time they gave him a break. The response was a shower of rotten fruit.

I said that at that moment he must have felt he might have been better off playing football. He said: 'No. I made the right choice. I like the stability and character of cricket. I was asked the other day what I would do if I was offered lots of money to leave Surrey. Well, I've been here since I was a kid. If someone offered me £50,000 I wouldn't want to move. Why? If people think money is the only thing worthwhile about playing sport then I think they have their priorities wrong.'

Like I said, there's something reassuring about Graham Thorpe, something that makes you optimistic about the future of our summer game.

20th May 1995

·28·

NICK FALDO

—

THE SCHOOLBOYS were twittering with excitement at the arrival of the world's greatest golfer. Nick Faldo selected a wedge, loosened up with a few purposeful swings, and then said: 'If you boys will tell me your golfing problems, then I'll try and show you what to do.'

A small child raised his hand. 'What's your problem?' asked Nick. 'Please, sir, I only have one arm,' said the boy. The golfer didn't blink. 'I can hit a ball with one hand. Let's have a competition,' he said.

The boy, frail and nervous as a chick, set up. His swing was rushed and excitable. Faldo re-aligned him, showed him how to turn, so he had a steeper swing. The boy swung again and hit the ball further than he had ever done before. Master and pupil beamed in satisfaction.

For more than an hour, in drenching rain, he taught and demonstrated. It was the best golf lesson they will ever have. Moreover, it was free. Faldo showed great charm and patience with the children.

In that respect he was like two other great athletes I have observed at close quarters – Boycott and Best – both of whom, like Faldo, have often been at conflict with the adult world. Their rapport with youngsters has something to do with the uncluttered enthusiasm of children, their genuine acceptance of heroes. Adults make pre-conceived judgments about people; children take as they find.

Nick Faldo drew the driver from his bag, unsheathing it in dramatic fashion as if revealing a magic sword. The children gibbered with excitement. He boomed a drive across the practice ground and over a hedge. 'That's in the swimming pool, sir,' said a boy hopping with delight.

Another majestic drive disappeared from sight. 'That's the greenhouse!' the boys squealed. 'Any requests?' he said. 'Can you hit the clock on the pavilion, sir?' was one. 'Better not, but I'll hit a low one, just over it,' he said. The balls screamed a yard or so over the clock, as nominated. But this time the boys were wetting themselves with joy.

'Heroes are important, aren't they?' said Nick Faldo later. 'If you're lucky, they inspire you. Mine were Nicklaus and Palmer. When I was young, I'd play imaginary games against them. I'd take four balls out. There'd be Jack, Arnie, Tom Weiskopf and me. I'd play their shots, try to emulate their swings. I'd imagine features on the courses at Welwyn that weren't there, like lakes and extra bunkers.

'I'd start at eight o'clock in the morning and play until dark. Thirty-six holes and then I'd practise. Sometimes, I'd play a hole backwards. In other words, if it was a three-wood, five-iron to the green, I'd take a five-iron off the tee and a three-wood to the green.

'They sent me on a scholarship to college in America. It's the kind of situation young golfers dream about. But it wasn't for me. Studies got in the way of golf. Also, they reckoned they worked us hard, but I was working four times as hard on my own at Welwyn. I just walked away from it.

'I was good at most games but as soon as I picked up a golf club at 14 I knew this was the game for me.

'I didn't like team games, so I tried swimming but that bored me. Swimming up and down the baths all day long, until you were blue and wrinkled, wasn't for me. Then I got into cycling and that was boring, too. A good practice was if you fell off your bike, exhausted, and puked. Again, not for me. The difference with golf is imagination. That's the reason I'm never bored when I practise. It's such a complex and difficult game but it's also artistic.

'I remember the first time I heard someone say: "He played a shot punched low under the wind." It stirred my imagination. I couldn't wait to get out on the practice range and interpret what I thought it meant.

'It's the reason I prefer fly fishing to ordinary fishing. The idea of chucking a line into murky water, and sitting and hoping, doesn't appeal. But the joy of casting in clear waters, where you can see the trout and the bugger can see you, is wonderful because it's a great skill and a marvellous contest.'

At 35 and at the top of the heap, Nick Faldo would appear to have it all. His wife, Gill, is strong-minded and encouraging, the children bounce happily around the house, and he has just been declared one of the wealthiest 500 men in Britain.

He is the archetypal working-class hero, the man who demonstrated that by hard work and dedication you could take on the world and be the best. He is tall, fit and strong, with boyish good looks, size 11 feet and beautiful hands.

He knows he is the best golfer in the world but he is no braggart; he has more money than he can spend but he is not flash about it. So why is it that he is not beloved like Frank Bruno, or Gary Lineker, or Sandy Lyle, even? Is it that we are uncomfortable with true greatness? Are we, perhaps, misinformed by mischievous elements in the media who, for one reason or another, have it in for the likes of Nick Faldo?

He says: 'I don't know what they say. First, I'm a loner. Well, if that means that I don't go into a bar at the end of the day and have a few drinks, then I suppose I am. But I don't see that makes me a bad person. I've always preferred to concentrate on my game. When I'm at a tournament, I'm at work. I don't drink at work. It's as simple as that.

'Then they say I'm a miserable bugger. I like to be focused, to concentrate. I find it difficult to smile and joke like some do. Let's imagine I've just shot six birdies on the trot and, at the seventh hole, I laugh and joke with the gallery and then make a bogey. I wouldn't know if it was because I'd mucked about with the spectators. So I try to eliminate all the risks.

'Also, I'm shy. I do find it difficult to relate to the spectators sometimes, because if I start chatting them up some might think I'm a big-headed sod who's showing off.

'They say I'm not like Seve. But, then, who is, and why should I be? He hits the ball into the trees on three consecutive holes and keeps on scoring, but that's the way he is. If I hit three balls into the trees, I'd give the game up. He has this happy-go-lucky reputation. But I'll tell you what, he doesn't look that happy coming down the 18th when he's scored 74. Who would? But they don't mention that, do they?

'Then they accuse me of being "Mechanical Man". This really gets my goat. Makes me sound like a battery toy. What my game is about is control. It's the ability to shape the ball at will, to make it behave just as I want it to. What's mechanical about that?

'The conclusion is that these people don't really want to know me. If they can't be bothered to take one step closer, to see the real person, then sod 'em.'

This is really what he was saying in that speech at Muirfield after winning his third Open. He remains unrepentant, pointing out he was merely trying to be funny, which is more than can be said for some of the media who appear unhappy that we have a genuine world champion among us.

To expect Faldo to take a more measured, philosophical approach to his detractors would be to misunderstand the man and what makes him tick.

He works harder than anyone he knows at getting things right. He leaves little to chance and genuinely cannot understand people who appear not to comprehend what he is striving for. It's not just mere mortals, either. He has been known to walk down a fairway, head tipped to heaven, addressing the Almighty: 'Dear God, how much harder do you want me to work to get it right?' is what he says.

Only a zealot could have decided, as Faldo did in 1985, to change his swing. It was as if Geoffrey Boycott decided in mid-career to bat left-handed, or Lester Piggott to make his come-back riding side saddle. Faldo was already recognized as a world-class player, but it obviously was not good enough. The demons inside him urged him to try for something else. What was it? 'Perfection,' I suggested.

'No such thing,' said Nick Faldo. 'What I was after, and still am, is control. I want to be in total charge of my game, hit, fade or draw, just as I visualize the shot. It was the right ambition, but it nearly brought me down. Those were the black days. I was very depressed. The mistake I made was in trying to play tournament golf while restructuring the swing.

'I didn't play well and they started writing me off. "We've seen the best of him," seemed to be the general tone.

'I'd arrive at an airport and I'd see some of the other pros waiting for their baggage and they'd be demonstrating my new swing or the exercises I had to do. They'd shake their heads as if they thought I'd gone mad.

'Everyone assumes that when I went to Lead [David Leadbetter, Faldo's coach] in search of a new swing, we had already designed one. Not true. It was an uncharted journey for both of us. I was a guinea pig.

'I'd hit 1,500 golf balls a day. I'd have to go for a swim halfway through in an attempt to relax my body. My fingers were so sore that they swelled up and I couldn't grip the club properly. I'd come home and Gill would have dinner ready and I'd sneak out because I would have a thought about what I was doing wrong. When I got back, dinner was ruined.'

Some sponsors lost faith and cancelled contracts. Nick Faldo knows where they live. The company providing his sweaters gave him a new contract. Nick Faldo will not forget the gesture. It was an unpleasant but important part of his young life. 'At least, at the end of it, I knew who my friends were,' he said.

Apart from the expert help he received, there was friendly advice from the public. One letter, for example, read: 'Dear Mr Faldo, I am a 16-handicap golfer but I am regarded as the best putter in my club and maybe I could give you a few tips.' Faldo laughs at the recollection and says: 'Mind you, you sometimes wonder if they might be right.'

One day in 1987 he went to Hattiesburg in America and shot four 67s. 'Everything fell into place,' he said. 'It was like sunshine.' It was a rebirth. In Britain the same year he won the first of his three Opens, and in '89 the US Masters for the first time. He wants two more American titles to complete the set. Then?

'I still have the desire to hit a golf ball and to win. I look forward to another 10 years at the very top. After that, who knows? The family is important. The kids say they have two dads and one is 'Nick Faldo the famous golfer'. I try to balance out the two Nick Faldos.

'I suppose that in the end I would just like people to say: "I saw that Faldo play and, by God, he was a good golfer." ' Whatever else they might say about Nick Faldo, that much is guaranteed.

1st May 1993

·29·

ROGER TAYLOR

—

IT IS a fair indication of Roger Taylor's love of a fight and his stubborn refusal to accept the notion of a lost cause that when he was asked to be coach of Britain's women tennis players he jumped at the chance. Tomorrow he takes the first steps on what will be an interesting journey when he accompanies some of our hopefuls to Bulgaria to see how they shape up in an international tournament.

When I tell you that the team includes Shirli-Ann Siddall, who is rated 211th in the world, and Julie Pullin, who is 285th, and that our best ranked player is Clare Wood at 181, with our national champion, Jo Ward, at 492, it becomes clear that Taylor faces something of an uphill battle.

Fortunately he relishes a scrap. Three times in the late Sixties and early Seventies he fought his way to a Wimbledon semi-final, the last British man to get that far.

He joined the rough and tumble of the early pro circuit where he sorted out the aggressive South African Bob Hewitt. 'Let us say I defended myself,' says Taylor, in more diplomatic mood nowadays.

He could look after himself on and off the court. When he retired at 35 he set up a tennis centre in the Algarve and started teaching middle-aged holidaymakers how to play while the British game cried out for his expertise at international level.

The trouble with mavericks is that they threaten the accepted order of things. The last thing an august and traditional body like the Lawn Tennis Association desires is anybody or anything designed to upset the tranquil routine of privilege, or to challenge the reassuring nepotism of jobs for the boys. Taylor is now 53, and for the past 18 years he has waited for the LTA to make a decent offer.

When Paul Hutchins ran the game, Taylor was given the job of looking after our Wightman Cup team. The Americans had King, Evert and Shriver; we had Wade and Barker. The Yanks were hot favourites but we won 4–3. 'I thought that might give me an in,' said Taylor. Not a bit of it. He went back to coaching holidaymakers. Why?

'Perhaps I made the mistake of winning the match. People told me I was too aggressive, difficult to work with. I only wanted to win, so what's difficult about that? The LTA system was very calm and quiet. Very smooth-running. Paul Hutchins was well organized. Loaded himself with graphs and technical support. When people asked what's wrong with British tennis, out would come pages of stuff. But the bottom line was we still were not producing the right kind of tennis players,' he said.

What will he be looking for? 'The right kind of personality and character. I want instinctive competitors. I'm looking for someone who refuses to be beaten, even on a bad day. Someone who doesn't say: "Oh, I don't feel like it today," and rolls over just because things are not going well. You can give young players all the coaching you want, spend a fortune on them, but if they haven't got the will to win you are wasting your time.

'It comes before physical strength or concentration and the rest you need to be a champion. Look at Jimmy Connors. No one walked away from a match he was in because no matter what the score, he was never beaten until the last gasp. That's what the players should learn from,' he said.

Can it be taught? 'I think you can help people find it. I think what I bring to the job is that I know how tough it is to play professional tennis. I will never be surprised how hard it is to get there. I have got to make them aware of what is needed.

'I remember when I was advising young Andrew Castle and he played Mats Wilander, who was then the world No.1, at Wimbledon. Andrew had never played Wimbledon before so he didn't know what to expect. He was sitting there waiting to go out, frightened to death and John Barratt passed by. He said: "Good luck Andrew, and remember to go out and enjoy it." I told Andrew to ignore that. It was said for the best possible reasons but it was the worst advice. It's a myth that you go out and have a jolly time.

'I have stood on Centre Court and been so nervous I couldn't get the ball out of my hand to throw it up. I have turned away from the cameras so they couldn't show my hands shaking. The test of character is to overcome all that and go on, not just to compete but to win. I can tell them what it is really like and perhaps that might be one of the more important aspects I can bring to the job,' he said.

Taylor looks 10 years younger than someone in his sixth decade. The hair might be thinning but the physique looks toned and hard. He learned his tennis in a local park in Sheffield and instead of following his dad into a steelworks came to London and lived in the YMCA in Wimbledon.

He reached the semi-final at Wimbledon in 1967 and received not a penny. He turned professional next year on the World Championship Tennis circuit and embarked on a crazy, exciting adventure that shaped the modern game.

It wasn't simply that Taylor and the others fought for players to be paid. They were the first players to wear coloured clothing, to use tie-breaks, to play on artificial turf. Most important of all, the Association of Tennis Professionals came directly out of the experiences of the players on the WCT tour.

According to Taylor, the players' organization was set up to control Ilie Nastase, who was then the top tennis player but someone who played with a different set of rules from the others. 'In the unlikely event of any of us looking like beating him, he would run off the court and sit between two beautiful girls. He did this to me once in Barcelona. He ignored the umpire, even the president of the club, who tried to persuade him back on court.

'There was uproar. Then, when he decided it was time, he came back on court. But it didn't end there. Before he served he mimicked the umpire trying to persuade him back and did impersonations of Charlie Chaplin. Finally, when he decided to serve, he had this trick where he would try to bounce the ball but would deliberately hit his foot. More uproar and off he'd go again. He was a significant figure in the game, was Nastase. Every rule about the abuse of umpires, ball and racket was due to him,' he said.

Talking to Taylor you sense a huge enjoyment of his career which he wants to share. At the same time he wants anyone thinking of following in his footsteps to be aware of what is required to achieve a comparable fulfilment.

'I remember when I was playing in Australia and I met Fred Trueman, who was over with the cricket team. He said to me: "Are you still playing that silly game?" The inference was: "Bloody pooftah game". But it's the opposite. It's as hard a game as there is. The trouble is that some of our young players don't understand that. You can see the aggression in rugby league and boxing and you can't see it in tennis but that doesn't mean it's not there.

'At the top level it is two guys trying to beat the other's brains out. Anyone doubting that should have played Ken Rosewall. He was the toughest guy I ever played. He was ruthless in a way you could only know if you played him. He never missed a ball, never gave you a sniff. He'd stretch you, pull you, torture you and put you through the wringer.

'Off the court he was the nicest man in the world. On the court he was as tough as old boots. Now we have some good young players in Britain at junior level but they can't make the transition. Perhaps it is because they don't realize what a hard game it is.

'We won't start finding champions until our juniors start winning major events at their level at Wimbledon or Paris. That's where it must start. We have run out of excuses. There is money in the game, there are the facilities about. All right, we must spread the net wider but the fact remains that our lack of success is not due to lack of money. It is about attitude. That is what we have to change,' he said.

In the past Taylor and the LTA have played footsie with each other. This new job could be their betrothal and it is to be hoped devoutly that the union is properly consummated as soon as possible.

Taylor would welcome the chance of a more permanent involvement with British tennis. His appointment would be yet another reason to believe that the people who run British sport – not just the LTA – are at last waking up to the idea that the future is too important to be left in the charge of willing amateurs.

Taylor has the hardest task of all. Our women tennis players are, frankly, an embarrassment. If he can change that he will have worked a miracle. He has the enthusiasm and the talent to make a considerable contribution. He just needs the time. As he says: 'Real life is not what happens in the *Rocky* movies.'

8th April 1995

·30·

DARREN GOUGH

—

I N THE last hour of that fabulous Test match in Sydney, with the spectators nervously applauding every ball survived by the Australian batsmen and the faces of the England players pale and tense with fatigue and exasperation, Darren Gough chased a ball to the boundary edge, galloping along with the carefree energy of someone who doesn't yet know how to be jaded.

He hurled the ball to the keeper, turned to bow to the Barmy Army and proceeded to make his way back to his mark by walking on his hands.

It was the action of a born showman and confirmation, if it be needed, that for the next 10 years or so, with Darren Gough around, cricket is unlikely to be dull.

There is, of course, more to Gough than the showman. He is a fine cricketer who loves hitting sixes and bowling fast. Again, there is more to his cricket than that. He is a good bowler and capable of developing into a great one. He is a useful bat with the talent to mature into a very good one.

He is being talked of as the next Ian Botham, which may be flattering in one sense but might cause concern in another. Inevitable comparisons are made with Fred Trueman, who was the last fast bowler/showman produced by Yorkshire.

If he becomes as great a Test bowler as Trueman we are in for a treat. But again, as with Botham, he might be better advised to work out what Fred did to hamper his career than try to define the gifts that furthered it.

His greatest and most difficult task will be to restore the reputation of Yorkshire cricket. For 20 years or more the county suffered serious decline. The envied reputation of the club began to seem like a sick joke.

Sadly, most of the damage was self-inflicted. The county was riven by internal strife and dispute. Petty jealousies and silly rivalries created an atmosphere in the dressing room something like Hitler's bunker in the final days of the Third Reich.

Four of the shrewdest analytical cricket brains the game has produced – Ray Illingworth, Brian Close, Fred Trueman and Geoff Boycott – were either unwilling or unable to work together to put things right.

The longer it lasted the more desperate became the search for a saviour, a great player to rescue the county.

The club turned, for the first time, to an overseas player, thereby breaking a tradition in a way that many thought would lead to the end of the world.

In a curious way it provided the solution but not in the expected manner.

Yorkshire hired Richie Richardson, the captain of the West Indies, who had an ordinary couple of seasons because his marvellous talent was inhibited by fatigue from the incessant programme of international cricket and his spirit drained by the unrelenting grind of the English county game.

There was, however, one inspirational moment. Yorkshire were playing Hampshire and Gough was bowling to Shaun Udal. At that time Darren Gough was not a happy cricketer. He was overweight, confused and unhappy. He wanted to bowl fast but lacked the confidence to let himself go, scared of going for eight an over.

Udal, who is far from being the best bat in the world, clouted him for four. Richardson said to Gough: 'I wouldn't let a batsman like him hit me for four.' Gough said: 'What would you do?' Richardson said: 'If I was a fast bowler I'd let him have it, put him on his arse.' Gough did and a legend began to take shape.

Since then he has never doubted his role in life. He went about preparing to be a fast bowler. He planned a healthy diet, lost his beer belly, started exercising to improve his upper body strength.

Today he stands 5ft 11in tall, weighs 12½ stone and is broad of shoulder and beam, with good strong legs. He is built for hard work. When he reaches the peak of his strength he will, like Fred before him, be a formidable and imposing physical presence.

Although comparisons with Trueman are unfair and wide of the mark, they are inevitable, particularly in Yorkshire.

In fact, they are very different people. Fred was the archetypal Yorkie: dark, glowering, resentful of authority, suspicious of the rest of the world.

What is more, he was put on earth to bowl fast and put the fear of God into batsmen. No one ever needed to tell Fred – as Richardson told Gough – to knock a batsman's head off. Fred took that in with his mother's milk.

Darren Gough might fill Fred's boot but he is a very different human being. He is a sunny young man with a big smile for the world and an infectious personality. If Fred was a rottweiler, powerful and menacing, Gough is a big soppy labrador forever wagging his tail.

And Gough is charming, which no one ever accused Fred of being.

Gough understands the comparisons that are made, even pretends to go along with them, but has no intention of becoming a carbon copy. It wasn't Fred Trueman's photograph pinned to his bedroom wall – it was Ian Botham's – and while Trueman was drawn to cricket like a moth to a flame, Gough wanted to play soccer for a living like his great hero, Glenn Hoddle of Spurs and England.

What he can't escape is the folklore surrounding the fast bowler, particularly the one born in Yorkshire. There are more stories told about Fred Trueman than anecdotes about Noël Coward. How many are true? I once asked Fred that question. 'Not many. But does it matter?' he said.

Of course not. Fast bowlers are the gunslingers of cricket, the hard men who ride into town trailing legend and myth.

Typical story: Fred Trueman bowling to a young university cricketer who is wearing a fancy hat. Trueman bowls him first ball. As the young toff passes Fred he says: 'My word, Trueman, that was a good ball.' Fred glowers and says: 'It was that, but it was wasted on thee.'

Fred in Australia being shown around Sydney. Aussie host points to the harbour bridge and says: 'A great Australian achievement.' Fred says: 'What do you mean a great Aussie achievement? That's a Yorkshire bridge built by Dorman Long, engineers of Middlesbrough in Yorkshire.' Long pause to let this sink in and then: 'What's more, you miserable buggers still haven't paid us for it.'

Fast bowlers carry with them a reputation and a fame that goes way beyond the normal boundaries of the world they occupy. My favourite Fred Trueman story is of him touring in some remote part of India when the train they were travelling in made an unscheduled stop at a tiny and remote outpost.

The players took the opportunity to stretch themselves and go for a leak. As Fred looked around for the toilet facilities he was approached by the station master, who said: 'Come this way, Mr Trueman, I have prepared a special facility for you.'

Whereupon he took Fred into his office and from behind a curtain produced an old Victorian chamber pot with 'F S Truemen' handpainted round the rim. 'I made this many years ago just in case you ever passed by,' he said. Or so Fred claimed. I was not convinced. 'Are you telling me the truth?' I asked. 'Would I tell you a lie?' said Fred.

Darren Gough has set off in the same direction but without being aware of what is at journey's end. The other day he wore a T-shirt bearing the legend: 'The Finest Fast Bowler That Ever Drew Bloody Breath' underneath the face of Fred Trueman.

He didn't know the provenance of that quote but I did. Many years ago I was asked to write Fred Trueman's biography. We thought of taking rooms above a brewery in Barnsley to create a pleasant working ambience but in the end had to call it off because Fred was too busy to sit down and tell it all. We did, however, discuss the title of the book.

I told Fred the title was important. It needed to be dynamic and exciting and must tempt people to buy his remarkable story. Above all, it should be brief and to the point.

'What do you think we should call the book?' I asked. He thought for a moment and then said: 'The book should be called *Fred, T'definitive Volume On T'best Fast Bowler That Ever Drew Breath.*' It never graced the spine of a book but it made a fabulous legend for a sweatshirt 30 years later.

The young man wearing the sweatshirt, the boy who has inherited the crown, is already on the way to creating a new fund of stories to be polished and improved by a succession of after-dinner speakers.

One already going the rounds which defies improvement is of Gough going to see a witch doctor in South Africa while touring with the England A team.

Gough told the witch doctor he wanted to bowl fast for Yorkshire and England. The witch doctor told Gough he would always bowl like the wind if, before every delivery, he kissed the ball and said the Lord's Prayer.

Gough told his team-mates and announced he would try the new system next match. Come the day and Darren Gough kissed the ball and set off on his run to the wicket praying aloud. The batsman whacked the ball for six.

When asked by his team-mates what had gone wrong the bowler confessed that he couldn't remember the Lord's Prayer and had run up chanting 'For what we are about to receive'.

What does the future hold for Darren Gough? I think he will become a huge world star of cricket, as big as – if not bigger than – the two he is presently compared with: Botham and Trueman.

It might be that he won't achieve the statistics of the other two – although barring accident he'll run them close – but I have little doubt that Gough will elicit more affection and admiration and from a wider cross-section of the general public.

Moreover, to the commercial and marketing experts who play such an important part in the modern game this good-looking, amiable extrovert from Yorkshire is a gift from heaven. He will do for English cricket what Shane Warne has done for the Australian game.

Together they will do wonders for cricket around the world.

8th January 1995

·31·

PHILIP DON

—

WHY WOULD anyone want to become a football referee? It remains one of life's great unsolved mysteries, like why people eat tripe, and the function of the human appendix. Even the most respected referees have the popularity rating of a man towing a caravan down a narrow road on a Bank Holiday weekend.

They certainly don't do it for the money. Today Philip Don will be at Maine Road, Manchester. The £300 he is paid will hardly make a dent in the gate receipts or enable him to contemplate a change of lifestyle. It is, however, considerably more than he receives for refereeing in Europe. Three hundred pounds more, to be precise. All he gets for being in charge of important games on the Continent is £75 per day living allowance.

He has been refereeing since he was 14. He is now 42 years old. In his time he has been punched by a player in the Chiswick Sunday League, smuggled out of Fratton Park in the back of a van and earned his own place in the Dictionary of Cheap Jibes (Referees' Edition) when Jimmy Greaves, commentating on the sending off of Tony Adams for a professional foul, said the Arsenal captain had been well and truly 'P Don' (geddit?).

If you didn't, the pupils at the South London school where P Don is headmaster most certainly did. The children are in favour of having a boss who is a famous referee. It gives them something to talk about. 'That was never a sending-off offence,' they say on Monday mornings. At parents' days and school functions the adults are more eager to talk football than discuss the academic progress of their children.

Philip Don lives with his wife, Judith, also a teacher, in a quiet cul-de-sac in Surrey. Judith doesn't enjoy going to football matches.

'I get upset at the names they call Philip,' she says. They have a daughter at Oxford and a son who is a member of the British triathlon team.

Philip Don is a slender, wiry man. He runs 20 miles a week to keep in shape.

Even on holiday he trained for 15 of the 21 days that they were away. He is attractive, has an affable manner, and is not the sort of person you would expect to be publicly reviled as a 'wanker' or a 'bastard', which he is, most Saturdays, as a matter of routine. Nor is he the kind of bloke you would imagine being escorted from a ground by a platoon of policemen to save him from being scragged by the mob.

The question is: why bother? 'I don't really have a good answer,' he says. 'It started when I was 14. I'd play soccer in the morning and then referee a game in the afternoon. When I was at college, I'd supplement my grant by refereeing three times a week.

'So was it the case I became a referee because I'm a mercenary Yorkshireman? Don't think so. Not even our worst enemies could accuse us of doing it for the money.'

He placed his fingertips together. He has neat hands. 'I've always been a methodical and organized person. I've always captained teams I've played in. Maybe refereeing is an extension of that. Power. Maybe that's it. Maybe I get a kick out of being in control.'

He was born in Hull. There is a trace of accent. His ambition to be a referee was sorely tested before his first game when he had to clean mountains of cow pats from the pitch before play could commence.

As he moved up the divisions, he observed the crowds became bigger and the surroundings more spectacular but the referee's status rarely improved on someone who was expected to shovel manure. At one League ground, Don had to ask for an air freshener because the room set aside for the referee was the annexe to a public urinal. At another, the officials changed in the laundry room and in another the pre-match briefing by the referee could be carried out only if the linesman stood in the shower.

The ultimate insult was invented by the club who built a palatial new stand and forgot to include a room for the officials in the plans.

Working in Europe, he discovered that visiting referees were treated with splendid generosity, which lasted only so long as the home team won.

In Oporto, he allowed a goal which the home team believed was offside. Oporto lost 2–1. That night at the official banquet, Philip Don and his linesmen were placed between two television sets screening continuous replays of the controversial goal all night long.

He thinks, however, that the status of the referee is changing for the better and the World Cup in the United States is responsible. 'It showed the crucial part referees have to play in the way the game is played,' he said. 'The laws weren't changed. All that FIFA did was to remind referees of what their responsibilities are.

'Something had to be done to make the game more entertaining. In this country, people were paying a lot of money and not much of what they saw was worth the price of admission. There seemed to be too much pressure on management and players to be negative and forget about the spectators.

'I believe FIFA and the referees changed all that. Most importantly, FIFA have allowed referees to appear in the media to explain their problems and what they're trying to do. I'm all in favour of it.

'At one time, all that referees were allowed to say was "no comment". Now we have a much more important profile and it can only lead to greater understanding between all of us responsible for making sure the game gives value for money.

'It will take a season or two for the game to come to terms with the new philosophy, and what we referees have to do in the meantime is achieve consistency. We have to convince managers and players that this is what we're after. If we do, then we'll have their full co-operation. As referees, we have to hold regular meetings, watch videos, work out a consistent approach. Most importantly, if we are wrong and the video evidence tells us we are, then we should own up.

'This question of consistency is where the argument for two referees on the field falls down. It's difficult enough with one but what sort of consistency would be achieved with two referees at the same game? It would be mayhem. My own view is that the system of three officials has stood the test of time.'

Hasn't the time come when being a referee should be considered a full-time job? Last season Philip Don had nine weeks' unpaid leave from his school. He was not recompensed for loss of earnings. He thinks there might be a case for paying referees more money but not for them becoming full-time officials.

'I'm sure that if I announced I had become a full-time referee, spectators and players alike would expect me to become a better referee overnight,' he said.

'The truth might be that if I had a five-year contract with good money, pensions, life assurance and all that, I might become complacent. As it is, on my present one-year contract, I'm always striving for perfection. I have to because I know that if I slip next year I'm officiating on Hackney Marshes.'

He thinks the greatest virtue of the present system is that it brings to the game people who possess skills and insights gained in a broad area of man-management. Nor does he believe, in the final analysis, that the job deserves full-time, professional status.

'I suppose that I was living like a full-time referee in America during the World Cup, in that I had nothing else to do,' he said. 'And that was the problem. After I had trained, looked at videos of my last game, prepared for the next, there was nothing left to do. It was boring.'

Nonetheless, it is a fact that the present system depends on the co-operation of employers and a satisfactory balance being maintained between a job and a hobby. It is this that has led to something of a crisis in Philip Don's life.

'My problem is that the hobby is taking over the job. I had nine weeks' unpaid leave last year and it's getting to the stage where the governors and staff might be saying that I'm not spending enough time at school. I'll have to sit down and think about what to do. I have already turned down one trip to Europe this year because it comes in school time. If I turn down too many games I'll be taken off the list. So what do I do, resign?'

He leaves the question unanswered. In the coming months, he has some serious thinking to do. But at the end of the day the reason why he decided to become a referee is much more fascinating and difficult to explain than why he is thinking about chucking in the job. So let's try again. Why on earth did you want to be a referee?

'When I was in charge of the Cup final my mother reminded me that when I was a teenager I'd told her that one day I'd referee a final at Wembley,' he said. 'I'd forgotten that.

'Obviously, the ambition has always been with me but I've never tried to explain it. Again I ask myself, is it power? Or might it be something else? I became a teacher because I had a sense of vocation. For a while, when I was young, I thought I might have a vocation for the priesthood. So maybe being a referee is vocational, too.'

He was smiling when he said it but he might be right. It could be that the most perplexing of questions has a simple answer: it is not that a man chooses to be a referee. The fact is, he can't help it.

27th August 1994

·32·

BRIAN BARNES

—

WHEN BRIAN Barnes, professional golfer, was Good Old Barnesy, professional pisspot, this is what he used to do. 'Let's say my tee-off time was 8.30 in the morning. When I awoke I'd stick the kettle on and have three or four brandies with my morning coffee. That would get me on to the putting green. Then I would fill a litre bottle with a mixture of two-thirds vodka and one-third orange juice. That would get me round the golf course,' he said. I asked him what he did when he had finished playing. 'That's when the serious drinking started,' he said.

Fifty today, he is this weekend in America seeking a new career on the Seniors Tour. It is in every sense a second chance for Brian Barnes because he hasn't had a drink for more than two years and there is time yet to make up for those wasted years both as a man and as a golfer. Drink brought him to the edge. Literally. Twice he drove to Beachy Head in the grip of a severe depression and contemplated committing suicide. He revved the car while he made the decision. 'Thank God I lacked the guts to do it,' he says.

The crucial incident that made him seek medical advice instead of oblivion through drink was when he drove his car at breakneck speeds through narrow country lanes near his home, angered by his wife's observation that he was too drunk to drive. 'I arrived at the pub, took one sip of a drink and was violently ill at the thought of what I had done,' he said.

'I went for treatment in a clinic. I had five weeks' group therapy. They told me that had I carried on I would have killed myself in three months. When I came out of the closet and confessed I was an alcoholic, colleagues who had played with me for years on the tour said: "We never saw you pissed." ' They were probably sparing his blushes. His reputation was that of a boozing, boisterous fellow whose sometimes bizarre behaviour on the golf course had more to do with an excess of drink than a genuinely eccentric nature.

When he shot 62 at Dalmahoy in the 1981 Players' Championship, the last of his 17 victories throughout the world in 30 years as a professional golfer, he enjoyed 'a little carry out' of six pints. He then downed another eight before winning the play-off. At the same course in the same year, when winning the Scottish Professional Championship, he marked his ball on the 18th green with a beer can. The officials shook their heads. The galleries laughed and called him 'Good Old Barnesy'.

He says: 'It was always "Good Old Barnesy. He's a lad isn't he?" In fact I was in deep trouble. I wasn't a fighting drunk. Booze made me easy-going, the life and soul of the party. In fact I am a shy person, lacking in confidence. I drank to feel better. Fact is I never had a hangover. When I was 13 I weighed 13 stone and stood 6ft 2in tall. I could drink six pints of scrumpy and not fall down.

'Golf was a very social game. I remember when I was a young pro going to a seminar about golfers and health. The doctor who was advising us said he thought that four to five pints a day wouldn't do us any harm, nor 20 to 30 cigs. Times change.'

He didn't have a festering ambition to play golf. He played his first games as a child in Germany where his father, who had the job of repatriating foreigners at the end of the war, built a golf course. Brian Barnes was a strong, athletic boy who loved cricket and rugby. He went on a sports scholarship to Millfield where R J O Meyer, the prescient headmaster, insisted he take up golf seriously. 'You will play golf whether you like to or not,' said 'Jack' Meyer. At 17, Barnes was down to a three handicap, two years later he was plus one.

When he joined the European Tour he danced many a merry jig. He was a swashbuckler on the course, smiting the ball miles off the tee, never taking a backward step when the time came to attack. It was a laugh a minute, the enjoyment shared by golfer and spectator alike. And the boy could play at the highest level and in the best of company.

In 1970 he played the American Tour. In 1975 he became the only man who can claim to have beaten Jack Nicklaus twice in one day in the Ryder Cup. Nicklaus remains a friend and a hero. Barnes has signed with the great man's management company for his latest venture in the States.

'Jack once gave me the most terrible bollocking for not choosing a career in the States. He said my game was made for American courses. He said it was a terrible waste,' he said. I asked him if he felt that he had chucked away his career. 'I don't think so. In fact I can't afford to look back. Who knows what might happen in the next 10 years.

'Sometimes I do wonder what might have been had I not been pissed most of the time. Gary Player once gave me a dressing down. Asked me if I ever thought what I could have achieved had I been different. I asked him if he'd ever considered what sort of golfer he might have been had he been 6ft 2in tall. He laughed.

'What I don't know is if I had enough guts in me to win a major. It takes guts you know. I used to like coming from the pack to win but I wonder if I could have done it from the front, leading all the way and winning. I have always suffered from never believing I had the ability. Most champions don't have self-doubt. Most champions are plain bloody selfish, don't give a toss. My problem has always been that I never liked to disappoint people.'

When I met Barnes he was practising his putting at West Chiltington Club in Sussex, which he designed and helped build. He is a tall man with a solid build and a face that smiles easily, the sort of man you would like to have a drink with at the local pub. We drove to his home nearby, through lanes thick with blossom and budding rhododendron, to a front door framed by wisteria.

His wife, Hilary, is slender, attractive and charming. It is difficult to imagine that anyone could become befuddled enough to want to leave all this and drive off Beachy Head. But then booze does terrible things to people.

Brian Barnes said: 'When it was at its worst there was no light at the end of the tunnel. I didn't want to get out of bed.' He paused, seeking the words to describe what it used to be like. Finally he said: 'It was a vicious thing.'

Nowadays, supported by family and friends, he treads the fragile tightrope that is never-ending for alcoholics. 'The best part is I now have the best possible get-out for leaving boring cocktail parties early,' he said. 'I have never liked cocktail chit-chat. When I was drinking I'd just get pissed. Now I've got a doctor's note so I leave early. So far stopping drinking has not been a problem . . . yet. That's a big word in an alcoholic's vocabulary . . . yet.'

It is not going to be easy for Brian Barnes as he seeks a new life and, I suspect, redemption, in America. 'People imagine it's going to be a pushover. In fact it is going to be really tough,' he said.

Golf apart, there are new pressures and temptations to combat. Barnes has taken a friend along who is as much a minder as a caddie. There will be a lot of people rooting for this agreeable and talented man, hoping that he succeeds and prospers.

'I hope it works out. I have worked harder recently than ever before. I am swinging better than at any time in my career. You could say I have mellowed,' he said. Better than ending up pickled, which is where he was heading.

3rd June 1995

·33·

MIKE GATTING

—

WHEN HE came in the restaurant he looked trim, fit and clear-eyed; like a contender. In fact, he had just been told that he wasn't in the tour party to the West Indies (which he expected), nor had he been chosen to lead the A team to South Africa (which he thought he might). So, Mike Gatting, what are your comments, please? He shrugged his shoulders: 'The door is shut on my Test career. I suppose that's what it means,' he said. Disappointed? 'Of course. I love playing for England. Goochie had some of his best years for England after he started going grey. Why shouldn't me and Gower do the same?

'On the other hand, it will be good to have a winter in England. I don't think the family will mind me being home for Christmas. I've had 15 years, good years at that, with England. So I can't complain,' he said. What will he do? 'Don't know. Look around. I used to be a plumber you know. Might take that up again.' You used to be what? 'Well, a plumber's mate really. When I was at school I used to work with this plumber. Learned a lot about it. It's all about organization really. Might set myself up doing central heating systems and the like.'

He likes organizing things, Mike Gatting. He thinks captaincy is about organizing players into the right place at the right time and in the right frame of mind. 'It will be a trying time for Mike Atherton in the West Indies. First of all, the quicks will be after him. The way they operate is seek and destroy the captain and demolish the side's confidence. He had better get used to the fact that he is not going to get many pitched in his own half.

'Then he has to convince the team that they are on tour playing cricket and not on holiday. That's a problem with every touring party, but it's a particular problem in the Windies where it seems like carnival time wherever you go. Sometimes it's difficult to organize net practice and very easy for players to drift off and not concentrate on the job in hand.

'I think they have been very brave picking a young side. I do think it might have been wiser to have taken at least one experienced player but there is no doubt that playing the West Indian pace bowlers is a job for quick eyes and lightning reflexes. If I was to offer any advice to Mike it would be to talk to his team, get them to think about the way they do things. It seems self-evident to say that different players need a different approach, but not every captain understands that.

'When I had Ian Botham in the team and we won the Ashes in Australia, he made a significant contribution because I think I handled him the right way. I didn't insist that he have nets every day or do all the physical training. I'm glad they've picked Chris Lewis. He bowled well in India without much luck. Had an unhappy series against Australia and got dropped. He needs talking to. . .understanding, then see him go.'

Michael Gatting learned in a tough school. The Middlesex record through the 1980s and 1990s is an excellent one with only the odd blip. It was achieved by good cricketers being well led. That much is certainly true of the present team, who have finished the season as the champion county.

Gatting is at home with players like Emburey, Fraser and Desmond Haynes. He admires the way they think about the game, talk about it. 'After a day's play we try to get all the players to sit down and talk about the game. We're looking for awareness, understanding. There's a tendency for some of the young players in county cricket to finish playing, put the gear on and go out dancing. That's sad,' he said.

What about one or two of the younger players in the Middlesex team who have a reputation for being difficult or temperamental? Ramprakash for instance. 'He has never tried it on with me.' Next question. What about Tufnell? He thought carefully about this one. 'He knows where he stands with me,' he said, eventually.

It is not inconceivable that Mike Gatting might have skippered England for as long as Allan Border captained Australia. There are few who doubt he is England's best county captain. He was the last England captain to win the Ashes in Australia, or anywhere else for that matter. The reason he did not emulate Border is the much-discussed incident at Faisalabad where he had a row with the Pakistan umpire Shakoor Rana.

'Worst mistake of my life. What I did was wrong in that you must never argue with an umpire. I think I should have come home. Perhaps the team should have pulled out. Something needed to be done. A lot was going on and nothing was being done about it.' What was going on? He smiled, sadly: 'I'm not going to say any more about it. I'd only get into more trouble. One day the truth will be told.'

Scyld Berry, the experienced cricket correspondent of the *Sunday Telegraph*, covered the tour and had no doubt what was happening. He wrote: 'The Faisalabad Affair has been almost buried, if not covered up, so that the essential truth of it has not been widely grasped. Beyond reasonable doubt the England players were right in thinking that the Test series was "fixed" by a Pakistan regime which has mercifully moved on. Pressure, direct and indirect, was put on the umpires to bring about a Pakistan victory in the first Test and to halt England in the second at Faisalabad. When Gatting exploded . . . most human beings would have done the same as he did, following the accumulated injustices. Gatting was as good as stitched up.'

The injustice rankles still, particularly because of a further demonstration of Rana's seedy nature. A year later the umpire, who was writing a book about the incident, turned up at Worcester, where Middlesex were playing, accompanied by a newspaper photographer. 'He was tapping on the window of my car saying he wanted to talk to me, to explain things. All the time the photographer was snapping away. A stunt. I didn't react. One day I'll give my version of events,' said Gatting.

Rana might be a clown, and worse, but he did for the captain of England. There is little doubt that when Gatting was deposed for behaving irresponsibly in inviting female company to his hotel room for a drink, the hierarchy had more on its mind than a mere dalliance with a barmaid. Gatting has no doubt. 'It was a back-dated punishment,' he said.

That led to Gatting going to South Africa. It might have made him a lot of money but it did little for his public relations. 'I felt left out and let down by the England set-up. Was I condemned to county cricket for the rest of my life? That uncertainty pushed me to South Africa.

'What it taught me was to do a bit of homework before jumping into a volatile situation. What it also showed me was how all sides used cricket as a propaganda weapon,' he said. What he miscalculated was the kind of madness stirred by an emotive issue like South Africa. His wife received death threats. He had to employ a security firm to guard the house.

When the authorities decided to pardon the rebels the scene was set for Gatting to write a satisfying final chapter to his career. Instead, he was part of the débâcle in India and Sri Lanka and an early casualty of the hammering by the Australians.

If he ever thought the gods were against him – and he had every reason to believe so – then the message of confirmation was delivered by Shane Warne in the Old Trafford Test. His first ball to Gatting pitched way outside leg stump, turned square and took Gatting's off bail. It announced an extraordinary new talent to Test cricket, triggered a series of events which led to a fundamental rethink of the England set-up and sealed the fate of stalwarts like Gower and Gatting.

'It's not the end of my cricket career. I might not play for England again but I am certainly going to go on playing for Middlesex. I reckon I have three to four more years in me. I still have an appetite for cricket. Even if I wasn't captain, I would play on as a member of the team if they wanted me. After that? Wouldn't mind a job as coach. Like to put something more back into the game,' he said.

Coming from someone else it sounds like a cliché. From Mike Gatting it is a statement of intent. It is good news for Middlesex that he is not disenchanted with the game. It gives the county a guarantee that for a few more years any victory for the opposition will be gained only over the dead body of Mike Gatting.

For all the tumult of his career, he has few regrets. 'What I would like to have done was play in that period of time when Compo and Edrich were at Lord's and the crowds spilled over on to the grass. That would have been nice. I'd have liked to have gone to Australia on a boat as they used to. Take your time getting there. It must have been wonderful to have played in a more leisurely era,' he said.

It may be that when he finally departs there is less of a lament than accompanied Ian Botham or is likely to be heard when David Gower goes. He is not the sort of cricketer to cause an extraordinary meeting of the MCC, nor the kind who would be comfortable sitting on stage telling anecdotes. And yet he is more durable than they, and his contribution to cricket – particularly his beloved county – is something few cricketers have achieved.

18th September 1993

·34·

STEVE REDGRAVE

—

WHEN HE was 14 Steve Redgrave stood well over 6 feet tall and weighed more than 14 stone. They stuck him in goal, working on the theory that his large frame would make it a much smaller target, but he found no satisfaction in the job. Similarly, when they picked him to play rugby they put him in the forwards where he was expected to make mincemeat of the opposition, while all he wanted to be was a silky stand-off.

Then they sat him in a boat and, quite by chance, found him the perfect mate. In sundry boats and various company he has won three Olympic gold medals, one bronze and five world champions'. If he and his partner, Matthew Pinsent, win gold at Atlanta in '96, Redgrave will prove himself the greatest Olympic oarsman of all time. There are some who would give him the title now and be done with it.

He is certainly the most successful Olympic athlete Britain has produced, which makes it strange that compared to other less successful athletes he is an unsung hero with a low media profile. It is almost as if we take him for granted.

'I find it particularly frustrating when I watch *Sports Review of the Year* on BBC and they dwell at length on cricket, rugby and soccer, where we might have not had such a great time, and then say: "Oh, and by the way, we do have 50 world champions," and get rid of the rest of us in 30 seconds of film.

'That's annoying. I've been nominated three times for the individual prize but have never been in the top three. I sometimes think that if we did badly we might get more press. Perhaps we might start losing and see what happens,' he mused.

'You wouldn't like it, though, would you?' I said.

'What?' he asked.

'Losing,' I said. He gave me an odd look.

It was a silly question. What separates Redgrave from the pack, what defines all great champions is that they find it impossible to contemplate the possibility of coming second.

Redgrave learned his lesson early on. 'I had a bad result in the world championships as a single scull in 1983. Up until that point everything seemed simple. Since I was 16 or 17, people had been predicting that I would be a world champion. It seemed all I had to do was sit long enough in a boat and it would happen naturally.

'Then I failed and thought: "How did that happen?" So I looked at methods of training, saw how swimmers trained, found out what was happening in East Germany. I changed my routine, did more work, set much higher endurance levels,' he said.

A year later he won his first Olympic gold medal, in the coxed four at the Los Angeles Olympics. He admits that for all his success his real ambition was to win gold as a single. 'I could go back to being a single sculler but it would take a year or two to prepare and would be a backward step. I don't think I could face two or three years of not winning, two or three years of coming second.

'I don't know why I didn't have the same success as a single scull. It's a lot more technical and maybe I'm too strong and try to muscle the boat along rather than scull it. Anyway, I don't know why I even bother thinking about it. Matthew and I are strong favourites to win gold at Atlanta. Who would want to give that up on a gamble?' he said.

He measures out his life in Olympic Games. When one finishes and he stands on the winners' podium with gold round his neck and the national anthem playing he is thinking four years ahead. He is convinced he has the will to suffer the routine of training that will take him and Pinsent to Atlanta rowing four seconds faster than the targets they set for Barcelona.

So far this year they have beaten their own world record by three seconds and won another world championship. They are ahead of schedule but that does not mean a slacking-off period. Every day, apart from a break of three weeks, they train from dawn to dusk, including four hours a day on the water rowing a total of 25 miles.

Then there is weight training, cycling, running and simulated rowing on ergometers, supervised by their East German coach, Jürgen Gröbler.

Redgrave broke away early from the training dictated by the national rowing coaches. One of them had the gall to say that she made him the success he is today. He bridles at the memory: 'She did, in that everything she told me to do I did the opposite,' he said. He is not by nature or inclination a squad person. He is a loner driven in pursuit of a fierce ambition.

He says of himself: 'I'm a private army in the squad system. I like looking after myself. I listen to the best possible advice and then I make up my own mind. When I'm 100 per cent sure I've got it right, then I dedicate myself to whatever it is I have decided upon.'

His single-minded, obsessive quality sometimes brought him into conflict with the rowing establishment, who regarded this son of a builder from Marlow as something of an unpredictable maverick.

I remember when I was a young man attending the Henley Regatta on behalf of my newspaper to find out about the chaps who ran rowing.

At the entrance to the Leander Club stood a man wearing one of those funny hats. He was perusing a clipboard. I told him I was a journalist and would like to ask him a question. He continued looking at his clipboard.

'Fire away,' he said. 'I would like to know what kind of people you won't let in this club,' I said. Without even looking at me he said: 'People like you.'

'That's Henley,' said Redgrave. 'Things are different now in the sport. A lot more women in rowing, for one thing, and there's a much bigger cross-section of people taking it up.'

What does not change is the struggle for people like Redgrave to get proper funding. Finding sponsorship, he says, has been the hardest task of his career.

He and Pinsent are adequately funded but the man with three gold medals and favourite to win a fourth is a pauper with a begging bowl compared to the likes of Linford Christie. He feels there should be a system whereby the winners of Olympic medals and world titles are assisted according to their performance.

'It needs a two-tier system. To start with, just enough to get you going, see what you're about. Then the big money should be granted to those people who prove they have it in them to be outstanding,' he said.

When you meet Redgrave you are immediately consumed by a resolve to give up drinking and take more exercise. He shames you with his fitness. He is 6ft 5in tall and weighs 15 stone. He looks immensely strong, without being intimidating.

He has a stealthy quality about him that is surprising in so large a man. He moves carefully in the relaxed manner of the athlete. When we ate, I half imagined he would eat a cow pie in the manner of Desperate Dan, horns and all. He settled for a little lamb, which he chewed fastidiously, and sipped water.

The menu might have caused him a problem. He has the odd difficulty reading and writing as he is dyslexic. Sometimes he sees a word and it means nothing. Other times it is perfectly familiar. Sometimes, when signing autographs, he has to stop and wonder which way round the letter D goes.

It hindered his school work. 'Being a big child helped in that they didn't take the mickey. Instead, my mates used to assist me,' he said.

Nowadays, because he has a couple of young children, he has set out to improve matters by reading to them. Even so he still struggles. He was holding up an alphabet letter for one of his daughters to identify and could not understand why she seemed mystified.

His wife passed by and pointed out he was holding the letter upside down. It had looked the right way up to him. 'Fortunately I have followed a lifestyle where my dyslexia isn't an issue,' he said.

People looking for wellsprings of Redgrave's obsession with winning might have a fruitful time examining a possible link with his disability. On the other hand they might get a more interesting insight studying his relationship with Andy Holmes and Pinsent, the two men who have been closest to his ambition.

It was reported that he and Holmes ended up hating each other. 'Not true,' he says. 'But it was a business relationship. With Matthew it's different. He's godfather to one of my children. We enjoy one another's company. We're friends. In many ways it's a strange relationship. I see more of Matthew than I do my wife.

'It's a very close, intense relationship. We're trying to be one person. Sometimes we sulk at each other. Once it flared into a shouting match. But in the final analysis we both know that if we are to achieve what we want, which is to be the best, we need each other.'

He talks easily, without bombast and in a gentle manner, except he mentions not once but thrice 'destroying opponents'. Is that what they do? 'Of course. We aim to beat them before they get to the start line. Every race we try to go out and dominate the opposition.

'If we can get it into their minds that we're the best, the favourites, there will come a crunch situation during the race when we make a move and the other crew will say: "Well, they are the favourites. That's what we expect." And they'll settle for second or third,' he said.

His mental strength is absolute, his physical strength legendary. He has been called a physical freak. His lung capacity is 10 per cent above the average of the top rowers, his energy stoked by a big heart. Approaching his fourth Olympics, the flame of ambition has lost none of its heat.

'I know that when we break records for speed someone will go faster. That's inevitable. The record I want to set is for events won. If I get gold at Atlanta that will make four gold and one bronze. No one has done that.'

He says that he will retire after Atlanta though there is nothing to stop him going to Sydney in 2000. 'I'd be 38 at the time of the Sydney Olympics. That's not too old to win a medal,' he said. So might he be tempted to go to Sydney, to compete in his fifth Olympics? 'No,' he said, looking out of the restaurant window at the river. 'Why?' I asked. 'It's enough,' he said. For the time being, at any rate.

22nd October 1994

·35·

MARK
McCORMACK
—

LET ME come clean. I have been a client of International Management Group for more than 25 years so am I the person to interview Mark Hume McCormack, the chief executive officer and chairman of the company? Well, in all that time I have lunched with him not more than half a dozen times so we can hardly claim an intimate relationship.

On the other hand I am still with him after 25 years so I cannot be expected to criticize the way he deals with clients nor find sympathy with the point of view once expressed by Curtis Strange, that to some people IMG is a four-letter word.

I understand what Mr Strange, himself a client, was saying. The announcement that you are represented by IMG brings an interesting reaction from people; some of whom swoon away while others take on that clenched-jawed, steely-eyed look of someone about to unblock a toilet.

The main criticism of IMG is that it is too powerful, that it packages and sells sport like fancy chocolates, that it creates spoiled and greedy monsters out of the athletes.

Wimbledon provides the perfect example for those who are critical of McCormack's influence in sport. It was he who started selling the television rights worldwide, creating the financial spiral which could lead to a situation where the price is too rich for the likes of the BBC. It was McCormack who first thought of the idea of selling corporate hospitality facilities at Wimbledon, who dreamed up the Wimbledon logo and created a multi-million pound industry against the wishes of the traditionalists who were fearful of big business swamping a sporting occasion.

Moreover, because he makes so much money for the tennis players who are his clients, he personally is held responsible for their behaviour whenever they step out of line and act like spoiled brats.

As you would expect, Mark McCormack takes a slightly different view. Wimebledon represents his ultimate achievement. He thinks it is the greatest sports spectacle that exists and is proud of the part he played in creating it. It is only one sector of the IMG empire which now has 62 offices in 26 nations, turns over about £600 million a year and includes a literary agency, an organization that manages and presents classical music artists, two international modelling agencies, a company building golf courses and the world's largest independent producer of televised sports programming.

Clients include Nick Faldo and the Mayo Clinic, Andre Agassi and the Nobel Foundation, Itzhak Perlman and the Open Championship. Greg Norman and the Pope are former clients.

So what is he like, the man who owns the entire kit and caboodle – the most powerful man in sport? In his tent at Wimbledon I doubt that you would pick him. The sleek and likely-looking candidates are either employees or clients. McCormack wears a tweed jacket and carries a battered briefcase. He looks like an absent-minded inventor. It is an effective disguise.

Similarly he never seems to be at the centre of things, always on the edge of the action as if, wherever he is, he has no intention of stopping for very long. When you meet him he doesn't so much look in your direction as inspect the goods. From that point on there is little eye contact.

For all the gently modulated voice, the benevolent manner, the feeling that in another time he would have been played by James Stewart, there is an edge to him and it is not far under the surface. He takes things personally. Thus when Greg Norman recently left the organization to go his own way McCormack's disappointment was as much based on what he perceived to be a personal slight as it was on losing a client of immense financial value.

I asked him if Norman's departure was a sign that the business of client management invented by IMG was over, that the big stars of the future, having learned what was necessary, would now go their own way?

'Greg Norman made a long-term bad decision. He has enough money – which we made for him – to do as he likes, but there's no way he can do it like we can. I will say that for a man in his 40th year who has won two major championships – the same as Hubert Green and Hale Irwin – we have done an extraordinary job for him. It represents one of the most mind-blowing jobs done in the history of sport.

'In my experience the biggest mistake people make is in thinking that because they have succeeded in one thing they can succeed at anything. That isn't the way the world works. Managing athletes is difficult,' he said. And getting more so.

McCormack's first client 30 years ago was Arnold Palmer. He, along with Jack

Nicklaus and Gary Player, were the foundation stones of IMG. McCormack retains a special affection for Palmer.

'The pefect role model for all athletes. Honest, honourable, bold personality. I played with him in the Bing Crosby tournament and we hit our shots to the green where there was a puddle close to the hole. In that situation you are allowed to pace to the flag and then pace out again the same distance to give yourself a clear putt. Arnie took eight normal paces to the flag and then ten giant strides back from the flag.

'He had turned a 15-foot putt into one 25 feet long. I said: "Arnie, what on earth are you doing?" He said: "Mark, there are hundreds of people around this green watching me. If any one of them went away thinking I had taken advantage of the situation, I couldn't live with myself." Golf has its good reputation because of people like Palmer. Young pros see what he did and they put something back into the game. Doesn't happen at tennis. Golfers sign autographs, are polite to sponsors. Not tennis players. They scream and yell. Not all of them but generally speaking,' he said.

I suggested he might be partly to blame in that he had created a situation where half-formed children were attracted to the prospect of vast riches and grew up knowing nothing of the court. He laughed without humour.

'What do we have to do with that situation? There has always been money in golf; players start earning large sums when they are young and they don't behave badly. I think the problem with young tennis players is parental. It has nothing to do with the tennis establishment or agents.

'Parents with children who possess a precocious talent for tennis want to maximize that talent. The kids associated with burnout are often from familes that are not very well off. The talented child offers financial security. It's a trade. Where we come in is to maximize the income and deal with other parts of the child's development. Do we support an age limit? Sure we do. If they say we can't approach the kids until they are 18 or whatever, that's fine. Providing the rest of the world doesn't talk to them either. Otherwise we end up without any clients,' he said.

For the past 30 years he has had a unique overview of sport. What does he see today?

'I have no doubt that all sports are better by miles than before. Partly due to diet, size of the athletes, equipment, but in any sport you can measure there is a vast difference. Johnny Weismuller's winning time at the 1936 Olympics wouldn't come close to qualifying for the women's event today. It's interesting to hear people philosophizing and becoming nostalgic about the way things were. I remember Bjorn Borg's coach was always going on about what tennis players were like in his day compared to the present, until one day Bjorn said to him: "I tell you what, I would never have been beaten by a man wearing long trousers."

'I think the Faldos, the Normans and the Prices would bury players of 20 years ago. Same with tennis. Pete Sampras is, in my view, the greatest tennis player that ever lived. He's the only player I have seen who doesn't have a weakness. Jean-Claude Killy says that Tomba is the greatest skier ever. I'll take Killy's word for it. I've always believed that Killy winning three gold medals at Grenoble in '68 was the greatest athletic achievement I've ever seen. It was accomplished in his own country and the pressure was immense. General de Gaulle turned up to present him with his third medal before he won it,' he said.

After 30 years does he still enjoy being an agent? 'To begin with I don't like the word "agent". An agent is someone who smokes a big cigar and books the band. I prefer manager. The fact is I do every day what people retire to do, so why should I give it up or tire of it? I often think that I do every week a thousand things, any one of which when I was 16 I would have considered an experience of a lifetime,' he says.

So the rumours he is about to give it all up are premature, the talk that he is going to sell his business to Rupert Murdoch, merely gossip.

When I thanked him for the interview he looked at his watch and told me there were still 10 minutes to go. I had forgotten he is a man who divides his day into carefully timed sections. He was once asked if he had difficulty getting to sleep. He said he didn't because he allowed four hours for sleep on his schedule and that being the case, went to bed and fell asleep. On the same subject his wife, Betsy, said her husband was an achiever and even when he was sleeping he was achieving rest. I used up my time asking him if he would swap his present situation, his influence, his immense wealth for one Open Championship. He treated the question with care. 'Not one, but five perhaps. Similarly I wouldn't swap what I've got for one Wimbledon title, but Bjorn's achievements might tempt me to do a deal,' he said.

Did he ever imagine 30 years ago that he would be known in the future as the most powerful man in sport? 'I knew two things in the early days. The first was that jet travel would make golf international, the second that television would change the sporting world. The smartest thing we did was to go international early. Then I was lucky. I had Jack, Arnie and Gary, and when the revolution occurred they were the stars,' he said.

On the way out he showed me a photograph of him standing next to Paul McCartney, his great hero. He carries the picture with him in his wallet along with photographs of his family. Ask him why and he says he admires talent, always has, always will. When we get outside into the street his car isn't there. He checks his watch. He is on schedule so what on earth has happened?

As I say goodbye he is standing outside his house looking a little lost, even confused. You would have a hard time convincing a stranger that this was a man who had built a billion-dollar empire. He would think him too modest of manner and appearance. A lot of people, some of whom might have been expected to know better, have made the same mistake.

2nd July 1994

·36·

DAVID LLOYD

—

I F YOU ask David Lloyd about heroes he says: 'Rohan Kanhai, Ken Platt, Garfield Sobers, Jimmy James, Keith Miller and Albert Modley.' When he arrives for a *Test Match Special* broadcast his briefcase contains the *Complete Stanley Holloway Monologues*. He can do 'Albert and the Lion' without looking at the book.

As if this was not enough, he thinks that George Formby was as good an all-rounder as Ian Botham and says that, if required, he would be prepared to fill the odd 20 minutes or so entertaining the listening public with his rendition of Formby's greatest hits. He tells you this with a straight face; but, like all deadpan comedians, the eyes are crafty and humorous.

When he decided to play cricket for a living, the Wheel Tappers and Shunters Club lost a good comic. What cricket gained was a player able enough to captain his county and almost captain his country, an umpire, a coach, a first-rate commentator and a top-class after-dinner speaker.

Cricket and David Lloyd were made for each other. The accents of cricket, its class system, its folklore and, most of all, its humour, were gift-wrapped for a boy from Accrington with a God-given appreciation of the absurd.

When we say Accrington we are talking serious Lancashire. It is like Rotherham to Yorkshire, pickled onions to pork pie. When they say: 'You can take the boy out of Accrington but not Accrington out of the boy,' it gives you a fair indication of what you might expect. When the boy never bothered to leave Accrington in the first place, then you know you are dealing with the genuine article.

I dwell on David Lloyd's background because it defines his ambitions and explains his style. He believes in Lancashire as a separate land with Accrington as its capital and a population of cricket-loving humorists who sleep in pyjamas covered in red roses. The 'enemy' lives in the south and, generally speaking, is soft in the head.

When David Lloyd commentates on cricket or makes a speech, neither the bluntness of his opinions nor the plump sounds of his accent leave any doubt about where he comes from or how he was brought up.

'Tell me, Bumble, do you think Gooch should be the England captain?' asked Johnners. 'No, I don't,' said Lloyd. Watching Merv Hughes in the field: 'He's a time-bomb, ticking away, waiting to go off.' Observing Dickie Bird remonstrating with players for running on the wicket: 'They say he's a sandwich short of a picnic, that Dickie Bird. Not him. He knows what's going on. He's got all his chairs at home, has Dickie. He's saying to 'em, "Ayup, get off that pitch or else I'll have you." Doesn't miss much. Good umpire.'

It's a toss-up whether Lloyd likes commentating as much as he liked playing the game. When you ask him he says he enjoyed being an umpire best of all. He says he gets the same thrill waking up in the morning and going to the commentary box as he did entering the pavilion as a player.

'I think about it the same way. How I'll approach the day, what I might say. I have in mind my father. He's 80 years old, cantankerous at times. He's sitting there saying, "Go on. Tell me what's happening. Entertain me."

'The other thing is being part of an institution. That's what *Test Match Special* is. Whenever I make speeches around the country I say, "If anything happens to *Test Match Special* there would be a national day of mourning," and it gets a round of applause. People care. It's part of their lives.'

He was a boy of 16 when he came to Old Trafford. He bowled left-arm spin, unorthodox, googlies and chinamen. 'You can't bowl like that,' they told him.

Now he is Lancashire's coach the words echo down through the years. 'Coaching isn't about changing people. Am I going to change the way Wasim Akram bowls? What I have to do is give the players confidence, to get them ready to go out and play to the best of their ability.

'I think the four-day game will improve standards. It'll cut out mediocrity. The best players will come through. The raw talent is there. Lots of good young players coming through the schools system. It's more efficient than it used to be. What I'm looking for now is a leg-spinner. Love leg-spinners. Always something might happen. Two or three bad balls then a jaffa. That's what I want to find, a leg-spinner . . . [a pause] . . . an English leg-spinner.'

Lloyd's Test career lasted 12 months. He started with an unbeaten double-century against India and then came across Lillee and Thomson in 1974–5. Bill Frindall, in his book on England Test cricketers, says Lloyd had his Test career and confidence wrecked by that tour.

David Lloyd disagreed. 'Searing pace, Thomson. Their version of Tyson. Mike Denness said, "We need a left-hander at the start of our innings to take Thomson." I thought that sounded like me. Got hit in the groin. Inverted the box. Next innings got one in the throat. But all things considered, I did pretty well against them. Didn't matter. My Test career was over. But it didn't get me down. Whenever they announced a Test team and they'd picked someone else in my place, I always used to say that he got the job because he was from down south. For no other reason.'

Does that still happen? I asked. He gave me a withering look. 'The people who run the England cricket team all live in the south within 20 miles of each other, don't they?' he said.

Nonetheless, he might have been captain of England. He had an outside chance in 1980 when he was brought back for the one-day internationals against the West Indies.

Lloyd's account of what happened is a perfect example of his droll style: 'I was told I'd be batting number seven and if I showed up well, got a few runs and handled the quicks okay I would be in with a chance with a couple of others when it came to the captaincy. I remember taking guard and watching Malcolm Marshall walking back to his bowling mark. I thought to myself, "I don't go that far on my holidays."

'He set off towards me. He was halfway there when I thought, "I bet he doesn't want me to play forward to this delivery." He let go this 90 mph thunderbolt at me and I played what I can only describe as a very hurried backward defensive prod. The ball smashed into my forearm and broke it in two places. As I was helped from the field I remember thinking, "I wonder if I've done enough." '

Why umpiring when he gave up cricket? 'Same game, different view. When I was a player Viv Richards would whack the cricket ball and I would have to run and fetch it. As an umpire I had the pleasure of watching Viv smash the ball all round the park and some other poor beggar would run after it.

'Fascinating, too, standing when great bowlers like Hadlee or Marshall were bowling, watching them set a batsman up, then do him. Great art. Watching great art, that's what it's all about. Also, because you've played the game you're on the same wavelength. They can't try it on. If they do they must know you'll have 'em.

'I remember Bill Alley when he was umpiring, catching our bowler, Peter Lee, picking the seam. He inspected the ball carefully, threw it back to Peter and said, "If you don't get seven for 20 with a ball like that I'll report you to Lord's."

'Some great characters, too. Arthur Jepson was a magnificent umpire and a tremendous character. He had a broad Nottinghamshire accent and a booming voice. We were playing Gloucestershire in that famous one-day game when it went pitch black. When the light was very bad Jackie Bond, our skipper, had a word with Arthur. "Light, light, what's wrong wi' t'light?" said Arthur. Bond pointed out they could barely see wicket to wicket.

'Jepson snorted dismissively. "What's that up there?" he bellowed, pointing his finger skywards. "The moon, Arthur," said Bond. "Well if tha' can see that bloody far, there can't be that much wrong wi' t'light?" said Arthur. In another match I was bowling and was halfway through an over when Arthur said, "I hope you don't mind me mentioning this but you are the worst bowler I've ever seen. Fred Price was a bad 'un, but you're worse than him."'

The folklore of cricket is in good hands so long as there are people like David Lloyd about. So is the game's pleasant nature. He is not without his critics. A Lancashire member once enquired if it could be right for someone with an accent as broad as Lloyd's to captain Lancashire. At times like that it helps to come from Accrington and be born with a sense of humour.

He doesn't please everyone on *Test Match Special*. This is not surprising since the programme's genius is to ensure such a mixture of accents and attitudes that someone, somewhere is bound to be upset before the day is over.

I asked Peter Baxter, producer of the programme, to sum him up. 'Self-deprecating, strong-minded and frank, above all funny,' he said. That would be a fair description of him, not only as a commentator but as a cricketer, umpire, after-dinner speaker, coach and man. With David Lloyd, what you hear is what you get.

12th June 1993

·37·

NAT LOFTHOUSE

—

THE DAY after war broke out in September 1939, Nat Lofthouse joined Bolton Wanderers Football Club. He is still there. He is in his 70th year but bright-eyed and fit-looking. He looks as solid as an oak, a bit gnarled maybe, but you don't have to possess a vivid imagination to see how he terrorized defenders and why he gained the title 'The Lion of Vienna' (it's a long way from Bolton to Vienna, as they say, and more of that later).

He was the most English of footballers, direct, uncompromising, fearless, hard but fair. Nothing distracted him from his job, which was to fill the net with footballs and, if necessary, goalkeepers.

In the 1958 final Bolton played Manchester United. This was the United recovering after the horror of Munich, borne to the Cup final on an engulfing wave of sympathy and emotion. Some teams had found it difficult to play against them, had felt compromised by the public's overwhelming desire that nothing but good should happen to what was left of the Busby Babes. Bolton and Lofthouse put paid to the dream by winning 2–0, with Lofthouse settling matters by shoulder-charging Harry Gregg into the net.

So much for sentiment. There was much debate about its legality, it certainly wasn't pretty but, by God, it was effective.

That expert judge of footballers (particularly if they were born and bred in Lancashire), H D Davies, wrote of him: 'Some like to get their effects by stealth, others by rank piracy. Nat is in the latter class and when he opens out all his guns he is a sight to see.'

It was on 25th May 1952, playing for England against Austria in Vienna, that Lofthouse demonstrated all the virtues Davies perceived in him, to win a famous victory in such a manner that from that moment to this, whenever you mention Nat Lofthouse, people say 'The Lion of Vienna'.

What made the game so special was its billing as the championship of Europe. We were a year or more away from meeting the Hungarians at Wembley and having our world turned upside-down.

In 1952 we were still a great soccer nation. Finney and Matthews were two of football's acknowledged stars. The game was given another dimension by the presence of several thousand soldiers who were garrisoned in Austria.

Lofthouse won the match several minutes from the end when he took a through-ball from Tom Finney, ran half the length of the field with the Austrians in pursuit and struck the ball home before colliding with the on-rushing Austrian goalkeeper and knocking himself out. The moment moved *The Times* to report: 'For anybody who has ever seen or read football, Lofthouse will always be known as The Lion of Vienna . . . It was his example all through the match that brought the scores of British soldiers pouring through the crowd at the end of the game to cheer him, lion-hearted, from the field.'

We don't call people 'lion-hearted' any more. Nowadays, we say 'they've got bottle'. We don't have centre-forwards any more. We call them strikers. It is not just the game that has changed, so has our way of thinking about it, of describing it. What would the fanzine of today make of the poem written by a fan to commemorate Nat's retirement from Bolton Wanderers:

Lofty the Lion of Vienna,
Has retired from t'football field.
It took a medical specialist
To make Lofthouse finally yield.
All t'best centre-halves in t'country
Tried their hand at stopping our Nat.
Nearly all had to give up the struggle,
You can blame mother nature for that.
Like a Centurian tank was our Nathan,
Wi' a turn of speed like a bomb.
Many a goalie's said sadly
'I wonder where that came from?'

Nat Lofthouse had a laugh when I read it to him in his office at Burnden Park. He'd forgotten it, but he liked the humour. 'Typically Bolton,' he said.

The same could be said about him. He works from an office at the club helping out with sponsors' deals, linking the club with the community. As soon as he gave up playing he came back to the club for a job. They made him second-team trainer. His first task was to clean the toilets. He had scored 255 goals for Bolton, been capped 33 times by England and scored 30 goals, and here he was working as a lavatory attendant at his old club.

It redefines loyalty. He doesn't make much of it. 'There wasn't anything else to do, so I had to muck in,' he said.

Sometimes people say that he has a cushy job nowadays and he has to smile. When he joined Bolton, he was given two white fivers as a signing-on fee. When he took them home his father, a coal bagger with the corporation, thought he had robbed a bank. The money represented a month's wages to his dad. During the war years he worked down the pit. It made him strong.

'I was lean and hard as nails. Not an ounce of fat on me,' he said. He played his first game for England against Yugoslavia in 1950 and scored twice. He felt pretty chuffed with himself. 'Head like a bucket,' he said.

He returned home and Bolton lost to Chelsea 3–1. Nat still thought he was the bee's knees. As he came off the field, George Taylor, the trainer said: 'See me 8.30 Monday morning.' Nat said: 'It's our day off, isn't it?' And Taylor said: 'It is for the rest of t'team but not for thee.'

Nat recalled: 'When I turned up he gave me the biggest dressing-down I ever had, told me not to be big-headed and then said something I never forgot. He said: "You can do three things. You can run, shoot and head. You couldn't trap a bag of washing. So don't get fancy.

' "When you play for England, you've got Matthews and Finney working for you; here at Bolton, you've got Bobbie Langton and Doug Holden. So all I want you to do in future is run, shoot and head."

'That's all I did really. I was fit and fast. Matthews and Finney used to put it on my forehead. Then there were players like Mannion and Carter. Finney was my favourite. I played with him 20-odd times and on 18 occasions his was the pass that I scored from. He and George Best were the two most complete players I ever saw,' he said.

He showed me the boardroom with his England caps in the display cabinet and then led me down the tunnel on to the pitch. When he played for Bolton Wanderers with the likes of Hartle and Banks, this was the walk that would test the nerve of the bravest opposition player.

'Ay, they didn't like playing here,' said Nat Lofthouse, looking across the pitch. I inspected the track around the ground where Tommy Banks would dump his victims. 'Gi' em a bit of gravel rash on the arse. Let 'em know who's the boss,' said Tommy.

It is reputed that his partner, Roy Hartle, would call out: 'When tha's finished kicking thi' man Tommy, chip him over here so I can have a go at him.'

Lofthouse says: 'I used to wear my shin pads on the backs of my calves with Tommy and Roy behind me. Mind you, we were all tough and there was a wonderful team spirit. If you kicked one of our team you had to kick the other 10. But I would have hated to have played against Banks and Hartle.

'I tell people that if Roy Hartle's mother had pulled a No. 11 shirt on and run out at Burnden Park with the opposition, he would have kicked her to death.'

He played his last game at Burnden Park in 1960. He played inside-right and nursemaid to a 16-year-old boy making his debut called Francis Lee. Lee crossed, Lofthouse scored with a header.

Lee embarked on a glittering career; Lofthouse started a new life cleaning toilets and polishing boots for players who weren't fit to lace his. But he wouldn't change too much of it. He thinks being a centre-forward is much harder work nowadays. 'Defensive tactics and patterns of play make it much more difficult to score goals. They have to do much more than run, shoot and head nowadays,' he said.

'Mind you, I'd very much like a modern team to go out just one more time and play with two backs, three half-backs and five forwards. It would be very interesting to see how the other teams coped.'

I ventured that this was how Tottenham had played under Ardiles and look what happened. 'Yes, but they didn't have Banks and Hartle in defence,' he said.

Nat Lofthouse and Bolton Wanderers have been together now for 55 years, a remarkable test of enduring fidelity at any level, but in soccer, where players and clubs often show little regard for loyalty, it is nothing short of amazing.

The fact is that as well as representing Bolton's past, Nat Lofthouse also stands for the future. There is much the players of today could learn from talking to him and nothing but good to be gained from such a decent and friendly man representing the club.

As I left, my taxi driver said: 'Who you been talking to?' 'Nat Lofthouse,' I said. I bet myself he would say 'The Lion of Vienna'. Instead, he said: 'A gentleman. Still takes the same cap size he did when he was a lad.' I can't improve on that.

25th February 1995

DON

BRADMAN

—

I HAVE travelled long and far in my search for Donald Bradman. It started nearly 50 years ago when I rode on my bike the 30 miles to Leeds to see his Australian team slaughter our lot.

Since the first glimpse I have been seeking an audience. I have telephoned, telegrammed (remember?), written, faxed, pleaded, ranted and cajoled. The answer has always been No.

I have offered money, attempted to lure him with limousines and expensive hotel suites, persuaded mutual friends to use their influence, even tried incense and prayer. I still haven't interviewed Sir Donald. Not even got close.

On the odd occasion when I have glimpsed him in the distance he vanished before I could reach him, like a mirage. Once or twice I have been somewhere only to be told he had just left. One time the host showed me the teacup he had been drinking from. The liquid was still warm. I felt like an explorer who had just found a fresh footprint of the Abominable Snowman.

Why so persistent? Because he was the greatest cricketer who ever lived and a significant man both in the history of the game and the development of his country. In cricket there have been two towering figures, two people who more than any other wrote the history of the game. They are W G Grace and D G Bradman. One is still with us and any journalist worth his salt has a duty to try to talk to him.

The other reason is much more selfish. In a lifetime of interviewing people I have talked to most of my heroes.

The two big ones who escaped were Frank Sinatra and Donald Bradman. I got closer to The Kid from Hoboken than I ever did to The Boy from Bowral.

But let us suppose that dreams come true and the interview has been arranged.

What do I ask The Don? Well, all else apart, what fascinates me about Bradman is his fame. Generally speaking, being famous is a bit like having measles.

It is a minor affliction and the rash soon disappears. But for some it never goes away. It dictates their life and shapes their circumstance. They and their family are forever on display.

They are isolated by a special kind of celebrity and become icons of their time. Sir Donald Bradman belongs in that category.

I went looking for him on Australia Day in Adelaide. You must admire my stamina. Adelaide is his lair, the cricket ground on the first day of a Test match one of his regular watering holes and therefore offering the best chance of a sighting.

A man I met said he would take me to have tea with Sir Donald in a box in the Bradman Stand. Overcome by emotion I clasped my new friend by the lapels and told him of my search for the Holy Grail.

A short time later he took me to one side and said he would have to ask Sir Donald if he minded having me in the box. I had obviously frightened him with my exuberance. He must have thought I was going to kidnap The Don or film him with a hidden camera picking his nose.

I told him not to bother Sir Donald with such petty problems and settled instead for a drink in the Bradman Bar looking at pictures of the great man and wondering if they sold such a thing as a Bradman Burger.

Mooching around the ground I came upon my old friend Keith Miller making one of his rare public appearances.

He had just been to see Sir Donald. How was he? 'Looks fit enough to still be playing,' said Keith.

He invited me to his caravan parked on the tennis courts. Whenever there is a Test match at Adelaide Keith Miller sets up office in a caravan belonging to a friend and entertains the world.

Life is never dull in his company. People are attracted to him like iron filings to a magnet. His personality embraces everyone from bookmakers to conductors of great orchestras, barmaids to brain surgeons, people who sell newspapers on London streets and men who commanded armies in time of war.

If I was allowed to organize a party of people I most love and admire to celebrate my last day on earth, Keith Ross Miller would be at the top of the list.

His meeting with Sir Donald was a significant one. It might be the last time the two of them get together. Keith is in his mid-seventies, Sir Donald 10 years older.

They played with and against each other and it was, at times, a fairly turbulent relationship; they were very different men. Miller was the maverick, Bradman the authoritarian.

Conflict was inevitable. In Sir Donald's last first-class game at Sydney, Miller greeted him with two bouncers. The first, of the harmless variety, was hit for four.

The second, preceded by a gesture to the press box declaring: 'If you think that was funny you ain't seen nothing yet,' nearly decapitated Sir Donald, who at the time happened to be chief selector.

The incident had nothing to do with the fact that Miller, then the world's greatest all-round cricketer, was not in the team to tour South Africa which was named a short time later.

Differences apart, what the two men have in common is a celebrity that travels far beyond the shoreline of Australia and represents much more than a reputation gained as flannelled fools.

What they symbolized in their prime, and still do today, is the Australian character at its very best. Bradman was the gifted Aussie battler, the man of few words but great deeds. Miller was the handsome, sun-kissed playboy who laughed at life and didn't give a stuff.

Bradman was the Outback and the fight against nature, Miller was Bondi Beach and a celebration of the good life.

There are a million funny anecdotes about Miller, not many about Don Bradman. The Bradman legend is built on stories underlining the prowess that set him apart from other men.

There is, for instance, the tale of Bill Black, an off-spin bowler playing for Lithgow who on a memorable day in 1931 bowled Bradman for 52. The umpire was so excited that when the ball hit Bradman's wicket he called out: 'Bill, you've got him.'

The ball was mounted and given to Bill Black as proof that he dismissed the greatest batsman in the world.

Later that season Don Bradman again played against Bill Black. As the bowler marked out his run, Don said to the wicket-keeper: 'What sort of bowler is this fellow?'

The wicket-keeper, a mischievous fellow like the rest of his tribe, replied: 'Don't you remember this bloke? He bowled you out a few weeks ago and has been boasting about it ever since.'

'Is that so?' said Bradman. Two overs later Bill Black pleaded with his skipper to be taken off. Bradman had hit him for 62 runs in two eight-ball overs. He made 100 in three overs and finished with 256 including 14 sixes and 29 fours.

The other side to his genius is demonstrated by an encounter with George Macauley, the feisty Yorkshire seam bowler, in 1930. It was Bradman's first tour of England and there was a popular rumour that the English wickets would sort him out. As an ardent subscriber to this theory Macauley couldn't wait to get at Bradman.

When Yorkshire played the Australians early in the tour Macauley demanded loudly of his captain: 'Let me have a go at this bugger.' His first over was a maiden.

Bradman then hit him for five fours in the second over and took 16 from the third. A spectator yelled: 'George, tha' should have kept thi' bloody trap shut.'

Macauley was not the only English bowler to suffer on that tour. Harold Larwood once told me of a famous encounter with Bradman at Leeds during the third Test of the series when the little man played one of his great innings. Harold said there was no doubt in his mind Bradman was the greatest batsman he ever bowled to.

'We worked on the theory he was uneasy against the short-pitched ball early on,' said Harold. 'Maurice [Tate] got Archie Jackson and they were two for one. I gave Bradman a short one first ball. He played at it and there was a nick. George Duckworth caught it. We thought we had him but the umpire didn't agree. Mind you we got him out shortly after.'

'How many had he got?' I asked, walking blindfold into the trap.

'Three hundred and thirty four,' replied Harold with a grin.

When I first wrote that story many years ago I received a letter from Sir Donald saying he was concerned I cast doubts on his sportsmanship. I had not intended to do so nor do I now. Indeed, Harold Larwood's telling of the story was done very much tongue in cheek and recounted to enhance the Bradman legend rather than diminish it. Nonetheless, Bradman's reaction was revealing.

It served as a reminder that for all his genius, or perhaps because of it, Bradman often seems a distant and remote hero, preferring to be admired rather than beloved. The statistical difference between him and other cricketers is not the only huge gap that exists betwixt Bradman and the game he adorned.

R S Whitington, who played under Bradman for South Australia and later became a writer and commentator on the game, once wrote: 'Bradman the man was not so easy to idolize as Bradman the batsman. He decided . . . to remain encased in a shell that any oyster would have envied.'

To this day – and Bradman is now 86 years old – the greatest cricketer of all time has never given the long, definitive television interview about his life and time; a legacy to be stored in the national archives for future generations to watch and study.

He did a series of interviews about his career for radio, and fascinating they are too. But like the books written about his life, including his autobiography, they provide only a simple sketch of the man. Why should Bradman bother to go any deeper? Because he is not only an important figure in the history of cricket but a significant man in the development of his country.

No Australian has done more to announce his nation's pride and ambition. His effect on Australians during the Depression years alone is worthy of a book. A parody of the Lord's Prayer at the time went:

Our Harbour which art in heaven
Sydney be its name
Our Bridge be done in 1930 or 1931
Give Us this day our daily Bradman
For ours is the harbour, the bridge and the Bradman for ever and ever.

The stories about Keith Miller are much more self-deprecating and whimsical. Alan Davidson, his colleague in the NSW team, told me of the time when Miller as captain took the team to Maitland for a one-day game. It was a big event for the town and the mayor officiated at a civic reception. When Miller stepped forward to make a reply he said: 'Mr Mayor, we are very pleased to be in this town, er . . . this city, er . . . where the bloody hell are we anyway?'

His forgetfulness was legendary, something he shared with his great adversary Denis Compton who popped into the caravan to have a yarn.

It was a poignant moment. These were the two great glamour figures of the immediate post-war years, the Brylcreem Boys whose image was plastered on posters throughout the England of my youth. The best of enemies, the greatest of friends.

Compton recalled the day rain stopped play during a Test match and Keith Miller joined him in the England dressing room for a serious game of cards.

The pot grew and when the umpires decided play could recommence the card school cut for a large jackpot which was won by Miller.

Compton went out to resume his innings and the first ball from his friend Miller scraped a layer of Brylcreem from his head. 'You've won the money. What do you want now, blood?' said the aggrieved Compton.

Denis got to see Bradman. So did Sir Tim Rice, who I fear will never stop telling me of the day he sat next to The Don at Adelaide Oval. How close did I get? Well, eventually I sat at one end of a box and he was 15 people away.

I know. I counted. In profile he looked like a kookaburra. It was interesting observing people's reaction to his presence.

Some sneaked photographs of him, while others blatantly turned their backs to the cricket and surveyed the great man.

I fell once more to contemplating the kind of fame attached to Sir Donald and began comparing it to Keith Miller's.

In the end it is the difference between being inspected and being celebrated. The trouble with national treasures is that they are often placed behind glass, isolated by protocol, protected by a self-appointed Papal Guard.

Sir Donald remains a remote and lonely figure whose life will be judged and assessed by archivists and historians for as long as the game of cricket is played. Keith Miller will be celebrated in song, joke and anecdote.

As I left the Adelaide Oval on Australia Day I was struck by the thought that any country capable of producing two such gifted and singular men has much to be proud of and great reason to celebrate.

29th January and 6th February 1995

·39·

JACKIE STEWART

—

URING A lifetime of meeting people I have no hesitation in appointing Jackie Stewart captain of my World Championship Extraordinary XI. I would choose him as leader because he would be the best man for the job. Also, I would be aware that if I didn't make him top dog it wouldn't make any difference; within 24 hours he would have become the boss in any case.

Most of us find life to be a maze of never-ending corridors leading nowhere in particular. We are baffled, bemused by it all. Not Mr Stewart. He plots a straight line to the horizon. He is a meticulous planner with a pernickety eye for detail. In military terms he is more Montgomery that Patton. I have little doubt that had he been in charge of the Gulf War it might have taken longer to get on the road, but, when it did, would have lasted about 24 hours.

Should you go to Silverstone today and visit the site of Paul Stewart Racing (Prop: J Stewart) you will see what I mean. First of all, the transporter will not only shine like a guardsman's toe-cap, but you will notice that each of its wheels will be meticulously positioned so the name of the tyre manufacturer runs across the top in perfect alignment. This is achieved by Mr Stewart persuading the driver to jack up the vehicle and rearrange the position of the tyres. 'You won't see another lorry like that,' says the boss. You bet. But why bother? 'Pride,' he says. 'If the driver bothers to get that right, I can guarantee he's looking after the important things.'

If you arrive early in the day and see a small figure picking up scraps of paper, searching for unsightly grease in the bay area, you will have seen one of the greatest racing drivers of all time practising what he calls 'attention to detail'. Similarly, visitors to his shooting school in Scotland have been amazed to see the owner picking weeds from the range.

It is not as if he had nothing else to do. In a normal year he flies more than 400,000 miles. Last year he made 43 trips to America. When I met him, he was dashing off to catch Concorde, spending a couple of nights in Detroit, returning for Silverstone and then going home to Geneva. During this time he will have met a couple of royals, half a dozen captains of industry and will count it a moderately slack week.

At the age of 54, 20 years after he retired from grand prix racing, he is working harder than ever (Ford, Rolex, Moët et Chandon, commentating, lecturing, raising money for charity, shooting school, racing team); making more money than ever (we are talking seven figures a year here) and offering a rebuke to those sporting heroes who give up on life when they stop competing.

Jackie Stewart retired at the top. It was the year he became world champion for the third time, after he had crossed the line first 27 times in 99 races. 'All famous sportsmen – racing drivers, Gazza, Pete Sampras, whoever – lead abnormal lives. We inhabit a silly little world where extraordinary things become commonplace. We take for granted first-class travel and hotels, private jets, helicopters. My son Paul has five dinner jackets because he's sponsored by a clothing firm. What do you want five dinner jackets for? When I was world champion I went to Buenos Aires. I had eight bodyguards. Eight! I ask you. The adulation is enormous, a scandal.

'Before I retired I had to figure out how I could survive in the real world. My first decision was that I could do without an entourage – a sign of weakness, an admission you can't go anywhere on your own. I gave myself five years to adapt to a new life. Now I can honestly say that I look back on what were supposed to be my halcyon days and think I've improved on the situation. It's better than it was when I was a racing driver. I've broadened out, I'm more fulfilled. I'm very happy with what I've done because it's more difficult than driving a motor car, I can tell you,' he said.

At one stage during his retirement he was offered $6 million to make a comeback. He wasn't remotely tempted: 'When I decided to give it up it wasn't something I did on the spur of the moment. For the two to three years before my retirement I had stopped being competitive in the sense of racing against other people. I was competing against Jackie Stewart. My biggest challenge was to discover the full potential between machine and man. More fun to that than challenging the frailty of another man.

'Then I came to the conclusion that I was going round in circles, so I retired. It wasn't fear, though it must be pointed out that when a racing driver makes a mistake it isn't to be compared with something like Nick Faldo finding a bunker with his tee shot. It wasn't the death of friends. It wasn't the effect it had on my children, though I was brought up short when Paul came home from school one day and asked: "When is daddy going to get killed?" What happened was that I had matured and with maturity came the realization that I shouldn't be doing it.'

What is it that makes a great racing driver? 'Mind management. At Silverstone there will be 26 drivers, all of whom have been champions in their sport at various categories. Six will be special talents, three extraordinary and one a genius. There will be men who can drive as fast as Ayrton Senna but do not have his mental capacity to win. More than that, they can't do it over 17 races in a season. It's not about passion. Passion is dangerous when you're driving a racing car.

'I was once accused by a critic of being too clinical as a driver. He said I was like a computer. I took it as a compliment. The more I did it, the more I thought about it, the more clinical I became. I have an affinity with a motor car. I can sit in a car and discover its personality, tell you its faults. That's what I do when I test for Ford Jaguar and Aston Martin. I find out what's wrong and offer a solution. Some suggestions are incorporated in the cars people drive.

'That gives me a fantastic feeling. I test drive these cars at 50 mph. You can feel more at that speed, it's like seeing more as a passenger. When I've driven the car I tell them what I think. I'm not an engineer, but I am good at explaining what I feel. I paint a vivid picture.'

No one articulated better the excitement and mystery of driving a racing car than Jackie Stewart. His detractors might accuse him of being a robot on the track, but off it he was a peerless witness. He once told me that he regarded racing motor cars as a drug. Living on the edge of life and death was, he said, the ultimate high.

'Once I was driving on a very hot day in a particularly hard race when I came round this corner and through all the heat and the smell in the cockpit, through the balaclava, all the protective clothing and the stink of oil and fuel came the clearest aroma of cut grass. It was as if someone had spilled a perfume all over me. I couldn't imagine where it came from until I saw that a car had left the course on that corner and skidded across the grass. It was such a strong smell that I might have been walking behind a mowing machine cutting the lawn. Instead I was in the cockpit of a racing car, sealed off from the outside world. How do you explain that, except to say that my entire system was stimulated to an extraordinary degree of awareness.'

I came somewhere near to understanding what he was talking about when he gave me a lift from the Italian Grand Prix at Monza. He was driving a hired family bone-shaker through heavy traffic at a speed which made any thought of hiring a helicopter superfluous. The aroma in the car when we reached our destination had more to do with fear than horticulture, but it was a small price to pay for a demonstration of the perfect marriage between man and machine.

Sitting next to him then, talking to him now, it is difficult to appreciate that as a child he was dismissed as (in his own words) 'a dunce, stupid, thick'. He was dyslexic in the days before they had a name for it. School was a disaster, he was made to feel second rate. 'I was almost suffocated by my inability to learn. I had a serious complex about not being clever,' he said. What pulled him through? 'Sport. Soccer first, then shooting. Then, when I worked in my father's garage I always had the cleanest forecourt, the most spotless grease bay.'

The man you might see picking up waste paper around the area of Paul Stewart Racing at Silverstone this weekend is not being eccentric, merely promulgating the lessons of a lifetime. He is richer and wiser than he was, but only because he never forgot what it was like when people wrote him off as a complete prat. Jackie Stewart proved them wrong, and, in a sense, he is still at it.

The five-year period he gave himself to make it in another world expired in the Seventies. In the Nineties he looks forward to the 21st century without ever contemplating slowing down. When you ask him about retiring, he says he did that 20 years ago.

Sport can be cruel to its heroes. The years of adulation are scant preparation for a lifetime in the shadows. The tragedies are well documented, the post-mortem a foregone conclusion. More often than not the success stories, like Jackie Stewart's, are unheeded, the lessons ignored. Which is why the drivers at Silverstone, lowly or eminent, would do well to look at Jackie Stewart and think hard about the example he sets.

More to the point, anyone fearing retirement or coming to the conclusion that they have reached an age when it might be prudent to creep into a corner and fade away, should also listen to him: 'In most cases, as people mature in years they become more expansive mentally because they have accumulated this enormous experience. This must surely be the most important part of our lives. When I meet elderly people who are still able to communicate I get excited by them. I want to die standing up, doing something that I'm planning tomorrow,' said Jackie Stewart. Having first swept the forecourt, no doubt.

10th July 1993

·40·

ALISTAIR
COOKE

—

ALISTAIR COOKE was 12 years old when he met Neville Cardus. He saw the great man walking around the ground at the Blackpool cricket festival. Cooke read Cardus every morning in the *Manchester Guardian* but never imagined they would meet.

He approached him and asked for his autograph. 'I had a little green autograph book. Cardus wore a floppy hat with the brim turned down like Crocodile Dundee, pipe, tweed jacket, flannels. He signed my book and if I close my eyes I can transcribe his signature,' he said.

It was 1920, the year that Prohibition was introduced in America and the writer and critic H L Mencken described the legislation as 'Puritanism, the haunting fear that someone, somewhere, might be happy'. Although he wasn't to know it, at the time, both America and Mencken were going to play a far more significant part in Cooke's life than Blackpool or Neville Cardus.

Thirty years later, after Cooke had reported in the *Manchester Guardian* on the epic fight in New York between Sugar Ray Robinson and Randolph Turpin, Cardus wrote a fan letter to Cooke. In it he said that he carried Cooke's article with him at all times and brought it out whenever people wanted to know how a boxing match should be reported. Flattered by the letter, Cooke replied saying that he had once, as a small boy, obtained Cardus's autograph. Came the reply: 'Dear Mr Cooke, many thanks for your letter. I am glad you have my autograph because now I have yours.'

Today, aged 86, Alistair Cooke allows himself a smile at the memory. He is spending some time in London meeting friends and publicizing a book called *Fun and Games with Alistair Cooke*. It is a collection of his sports writing and includes the report that so impressed Cardus. People might be surprised at Cooke's range of sporting interests. In the book he writes about cricket, soccer, boxing, baseball, horse racing and, best and most lovingly of all, about golf.

He says in his introduction: 'For more than fifty years I can truly say that scarcely has a day gone by when I didn't think about government, its plethora of ailments and its depressing range of failed panaceas. In games the problems are solved, somebody wins. Hence the "isle of joy" offered by sport in an ocean of anxieties. I have come to feel a deep, unspoken pity for people who have no attachment to a single sport, almost as sorry for them as I am for teetotallers.'

I have known him a good few years now and when people ask: 'What is he like?' I can only answer that what you hear is what you get. In conversation he shapes stories and observations exactly as he does on radio in *Letter From America*. He starts with a simple thought, wanders around the world and then returns to base. It is like watching a wonderful piece of pottery being shaped before your eyes. He looks an inquisitive man, long sharp nose, watchful pale eyes. The body is bent but still stoking enough energy to play a regular round of golf and, of course, work.

Next year Alistair Cooke will celebrate embarking upon his 50th year of *Letter From America*. The series is the longest running one-man programme in the history of broadcasting and it is heard in 52 countries. It is a weekly demonstration of the craft of a born journalist blessed with a unique style. Kenneth Tynan said: 'Cooke is one of the great reporters. Nobody can reproduce the events, giving it feel as well as the facts, the pith as well as the husk, with greater clarity or gentler wit.' Paraphrasing Tynan's observation about a great actor I once wrote: 'If there is a tightrope bridging the gap between a good journalist and a great one, Alistair Cooke would make the trip in white tie and tails with a cocktail in one hand and a quill in the other.'

When we met he was wearing an old cardigan with a hole in the left elbow. He made it look as much a fashion accessory as torn jeans. I told him that I remembered the report of the Robinson–Turpin fight and it stayed in my mind as it had with Cardus. He said: 'It was 1951 and I was in California covering the Japanese peace talks. At the time there was another marvellous story in the area called the Central Valley Project where they were reversing the flow of two rivers to provide power in California. At the same time Sugar Ray was fighting Turpin in New York. I cabled A P Wadsworth, the editor of the *Manchester Guardian*, a marvellous man with a great sense of humour. I told him I intended to stay in California to report "the greatest hydro-electric project there has been" rather than cover a prizefight. He cabled back: "Go to New York immediately. In this country blood is thicker than water."'

Wadsworth was right because Cooke's report of the fight would justify its place in any anthology of sports writing you care to mention. It is not only great reporting, it is memorable prose. 'Turpin seemed almost sick with the concentration of his own frenzy. But he stayed with it and flung all he knew. His left eye was showering blood so that the four gloves looked as if they had been dipped in paint. Turpin's gloves were up against the hail-stones rattling round his head. Then they were down, and limp and gone forever. Two, three, four more rocketing blows and Turpin was slipping against the rope, baying mutely at the nearly full moon and the roaring thousands up against it. And then the man in white came in. And it was all over.'

I asked Cooke if Cardus had been an influence in his career. 'Well, I read him as a young person so I suppose so but I wasn't persuaded to copy his style. Very high style, wasn't it? Typical of the *Guardian* at the time. Very literary. Don't think it would work nowadays. James Agate was a great devotee of Cardus. I once sat with C B Fry, Plum Warner and Agate at Lord's and we started picking the All Time England cricket team. We all put Frank Woolley, the great Kent stylist, in the team. Then Agate came out with this theory that Woolley never existed, that he was an invention of the wretched Cardus. Cardus created him out of descriptions like "in the butterfly melancholy of the evening Woolley came to the crease. His strokes had all the beauty of Debussy". Well I saw him bat three times and I didn't hear any Debussy.'

The man who had as much as anyone to do with the shaping of Cooke's style was one of his tutors at Cambridge, Arthur Quiller Couch, who wrote under the name 'Q'. Cooke remembers: 'One day I went to collect an essay I had sent to him, convinced that it was the most brilliant article that he, Q, or anyone else, had ever written on the subject. He was dressing for dinner and he dressed down, which is to say he started at the neck and clothed himself downwards. Therefore he was fully dressed except for shoes and trousers as he flicked through my essay. He came to the third page which I knew was the greatest piece of writing ever committed to one page of paper. He studied it and shook his head. "My dear Cooke," he said, "you must learn how to murder your darlings." I have never forgotten that advice, the best any writer, particularly a journalist, can ever receive.'

But back to Cardus. There is little doubt that he and Cooke were the greatest names the *Guardian* possessed. Cardus was the first to be knighted. Cooke, because he is an American citizen, was granted an honorary KBE. It means he can put the initials after his name but not 'Sir' before it.

His best story about Cardus concerns Emmott Robinson, the aggressive Yorkshire bowler of the Twenties whom he admired for his resolute spirit and feisty temperament.

Nonetheless it didn't stop Cardus criticizing the bowler nor offering him advice on technical matters. After one such article in which Cardus made several observations on how Robinson might amend his technique, the bowler was sitting watching play when a friend sat next to him and asked: 'Did you see what Cardus wrote about you this morning?' And Emmott said: 'I did that.' His friend asked: 'And what did you think about it?' and Emmott paused and thought for a long time and then said: 'I'd like to bowl at t'bugger.'

Alistair Cooke took up golf in his fifties. It was his wife who persuaded him, saying that if he didn't he would end up 'a typewriter arthritic'. His teacher on Long Island was an old Scottish pro called George Heron.

When he first went to meet Mr Heron, he watched a while as the pro gave a putting lesson to a small, thickset man in a white cap.

'I was fascinated,' said Cooke. 'I didn't realize you needed a lesson to putt. At the end Heron said: "I hope that has been a help, Ben." Of course the pupil was the great Ben Hogan. Some time later I read Ben Hogan's statement that if you were to pick up a golf club and swing it in a natural manner you would become the worst golfer in the world. He said you had to learn to master 12 unnatural muscular movements. I was much taken by that. Then I saw Hogan after he had won the US Open by six strokes standing on the practice tee hitting shot after shot at the pin. Everyone had gone home but here was the man who had won still practising. When asked why he said: "I hit a bad seven iron on the 12th hole and I'm just putting things right." So with all that in mind I learned to play the game correctly and well.

'When I was 58 years old I reached 11 handicap. George Heron said there wasn't any earthly reason why I should ever play above 12. But it didn't happen. I remember the period when not breaking 90 was a disaster. Nowadays if I couldn't putt I'd never break 100,' he said. He says that his great friend and 'guru', the writer and critic H L Mencken, wrote the pithiest epigram about golf. 'He said, "If I had my way anyone guilty of golf would be denied all offices of trust under these United States." When he was dying I sat down and wrote through the night an appreciation for the *Manchester Guardian*.

'It was 5,000 words long. It was 1948 and in those days papers were rationed. Four pages for half the week but on Tuesday, Thursday and Saturday increased to six pages. I cabled Wadsworth, my editor, warning him my appreciation to be published upon the announcement of my friend's death was a long one. He cabled back: "Hope he dies Monday, Wednesday or Friday." '

He ponders the decline of public manners. 'Here's an old man's statement: "The young today are casual, bad mannered and have no respect for the old." Well I didn't make that up. Socrates did. So it's been a problem for a long time now,' he said.

Nonetheless he wonders about the effect that fame and fortune (mainly fortune) can have on even intelligent stars like Boris Becker, whom he started off admiring and now regards as a 'nuisance'. He recalls that he was once talking to Jack Nicklaus about John McEnroe's appalling conduct on court. Nicklaus said: 'The guy to blame is the father. When I was about 11 years old I threw a club. My father said: "Jack, if you do that again you won't play golf for six months." I sulked and went to my room. He came after me, opened the door and said: "What would Mr Jones think?" Bobby Jones was my dad's idol. I never threw another club."

What Nicklaus said gave Alistair Cooke an idea. He remembered a sentence and wrote to Mr McEnroe Snr. 'I said: "Here is a sentence once written by the immortal Bobby Jones. I thought you might like to have it done in needlepoint and mounted in a suitable frame to hang over Little John's bed. It says: "The rewards of golf – and of life too, I expect – are worth very little if you don't play the game by the etiquette as well as the rules." I never heard back from Mr McEnroe Snr. I can only assume the letter went astray.'

I don't think you can interview Alistair Cooke. Rather you let him muse about the nature of things for a while. He has one such final musing before I leave. It concerns his friend and golfing partner Manheim.

They planned a golfing holiday and were given an introduction through a friend to a very select club. Alistair called to make the booking. 'Pleasure to have you with us Mr Cooke,' the secretary said. 'What is the name of your partner?' Alistair told him his friend was called Manheim. A short time later the secretary called him back. 'We have been looking through our register of players and we don't appear to have any of the sort of gentleman you describe as members of the club,' he said. 'I didn't describe my friend, as a matter of fact. But he is Jewish so if you don't want Jews at your club then we shall go and play elsewhere,' said Cooke.

Some time later Manheim was told by a friend that he could arrange for him to play at the exclusive Jewish Club in Palm Beach. Manheim called: 'Certainly Mr Manheim,' they said. 'And your friend's name?' 'Cooke,' said Manheim, 'Alistair Cooke.' There was a sharp intake of breath at the other end of the line. 'Oh dear, that could be trouble,' they said.

Cooke shrugs and smiles at the sheer bloody stupidity of it all. But that's the way it is and, no doubt, the way it will always be. Like all the best commentators he is critical but rarely censorious, a fastidious man but not po-faced. He keeps a wise and amused eye on the world.

Any ambitions left? I ask. Ordinarily it would be daft to ask this question of an 86-year-old but not of Alistair Cooke. 'I hope in 14 years' time to play to my age round a golf course,' he said.

19th November 1994

·41·

DAVID GOWER

—

THE MAN on the gate asked what I was doing. When I told him I had come to interview David Gower he said: 'Make sure you write something nice about him.'

The lady in the tea room had much the same advice. A man called Brian, jumpy as a ferret, sought me out, anxious that the interview would not dwell too much on the possibility that Gower might be thinking of retiring after this season.

'Our job is to get him back in the England side, then on the tour of the West Indies. He needs to be encouraged to have positive thoughts,' he said. I asked him if, perchance, he was related to Donald Trelford. He said he wasn't. He was a retired businessman who had volunteered to help Gower by looking after his mental welfare. I inspected him for cracks. He seemed all right, which is remarkable considering that cricket is littered with gibbering wrecks of people who have tried to fathom what goes on in Gower's head.

The public concern for Gower is as touching as it is extraordinary. Of the athletes I have known, only George Best aroused the same emotions in people and even he, in his pomp, would have been hard pushed to fill City Hall, Westminster, with people demanding that Tommy Docherty stop playing silly sods with his career.

Apart from blessed talent the two men have one other thing in common. It is that once you start asking them to explain themselves the mystery deepens. I had the first evidence of the enigmatic part of Gower's personality at the beginning of his career. It was 1975 and his first season with Leicestershire. I was having a talk with Ray Illingworth, then captain of the county, about new talent and he said: 'I've a young boy in my team who will one day play for England. In all my years in cricket I've not seen many who can time a ball like this lad.'

This was worth noting because Illingworth is as good a judge of a cricketer as ever lived. What is more, he doesn't often wax lyrical. He added: 'His name is David Gower. He'll go all the way, providing he wants to.' That note of caution was the earliest indication of the problem Gower has always had of convincing people that he possessed the depth of will to underpin his matchless talent.

Illingworth's caution was probably due to an incident early in Gower's career when he turned up for a game wearing odd shoes, one brown, the other black. This provoked a telling off from Illingworth and a lecture on the importance of always being smart and well turned out.

The captain was seated at breakfast on the morning of the next match when Gower strode into the dining room dressed in dark blue dinner suit, bow tie and highly polished black shoes. Illingworth looked aghast at his player and said: 'Bloody hell, Gower, have you just come in?'

More than 8,000 Test runs and countless japes later Illingworth's protégé sits in the Hampshire dressing room achieving the impossible, namely, looking elegant in a tracksuit. He seems happy and at ease.

Mark Nicholas says that during the past few weeks Gower has been as relaxed and content as he has ever known him to be. Why? Has he been told to ready himself for a trip to the West Indies? Alternatively, has he decided that this is his last season and is he smiling at the prospect of not having to play county cricket seven days a week? Perhaps he has concluded that he owes Hampshire something, and is trying even harder to support Nicholas and his team.

We are here to find out. First the question of a return to the England team. 'Earlier in the season I thought I had a real chance. I made 153 against Notts and felt good. Then I cracked my rib. End of story. After the reshuffle in the Test team I think my chances of being recalled have lessened.

'Let's be frank, I don't want to bat at No. 7 for England. Being positive, I suppose you could argue that if there was one reshuffle there could be another. If there is I could be in with a chance. I am in the lucky position of having so many people taking up my case on my behalf. Is that an added pressure to do well? Maybe, but it's much more pleasant than having people gunning for you.

'Will I retire if I don't get picked for the Windies? I wouldn't rule it out. It's the usual conundrum, when to go. The first time it was suggested I might retire was in 1986. We were touring Australia, I had lost the captaincy and was feeling low and the press started speculating I might leave the game. A trifle premature, I thought. I wasn't even 30. Now I'm 36 and the prospect of retirement is obviously more real.

'I suppose if county cricket was designed differently I might contemplate a longer career than I do. It's no secret I don't enjoy playing cricket seven days a week. I don't like the Sunday game because of its artificiality. What would suit me would be one four-day game every two weeks,' he said. I must have looked surprised. 'All right, make that one four-day game a week and no Sunday games,' he said.

'In any event I don't want to drag out the end. I don't want my career to die a dismal death. Ideally I'd like to go out in a Test match or a NatWest final.

Something meaningful. Seems unlikely. I wonder if I could persuade Ted [Dexter, chairman of England selectors] to arrange to pick me for the last Test to make my grand exit. What do you think?'

I said the current England selectors were not renowned for flamboyant gestures. 'Perhaps we could persuade the MCC to invent some centenary game or we might have a special farewell match at Lord's for the David Gower Relief Fund. Seriously, though, it doesn't happen like that, does it? I think you wake up one morning and say: "Well, that's it. That's life. Time to go." '

We were talking before Ian Botham made his exit. I imagine that his departure from the scene would be regarded as another indication to Gower that this season might well be his last. Botham is a soulmate, someone who, like Gower, has no difficulty in being persuaded that while cricket is a wonderful and uplifting occupation there are other things in life as intoxicating, perhaps more so.

With his departure and Allan Lamb no longer an England player, Gower must feel increasingly that he might be overstaying his welcome. The three of them played their cricket the same way and shared a distaste for the squat-thrust and push-up regime of the England team of recent years. Gower says in his auto-biography that he would like the words 'Fun, style and excellence' as his epitaph. It was a philosophy he lived by. It won him a million friends but in the end it did for him.

When did he realize that his philosophy was also his undoing? 'Tiger Moth. Need I say more? When I sat down in a room afterwards with Gooch and Stewart and talked about the meaning of life and they put to me their disenchantment and I did the same I realized that this was the end of the road.

'There is still some of the atmosphere of that meeting hanging in the air. I feel that I haven't been picked for England on occasions for the sake of a few runs at the right time, whereas my record and reputation as a Test player has not been taken into account. It makes you think when many good judges say you should have played more. But I don't like moaning. Let's just say that, when you introduce a regimen, bravado disappears,' he said.

What he likes about Hampshire is that under the tolerant and kindly eye of Mark Nicholas his vagaries have been accommodated. Does he owe them a debt? 'I don't think I do. The club has been understanding and I am grateful but I think I've made a contribution in the last three years. Not just statistics either. I think I've played my part in the dressing room, trying to keep part of it sane.'

So will he be there next season or will he be in a commentary box with his sparring partner, Geoffrey Boycott, the man who once said that the perfect player would have Gower's talent and Boycott's brain? Gower replied to this theory by agreeing that while he might have scored more Test runs he would not have ended up with as many friends.

When he goes he will make many people very sad. All of us will have special memories. My own is Sydney in the tour of 1990–1 and Gower playing an innings of incomparable charm and beauty. It might be, of course, that between now and the end of the season he will do enough to convince the selectors that they must take him to the West Indies. I wonder.

Although he denies it, I have the feeling that Gower has already made up his mind. Before our interview I watched him bat against Worcestershire. He scored 30-odd in his inimitable manner before touching a lifter to slip.

When he came in he signed autographs patiently and willingly. During our talk he was approached and interrupted many times, sometimes with foolish requests.

Never once was he less than courteous and obliging. I was reminded, not for the first time, that I have always been as impressed by Gower's manners as I have by his talent.

Talking to him the other day I was made aware, for the first time, that I have witnessed all of Gower's career in cricket, from Illingworth and the first predictions of glory to Portsmouth and the first intimations of retirement.

When I tell my grandchildren about David Gower I will say that apart from the obvious glories of his batting, what I was most grateful for was that he never gave me cause to be concerned about or ashamed of the game of cricket.

In everything he did, on and off the field, he embodied the qualities of the greatest of games. And when he chooses the moment and the setting of his leaving we can be sure it will be done in great style, with perfect timing.

4th July 1993

·42·

DALE GIBSON

—

WHEN STEPHEN Wood was killed in a fall at Lingfield Park, fellow jockey Paul Eddery, who was in the fatal race, was asked what sort of man he was. Eddery replied that his colleague was not a famous man but just an ordinary working jockey, hard-working, conscientious, struggling to make a living in a dangerous and difficult occupation. I don't know why, but I was strangely moved by what Eddery said.

What we see are the jockeys at the top of the profession, highly paid men with enviable lifestyles enjoying a celebrity which opens the doors to many lucrative commercial opportunities. We forget there are 120 registered jockeys in Britain, 90 per cent of whom struggle to make living. I spent a day with one of them.

If Loyd Grossman ever peered Through the Keyhole into Dale and Julie Gibson's house, he would have little difficulty in detecting that the occupiers were into horses, but seriously so.

There are photographs and drawings of horses on every wall, the library contains every Dick Francis book ever published as well as several autobiographies of leading jockeys and enough form books to satisfy the most demanding student of the turf. In the bathroom, next to the toilet, there is a race card from a meeting at Wolverhampton.

Dale Gibson is 26, 5ft 7in tall and weighs 7st 7lb stripped. While Michelangelo would find little inspiration in his physique, any sculptor would love his gaunt face with its fascinating planes and angles. When he greets you, his hands are firm and strong. They need to be. His job is steering horses weighing half a ton at high speeds around race tracks. His wife Julie is bright and bonny. They were married early this year and recently moved from their home in the south for Dale to try his luck on the northern racing circuit.

It is the day before the Derby and Dale has two rides at Redcar. He had four but one horse was withdrawn and he was jocked off the other. He was due to ride Ned's Bonanza in the third race but Jason Weaver got the ride. Dale had ridden the horse

177

before and enjoyed the trip. He thought he had performed well and was not pleased at being replaced.

He was left with Karseam in the first – 'To be realistic not much chance; outclassed, I think,' he said – and Watch Me Go in the last – 'Nice horse. We'll see.' He would earn £110 for his day's work – £55 a ride – plus seven per cent of the prize-money if his horse won.

The total purse involved in the two races was much less than Eric Cantona earns in a week and would not be sufficient to persuade a golfer or a tennis player to set the alarm clock, never mind get out of bed.

'I reckon I need 350 rides a year to break even,' he said. 'I work 50 weeks of the year, seven days a week as a jockey. Whatever you say, you can't accuse us of not working for a living. It's a very demanding job. When I'm not racing I'm riding out or looking for work. To make a living at this game you have to be very professional and be involved all the time. It's no good just waiting for the phone to ring.'

Nowadays, jockeys employ agents to get them work. Dale Gibson's agent is his wife.

We drove to Redcar in Dale's car. He travels more than 60,000 miles a year by road, plus whatever he does by rail and air. Today, it's a simple trip from their home near Wetherby, up the A1 past the ghastly tangle of steel and smoke at Wilton that scars the landscape and sours the air.

There's something homely about Redcar racecourse. It's like the snug at the local. In the jockeys' room there is an old fireplace, polished postbox red, and a central table where the valets work. Dale cleans his own gear. Saves money. He borrows the valet's brushes to clean his street shoes. Waste not, want not.

There is a smell of cigarettes in the room mixed with the odd whiff of cigar smoke. Jockeys smoke to deaden their appetite as well as to soothe the nerves. They wander round the room, getting undressed, looking like super-waifs.

Compared to Dale Gibson, Kate Moss is overweight. Recently, he went to have his fitness assessed by scientists studying the physique of Olympic athletes. They nearly had to admit defeat after being unable to find any part of Gibson's torso with enough spare flesh to clip an electrode on.

A couple of jockeys emerge from a morning in the sauna, looking knackered. They arrange themselves on uncomfortable benches and sleep. Later in the afternoon, one jockey wakes up late for his ride and runs in a panic to the door. He returns immediately, having forgotten his whip. He has also forgotten to tuck his shirt into his pants and he runs towards the saddling enclosure with silks billowing and cap in hand like a schoolboy chasing a departing bus.

Jockeys look odd, bird-like figures in the dressing room. It is only when they mount their horses they make sense. Then they form a partnership with the animal that is, at its best, a most perfect symmetry.

Dale says: 'Once you ride a racehorse you're bitten by the bug. There isn't another buzz like it. Jockeys love horses. I only say that because sometimes you see it suggested that they don't. The understanding between horse and jockey is essential for success. Equally, there is sometimes an antipathy between animal and rider you can do nothing about.'

In his first race on Karseam there didn't appear to be much empathy 'twixt horse and rider. Dale tried hard but nothing happened. The horse came fifth out of seven runners. He was disappointed but it was very much what he had expected. He could do with a winner.

In May, he had 40 rides, five winners and a few places. So far this season he has ridden about 130 races with seven winners and a total of 20 seconds or thirds. His worst period was when he rode 100 consecutive losers. He says that what sustains him is the belief in his own ability, the knowledge that he is good at his job and that all he needs are the breaks.

He was born into racing. His grandfather was head lad to Noel Murless, his mother a riding instructor, he was brought up around Newmarket. He was good at all sports at school, becoming junior table tennis champion of Suffolk at the age of 12. He began his apprenticeship with William Hastings Bass, now Lord Huntingdon. He had a successful apprenticeship, particularly in 1989 and 1990 when he rode a total of 60 winners including five in the Queen's colours, the Steward's Cup on Very Adjacent and the Irish November Handicap at Leopardstown.

In 1989 he was third leading apprentice behind Frankie Dettori and Alan Munro. They were booked to ride in this year's Derby. Gibson wasn't. Why?

'They were exceptional. I was a less fashionable jockey. But don't get me wrong, I'm just as ambitious. I dream about winning the Derby,' he said.

Jason Weaver, the jockey who had replaced Dale on Ned's Bonanza in the third race, and was on the eve of his first Derby, stops by for a chat. What about, I ask? 'He wanted to know about Ned's Bonanza. I told him to watch out in the stalls, that it didn't like being kept hanging about. And I told him one or two other things about how the horse handles,' he said.

I remarked it was pretty damned sporting of him to help the man who had jocked him off. 'Not Jason's fault I lost the ride,' he replied. 'In any case, he's riding with so much confidence he could win a race on a hairy dog.'

His advice was prophetic. Ned's Bonanza nearly took his jockey under the starting gate. It finished fifth. 'At least it proved that when I rode it and it didn't do well it wasn't my fault,' said Dale, with quiet satisfaction. In a corner of the room the veteran jockey Bruce Raymond, at 52 twice Dale's age, relaxed quietly before going out to win on Jundi. Does Dale Gibson envisage sitting in a corner at Redcar races in 26 years' time? 'Don't see why not,' he said. 'I admire jocks like Bruce. Great professionals. I want to ride as many winners as I can, to become a top jockey no matter how long it takes. You're soon forgotten in this game if you don't keep on striving.

'In any case, being a jockey is all I ever wanted to be, so I don't contemplate anything else.'

He attempted to further his ambition riding Watch Me Go in the last race, the Dormanstown Handicap Stakes (Class E) for three-year-olds and upwards, £3,570 added to stakes. The horse was trained by Michael Dods. Gibson enjoys working with the Darlington trainer.

'I think he's a good trainer,' he said. 'He's also very straight and honest with people. No bullshit.'

The horse ran well but didn't get in the frame. One of the owners said: 'It needs another gear.' Dale said: 'Question is: does it have one? It ran as well as it can. The owner and trainer were happy. Can't ask for more.'

We drove home and ate boiled fish, pasta and salad. I had a glass or two of wine. So did Julie Gibson. Dale drank water. Me and Julie watched *Brookside*. Dale Gibson studied the form book. How would he sum up the day? 'Run of the mill,' he said.

He went to bed, up the stairs, past the pictures of racehorses and dreamed about riding in the morrow's Derby.

The next day he rose at 6.30 and rode out for Richard Whittaker, the Wetherby trainer. It was a glorious morning, smelling of cut grass and farmyards.

I asked Mr Whittaker how he rated Dale Gibson. 'Good jockey, intelligent bloke,' he said. 'Out of 10 as a jockey? Eight-and-a-half. There's a lot of them around like that. My jockey, Tony Culhane, for instance. All they need is the big chance.

'If they were riding for the big owners they'd be on Rolls Royce horses, getting five rides a meeting. They'd soon learn and get the necessary confidence. Then they might make the nine-and-a-half out of 10, which is where the very top few jockeys are.

'In a sense it's much harder for jockeys like Tony and Dale than it is for the men at the top. But there's no easy road in this game.'

Culhane makes ends meet by working the winter months in India. I asked him why India. He thought for a moment and then said: 'Because I like the food.'

Dale Gibson doesn't fancy working abroad. He reckons he can get enough work at home and that Sunday racing will be a bonus for freelance jockeys. 'Widens the circle,' he said.

He set off to drive to Yarmouth where he had three rides. While Willie Carson was entertaining the Epsom multitudes by bringing Erhaab so thrillingly home, Dale Gibson was trying to persuade horseflesh of a different calibre to do its best in front of a few holidaymakers.

His first horse came last, his second ride sixth out of 19 runners and his third horse, a 25–1 shot called Top Anna came a respectable fourth. That was a bonus. He will ride the horse again at Hamilton and reckons it has a chance.

So how was his day? 'You could say I knew I'd been to Yarmouth,' he said after driving for nearly eight hours to and from work.

Looking ahead, he was greatly impressed by the fact that there were four riders in the Derby over the age of 50, including three grandfathers. Time yet for miracles. Dream on.

4th June 1994

·43·

MICHAEL ATHERTON

—

I WASN'T going to say anything but Michael Atherton brought it up. Had I seen the promotions for the forthcoming television coverage of England's tour to the West Indies?

I said I had but I wasn't going to mention it, since it featured shots of various English batsmen trying to avoid being decapitated by the West Indies quicks. He laughed and said he thought it was pretty funny. I said it might be difficult to remain jolly once the video became reality, particularly since it seemed likely that his head might become a prime target.

He said that as captain and opening bat he expected to be given special treatment by the bowlers and he wasn't anticipating getting too many deliveries he could stroke through the covers off the front foot.

'The tour will test all of us. We will discover who has bottle and who hasn't,' he said. It gave me an opportunity to ask a professional sportsman what I'd been dying to ask ever since the word 'bottle' became the most over-used word in the sporting vocabulary, apart from 'pressure'.

'It's about not being afraid of getting hit. That's the obvious definition. Then, just as importantly, it means mental strength. It's the ability to face up to hour after hour of unrelenting concentration, of being able to conquer your nerves on the first day of a Test match so you don't arrive at the wicket a gibbering wreck,' he said.

God-given or can it be acquired? I asked. 'You can certainly learn it. Look at Goochie. Became a much better player the longer his career lasted, primarily because he had a much tougher mental frame of mind. Do I have it? Well, I hope so. I'm getting better at preparing myself for an innings. I learnt a lot from Gooch about how to concentrate and build a score.

'I think I'm a reasonable player and I think I'll get better: I've worked with Geoffrey Boycott, who has a marvellous technical eye. He's as good a coach as there is. He doesn't spare you either. He is too tough for some. They don't like being bollocked or called a twerp or worse. I don't mind a bit. One of my strengths is that I can take a lot of criticism if I know it will do me good,' he said.

He is an interesting cove, is the new captain of England. He has the natural good manners of a boy raised by sensible parents, the pleasant social grace acquired from the best of educations. He is the most charming of company, intelligent, easy-going with a ready sense of humour.

This makes him sound like a Deb's Delight and does little to explain why he might make a leader of men, except to say that it does the heart good to meet an England captain who is delighted to have the job and whose demeanour is free of weary despair.

The clues to the Michael Atherton who might lick a team into shape using sterner qualities than charm come from those who play with him.

One of his Lancashire team-mates told me: 'He's a tough bastard. Don't let the quiet manner fool you. He knows what he wants and if he doesn't get it then look out.'

Mark Nicholas, captain of Hampshire and a friend of Atherton, says: 'He is very stubborn. Maybe dangerously so. He has absolute belief in his own ideals. He is very bright, but not in a flashy way. He is a good judge of players, with a sharp eye and low tolerance for those who fall short of his own high standards.'

If Nicholas has a doubt about his friend it is that, at 25, he might be a little young for the job. Atherton says: 'Maybe being young is an advantage. I have grown up with most of the players in the present team. They are comfortable in my presence. They know they can talk to me. I like being captain, it makes me concentrate more, stops me getting bored in the middle, makes me a better player.

'I like making things happen and captains have that in their power. I think captaincy is common sense, but there is a part of it that's intuitive.

'People ask who influenced me. Answer is I haven't played under enough captains to make a real judgment. David Hughes always impressed me. He was an older man, aged 40 when he skippered Lancashire, and he carried a lot of authority.

'I learnt a lot from that tour to India. By default you might say. [He missed the first Test through illness, wasn't selected for the second, was left out in Sri Lanka, ignored by the management.]

'When I sought out Goochie and Fletch and asked them what was going on it became apparent it had never happened to them in their careers. Nobody had treated them as badly as the management were treating me and one or two others on the tour who were ignored and who wasted their talents sitting on their backsides instead of playing cricket. It was heartbreaking.

'It was a really wretched time. Soul-destroying. Such neglect can ruin a player's career. I was very angry and upset but I simply resolved that if ever I was in charge I would do things differently. Every member of the team going to the West Indies feels part of the whole. There's no question of some going to play in one-day games and others in the Tests.

'The previous England management didn't think I could play one-day cricket so I was left out. What nonsense to suppose that anyone good enough to play a Test match can't play the one-day game. I can tell you I'm not going to the West Indies to drop myself for the first one-day fixture.'

There were signs in the last Test against Australia that Atherton might be the man to arrest a decline in our reputation which has placed the England cricket team in the same category as Zimbabwe and the Cocos Islands.

Moreover, it stirred the blood to see the man in charge actually enjoying himself after those dreary years of lugubrious leadership on the field accompanied by a management style totally bereft of charm and, more often than not, sense.

We mustn't become too excited. Selecting the team he wants for the West Indies is one thing. Will he get the chairman he wants in future if he survives intact? Will he be happy with the other selectors, yet to be announced.

Brian Bolus was one name mentioned. Might there not be a case, now we have a young captain, for choosing more youthful selectors rather than men who remember how Brian Sellars ran things?

Michael Atherton was politely unforthcoming on the subject. He said, quite rightly, that he had more imminent problems to address. But what is clear to anyone who has observed him is that if he makes the England captaincy his own in years to come, he will present a much more persuasive and forthright argument for change than the executive has encountered hitherto.

A lot has happened to Michael Atherton in the short time since he became a professional. He has battled poor form, bad injury, insensitive management with a steady resolve. His biggest challenge lies in the West Indies. 'I'm looking forward to it. The defeatist attitude of some people amazes me. We are going there to win. The West Indies are a good side but not a vintage one. We have got to be like the England rugby team against New Zealand. They were up against the best but they refused to be second best. That has to be our frame of mind.

'Goochie upset a lot of players last season when he said they didn't hurt enough when England lost. Anyone who plays for his country hurts badly when things go wrong. People suffer differently. Some kick the dressing-room door in, others sit quietly in a corner.

'When I'm down and need a lift I look at the sweater with the three lions and I think: "They don't give them away to people who can't play. What's more, you can't buy them at corner shops." Just to remind myself what's at stake,' he said.

It's a tough road ahead but he is looking forward with the bold confidence of youth and the quiet authority of someone who is very much his own man.

It might well be that Michael Atherton has a lot to learn, but my hunch is that he will do so while advancing. His determination reminds me of something Scott Fitzgerald wrote: 'If you are strong enough, there are no precedents.'

18th December 1993

·44·

GEOFFREY BOYCOTT

—

PEOPLE REACT strongly to Geoffrey Boycott. There are two main schools of thought. One is that he is self-centred, selfish, remote, socially clumsy, indifferent to the conventions that help us rub along with our fellow human beings. In other words a pain in the backside. The other point of view is that he is refreshingly frank, blessedly free of cant and a greatly gifted coach and communicator.

Moreover, his friends will tell you he is loyal and steadfast, honest in his feelings and harshly judged. The trouble with being Geoffrey Boycott, as David Bairstow, the former Yorkshire and England wicket-keeper shrewdly observed, is that people are too busy finding fault with the man to ever consider what they might learn by listening to him.

Mind you, things are changing. Boycott's career on television and radio, his trenchant observations in the *Sun*, have created a wide audience of people who now believe that he talks more sense than most about cricket and that if there is anything wrong with our game – and there most demonstrably is – then he should be one of the first men called in to fix things.

And those who believe that his supporters merely comprise ratbags and malcontents intent on undermining the establishment should know that in a recent balloon debate held at Lord's the audience decided that Len Hutton should be sacrificed before Geoffrey Boycott. A straw in the wind? Maybe, but as Geoffrey Boycott's advocate on this occasion, I must inform you it ranks as one of my greatest achievements.

Let us suppose for just a moment that Lord's called upon Geoffrey Boycott to tell them what was wrong with cricket and how they might put things right. What would he tell them? 'County cricket is tame. That's a good way to describe it. Tame. It's very comfortable for the players. Not a lot of competition, not many good players around. Schools aren't playing cricket, clubs are struggling. Cricket is a package. No good attempting to get county cricket right if schools and clubs aren't playing a full part. What it means is that where there were once five guys after a county place, there are two now. They are playing on flat and boring pitches. Stewart and Dexter said that four-day cricket would make better cricketers. It hasn't. Bowlers are cannon fodder. The argument that four-day cricket on flat tracks would produce spin bowlers has been proved wrong. They have just set up a sub-committee at Lord's to find out why spinners are bowling less.

'What a spinner wants is the odd pitch that turns so he can take five for 25 and get a bit of confidence. We want uncovered pitches, make them bowl more overs, get the buggers moving. There's no urgency in the game nowadays. Brian Close used to say that the best cricketers are thinking cricketers. He was right but you have to give them something to think about, pitches that stimulate the imagination and challenge technique. When I played on uncovered tracks it led to a variety of problems to be solved by varied thinking.

'Nowadays, because of their obsession with Surrey loam and all pitches being like the Oval, the TCCB have changed the nature of pitches. Yorkshire, Lancashire, Essex, Worcestershire all had different characteristics. Not nowadays. What they have in common at present is uneven bounce. No good to anyone.

'Then there is the coaching. It is very moderate at county level. If it is wrong at county level it has to be wrong at Test level. The counties haven't moved forward in thinking about coaching. Still one coach for the team. No single person can teach all the skills of cricket. Every county should have individual, specific coaches for fast bowling, spin bowling, batting, wicket-keeping and fielding. We should learn from other sports like American football. Special coaches for special skills.

'England should have the same set-up. I wouldn't call them coaches at this level. I'd prefer them to be "consultants". You need continuity to be effective to change things. So what should happen is that the consultants and the England team come together in April, then for two days before every Test match, on other odd days throughout the season and before tours. And that should also include the next best batch of players, the most promising young cricketers in England. We are not doing that. The Aussies are.

'What the Aussies also teach us is how to use the big names from the past to help the future. I am not saying that a great player automatically makes a great coach but I am claiming that players who have had distinguished and long Test careers have something extra to offer. We seem afraid of our best players particularly if they are outspoken or work for the media.

'Aussies don't have that problem. Dennis Lillee kicked Miandad up the arse but the Aussies didn't boot him into touch. He coaches at the Academy. Rod Marsh has a reputation as a larrikin. Look at the job he is doing. Greg Chappell works as a commentator for television. Didn't stop him being appointed manager of the Australian A team in the one-day series. We must do the same. When you talk about encouraging youngsters, who are they going to be inspired by – some ordinary trundler from the county circuit or a legend?

'Finally, there's the county system itself. I'd keep the same number of counties but I think we play one or maybe two one-day competitions too many. Also, it is absurd we don't play proper cricket on Saturday and Sunday. That must happen,' he said.

Thanks, Geoff, for spelling it out. Now what are you going to do about it? 'Well, if they took me into a committee room at Lord's and asked me what was wrong I'd tell them straight. But would they listen? Would they want to hear it? In any case I don't think they'd ever let me in. I'm too strong-minded, opinionated, truculent sometimes. They say I am difficult, I believe I am different.

'People shrink away from frankness. I am not diplomatic because I think that diplomacy sometimes means avoiding the truth. What is interesting is that if saying what I believe in is a fault in one sense, it is a strength in my television commentary. It is also an asset when I am coaching. I love the game passionately, that is what I try to get across. I have never been bored with the game. Never. Some commentators and coaches are bored. You can see it. They just turn up and take the money. If that ever happened to me I'd be out, no matter what they offered,' he said.

He has just signed a four-year contract with BBC Television. He has parted company with Sky and is sorely missed. It will be a while before a game throws up another player with Boycott's clear eye for faults in tactics and technique and his simple and uncomplicated way of explaining a very complex and difficult game. His mentors were Jim Laker and Richie Benaud and he learned well. On the other hand, whenever he spots a flaw in a player's game and describes it with such precision I am always struck by the thought of how much better it would be if he was employed to tell the cricketer about it rather than a television audience.

Geoffrey Boycott has been retired from the game for 10 years, is financially well off, in demand, has a lovely house in Yorkshire, is as fit-looking at 54 as he was in his playing career; why at times does it still seem like Geoffrey Boycott versus the world?

'I have always felt that life was an uphill struggle. I am a solitary person and I think that makes me different. When I am working at a cricket match I don't go box-hopping or drinking wine in the sponsors' tent. Brian Sellars, my old chairman at Yorkshire, was once talking to Alec Bedser when he was chairman of selectors.

Alec was asking him about me and Brian said: "Oh he can play cricket all right. But nobody can bloody understand him." I like that,' he said.

He resists even the most skilled probing into the question of what makes Geoffrey Boycott tick. Invited to appear on Radio 4's *In The Psychiatrist's Chair*, where he was interviewed by Anthony Clare, he responded to the doctor's persuasive questions by saying: 'You'll get nowt from me.'

Anthony Clare thought he knew something about the infinite possibilities of the human personality until he encountered Geoffrey Boycott at his most enigmatic. Boycott smiles at the memory. 'He has contacted me since. He said he believed the saying "no man is an island" until he met me.' It is for certain that had John Donne ever opened an innings with Geoffrey Boycott, he might never have been inspired to write his immortal line.

I said I found it curious that since his retirement he had steadfastly refused to play a game of cricket. Why? 'Because I don't want to play rubbish cricket and because I don't want to play rubbish myself. I loved the game too much to play it badly. I have never picked up a bat since I retired and I never will. People can't believe it, but that only shows that people don't know or understand me.'

So how does he see the future? 'When I look ahead I can only think about not playing. Cricket is such a lovely and intricate game and I loved every minute of my playing career. Nothing can ever replace that in my life. I don't have heroes but the man I most admire in history is Alexander the Great. The gods asked him if he was given the choice of having a long and peaceful reign, or conquering the world and dying young, what would it be? And he chose to conquer the world. I often think about that, because if the gods offered me the choice of a long life or five more years playing first-class cricket I'd take the five years. After that I wouldn't bloody care what they did with me. Just five more years scoring runs for Yorkshire and England. That would be something. That would do me,' he said wistfully.

He is a very singular man.

28th January 1995

·45·

BRIAN CLOSE

—

WHENEVER I go to Headingley I seek out Brian Close. For my generation he symbolized the might of Yorkshire cricket. I still remember the pride I felt, the sense of belonging to a privileged tribe, when he walked on to the field and behind him Trueman, Illingworth, Boycott, Binks, Wilson, Nicholson, Sharpe, Padgett, Stott, Hampshire and the rest who made up that formidable Yorkshire team of the Sixties.

It was as tough and talented a team as ever competed for the county championship and led by a captain who could stand comparison with the very best who ever skippered Yorkshire, Somerset, England or anywhere else on the planet.

Since the Sixties it has been Yorkshire's desire to find the same kind of success, an ambition thwarted by a mixture of circumstances, some beyond the control of the Yorkshire executive, and some entirely due to the tribal warfare and petty squabbling that occurs whenever more than two Yorkshiremen gather.

Nowadays, fingers crossed, there are signs that Yorkshire cricket is on the way back to where it belongs. A lot has to do with the attention given to the grass roots of the game in the county by Steve Oldham, the director of coaching. Oldham and his staff trawl the county with a fine mesh, unable to rely, as they once could, on the catch willingly giving itself up.

At the pinnacle of the system is the Yorkshire Cricket Academy. While the rest prevaricated, Yorkshire acted and already the future is strengthened by what the Academy is producing.

The link between the past and the future is Brian Close. Through all the blood-letting and betrayals, in spite of being cruelly treated by the club when he was sacked and went to Somerset, he remains the man people look to when they talk of Yorkshire cricket and success.

Being a practical man, Close believes in action not legends, which is why on certain Saturdays you might find this 64-year-old battle-scarred veteran leading out the Academy side to play a local team.

Typically Close makes no concessions to age, either his own or the players. He refuses to bat lower down the order than No. 6 and any young man in his team who imagines he is taking a walk in the park with a pensioner is in for a nasty shock.

One young player who batted for some time with Close was sought out by his father at the end of his innings. 'What was it like batting with the great man?' he asked. 'Alright,' said his son. 'I saw him talking to you during your innings. What advice did he give you?' his father wanted to know. 'All he said to me was "I'm dying for a fag," ' said his son.

Ian Botham and Geoffrey Boycott both agree that Close is the toughest man they ever played with or against. Boycott says that the 'team discussions' of his day often deteriorated into heated argument which Close would settle by offering to thump anyone who disagreed. There were few takers because Close was not only physically strong but also a man of his word.

He once lifted Boycott up with one hand and was about to nail him to the dressing-room door when Illingworth and Trueman intervened and saved Geoffrey's life, a course of action which, in view of later developments, they might now regret.

Botham remembers that Close would declare that if he fought Ali over 15 rounds he wouldn't be knocked out. Other players remember that he made the same claim about Joe Frazier and I have no doubt in my mind, having watched both men in action, that he would be a serious threat to Frank Bruno. When he captained Somerset he became so angry at the way Allan Jones was bowling that he sent the player off the field. The decision was without precedent but Close cared little for that.

He was born to leadership. It transformed him from a talented but wayward cricketer to the man who led the most successful Yorkshire team of modern times, transformed Somerset from a social club to a winning outfit and won six of seven games when they allowed him to captain the national side.

He should have captained England for many more years, and Yorkshire, too, but Close was never favoured by the rub of the green. He was too instinctive to be a political animal, too much a reactor to be the diplomat, too certain of the way he wanted things done to curry favour.

The good news is that he has survived. He is still with his beloved Yorkshire, still talking provocatively and argumentatively about the game he loves. Boycott, who is not renowned for swooning over his captains, once wrote: 'I respected him totally . . . he influenced me more than anyone else.'

That's because he was the ultimate pro. Still is, come to that. As the boys from the Academy are finding out.

Thinking about Brian Close reminds me I must start preparing for one of the two cricket matches I play each season. He always turns out in one of them, which takes place at Victor Blank's lovely home at Chippinghurst in Oxfordshire.

It was here, having been hit for two sixes and four fours by Imran Khan – delightful blows hit with a full swing of the bat – that Brian left the field telling all and sundry: 'I never could bowl against bloody sloggers.'

Next season Shane Warne turned out for the opposition. This was his first game in England, a chance for us to have a privileged private view of the new sensation. When Brian went out to bat he thrust a large right leg down the wicket and played Warne with his pads exactly as he would do if saving England in the last half-hour of a Test match to win the series.

As it was we were taking part in a charity game in an Oxford meadow to the murmur of gentle midsummer. The Archbishop of Canterbury was the umpire at Warne's end and he no doubt found inspiration for several sermons in the ability of one man to change a pastoral idyll into a battlefield.

Warne thought it great fun as flipper, leg break and googly crashed into the batsman's pad followed by Brian's observation: 'This fellow will never get me out.' After playing out time with four or five maiden overs, Close walked from the field in triumph. 'Told you,' he said. I see he is down to play this year, as is Warne. I could have a significant role in the renewal of their contest as I have joined the list of umpires.

Upon reaching 60 and reading that the combined age of the Yorkshire openers is 39, I decided the game had passed me by, as had the chance of being awarded my county cap. Time to put on the umpire's jacket given to me by my old friend Dickie Bird.

Anyone who thinks that becoming an umpire is the easy way out should see what it has done to Mr Bird over the years. Give Dickie a light meter, low cloud and a light drizzle and no one, not even the Greeks, could concoct more drama and tragedy from the occasion.

At least I was properly attired and equipped as I made my debut as an umpire at Blenheim Palace in a friendly. I had a penknife for extracting impediments from the bowler's hooves, six shiny pebbles for counting and surgical dressing in case of an outbreak of violence.

My greatest problem was maintaining concentration. Players can dream awhile but not umpires. My first mistake came when I took a catch. I was standing at square leg trying to work out what it must cost to heat Blenheim Palace when I saw the ball lobbing towards me. Instinctively I caught it and threw it triumphantly in the air. It was then I realized what I had done and I let the ball fall to earth. There was an embarrassed silence with the batsmen standing in the middle of the wicket wondering what the next move might be. 'No ball,' I shouted, unconvincingly.

Worse was to follow. Half an hour later, concentrating like mad, I was standing at the bowler's end when he bowled a snorter which hit the batsman on the pad. 'Owzat,' I yelled, leaping in the air. What is more I had my finger up at the time, thereby simultaneously asking the question and giving the verdict. The batsman was plumb but that wasn't the point. It was at that moment I realized I would probably have failed my umpire's examination.

Thinking about what happened I was consoled that my late and revered father once stood as umpire in a game I played in and when I was bowling appealed on my behalf for lbw. Sadly he was the only person who did so, the ball having obviously hit the bat before the pad.

As the echo of his appeal faded he gathered his dignity around him like a robe. 'Not out, you silly old sod,' he declared. Like father, like son. Madness, like cricket, must run in our family.

12th June 1995

·46·

ROBIN SMITH

—

As Maurice Leyland once famously observed – and we must never tire of quoting the classics – 'None of us like fast bowling, but some of us don't let on.' Robin Smith is someone who doesn't let on. Indeed he will tell you that he enjoys the quicks trying to knock his block off. He is not being boastful, for that is not his nature. Neither is he whistling to keep his spirits high. He regards the challenge hurled down by the West Indian fast bowlers as the supreme test of nerve and sinew. So far this season at Lord's and Edgbaston, he has spent a total of 14 hours at the crease facing Bishop, Walsh and Ambrose, who have paid him the rather dubious compliment of bowling to him as if his was the prize scalp.

The steepling bounce at Edgbaston and the line of the West Indian attack – particularly when Walsh bowled round the wicket – caused many to wonder if the damage they intended to inflict was more serious and painful than the batsman losing his middle stump. Smith has no doubt they were trying to hit him. 'From that point of view, I didn't think they bowled well at me. They seemed more intent on letting me have it than getting me out. I don't mind that, I'll duck and dive all day. It gives me great satisfaction to sway back and see the maker's name on the ball as it goes past at 100 miles an hour. They will have to bowl faster than that to break me,' he said.

We met and talked at Sunningdale Golf Club in the company of Smith's Hampshire captain and close friend, Mark Nicholas, and Michael Hughesdon, a formidable golfer who prowls the fairways at major golf events for BBC Television. Mr Nicholas chose me for his partner, which was a bad mistake. He would have stood more chance of winning had he picked Dolly Parton. I played so badly I am thinking of reforming the Anti-Golf Society, which prospered under my leadership until I foolishly succumbed to fairway fever.

Mr Smith, who alleges his handicap is 18, has never had a lesson and plays only an occasional round, soon had the caddies making appreciative chortling noises with his long hitting. If there is such a thing as reincarnation, I most definitely do not want to return as one of Robin Smith's golf balls. For instance, at the 14th hole on the Old Course, which is a par-five measuring 480 yards, he hit a driver and an eight-iron to reach the green in two. He reduced the 16th, which is 423 yards long, to a three-iron and an eight-iron. He hit one nine-iron 170 yards, and took a five-iron for a shot of 230 yards.

He has forearms like York hams, and the same gloriously uninhibited way of striking the ball that we have seen over the years in his cricket. Mark Nicholas said that when he first came to Hampshire, the then coach, Peter Sainsbury, had to ban Smith from whacking the ball out of the ground during practice at Southampton. 'There goes another thirty bloody quid,' Sainsbury would say as the young Smith crashed the ball over the bowler's head in the general direction of Portsmouth.

While he strives to be assertive and dominant on the field of play, he seems strangely shy and uncertain about himself in other areas. In an age when top athletes are encouraged to be loud and arrogant, and are often rewarded for behaving like spoilt children, it is refreshing to meet someone as modest and pleasant as Smith. 'Take him anywhere,' says his captain. And you know what he means.

There was never any doubt he was going to be a professional sportsman. His father told him not to worry about getting poor results at school, but to concentrate on sport. Dad was proved right in his hunch, but his son seems sensitive to the fact that perhaps he is not as well educated as he might be. When we were talking about what he might do when he finished playing cricket, he said: 'I am not clever enough to write about sport, and I am not articulate enough to commentate.'

It is my guess he might be proven wrong in at least one of those assumptions, because he talks engagingly about cricket, particularly on the subject we all want to know about: what is it like batting for long periods against quick bowling of unflagging pace and unremitting hostility?

'I know people are going to say I am having them on, but the fact is I enjoyed Edgbaston. It wasn't a great pitch. The trouble with the uneven bounce was that it went up and up. At Lord's it was up and down. The worst part of batting against short-pitched bowling is that you can be out there for 45 minutes and think you are playing quite well until you look at the scoreboard and realize you haven't scored a run in that time.

'Bishop is the quickest bowler I have ever faced – he is as quick now as he was four years ago – and he was at his fastest at Edgbaston. He has genuine pace, and he seems to accelerate from the pitch. There were a couple of times out there when I wondered if I had sufficient life insurance.

'The other thought I had when I was batting was, strangely enough, a business concern. I have a company making cricket helmets, and I remember thinking when they were whizzing the ball past my head whether my helmets were any good, and hoping to God they stood the test. I wore a visor for only the second time in my career, but I think I might stick with it. You look at players who have been smashed in the face and see what it has done to them, not just physically but mentally, too.

'It was a pity we didn't have a different kind of wicket after Lord's. We were on such a high that what we needed ideally was a five-day featherbed where we could consolidate our confidence and make them work hard. If our wickets have any bounce in them, uneven or otherwise, the West Indies are going to have a big advantage over us. When I was at the other end watching our players, I could see the concern in the eyes of one or two of them. Not fear, but worry about what they were being required to do.

'You have to understand what it is like out there in the middle. It's a street fight, and they never stop coming at you. They play the game bloody hard, but that's the way I like it, because if you play well against them then you have passed the ultimate test. Curiously, their fast bowlers are some of the nicest guys in their team. I have played 20 Tests against them and I have never been sledged. They play it tough, but I think they respect opponents who fight back.

'When I was batting at Edgbaston, Brian Lara came up to me and said: "Well played." I pointed out I wasn't scoring many. He said: "I think you are batting really well." I'm glad we have this break now before Old Trafford. There's a new spirit in the team, different from the time when Keith Fletcher was in charge. I'm not bagging Fletcher, but it is much more positive and agreeable nowadays. Illy has changed things for the better, and I value the advice that John Edrich has given me. I just hope we can mend the bones and hang on to the confidence we found at Lord's.

'It is difficult to recuperate given the amount of cricket we play. After batting at Lord's for 8½ hours against the West Indies I went with Hampshire to play Derbyshire on what might be called a sporting wicket. I had a day of Devon [Malcolm] charging in at me. Then Edgbaston, and 5½ hours of ducking and weaving. By this time I'd forgotten what a half volley looked like.

'There is a different kind of concentration needed when you are playing high pace for long periods of time. It requires a special focus. What does concentrate the mind is if you happen to have a lapse of concentration against a spinner, the worst thing that can happen is being caught bat-pad, whereas if you make a mistake against a ball flying at your head, the consequences are a bit more serious,' he said. Does all that sound like someone who has trouble articulating his sport?

Watching Smith in the last two Test Matches was to be reminded of what some had forgotten: that he is our best middle-order batsman. He was hurt and upset about being left out of the team to tour Australia, but reckons now it was a blessing in disguise. It enabled him to have a second operation on his troubled right arm and gave him time to take stock of his future. He says he has never been happier playing the game than now.

His ambition is to play for England in South Africa. 'That would be special. To play in Durban, my home town, and see what kind of reception I receive is a great ambition. Then the World Cup. I do hope this nonsense that I can't play spinners is not held against me. Great leg-spin bowlers like Shane Warne trouble me, but then they trouble most players. All right, perhaps I am not the greatest player of spin bowling, but I'm not that bad.

'All I can tell you is that whenever we play Sussex, the first thing they do when I walk out is put Ian Salisbury on to bowl. You might be interested to know that so far I have scored nine first-class centuries against Sussex, and three hundreds in one-day games. What is more – and this is my big plug for the World Cup in India – in 38 one-day games I have played in India, Pakistan and Sri Lanka, I average 48, as against my overall average of 41.' Mr Illingworth, please note.

What was impressive was that he did most of the interview while playing majestic golf. Mr Hughesdon, who knows about these things, is seriously thinking of adopting him and sees no reason why he shouldn't be a single-figure golfer in double-quick time. Mr Nicholas and your correspondent want it to be known that if anyone called Robin Smith turns up at your golf club and says he plays off 18, either grab him as a partner or laugh in his face. Whatever you do, don't play him for money.

The last hole on the Old Course at Sunningdale is uphill and 414 yards long. Smith took his driver and gave the ball the most appalling spank. 'I lacerated that one,' is what he said. We reached the ball after a two-day walk. His partner asked him what club he had selected for his second shot. 'A sand iron,' said Smith. Mr Hughesdon smiled. 'How far is it to the hole?' Smith asked. 'Just hit your sand iron. If I told you how far it was, you'd die of fright,' said Mr Hughesdon. Smith plonked the ball on the green 15 ft from the pin, and made his par. I wish we played the West Indies at golf.

15th July 1995

·47·

GARY PLAYER

—

There's not much of Gary Player (5ft 7ins tall, 10st 7lbs wet through) but what there is has lasted a long time and journeyed a long way. He has been a golf pro for more than 40 years and in that time has travelled nine million miles.

He has the knack of turning the most gracious home into something resembling the departure lounge of a busy airport. We met in an elegant house at Ascot and picked our way to the garden over an assault course of strewn baggage. He had just returned from St Andrews, was spending a day at Wentworth raising money for charity and then going to Ireland, with visits to Japan, Singapore, Jakarta, Hong Kong, China, France, Taiwan, Germany, the United States and Africa planned before the end of the year.

He will be 60 in November, with business interests the world over that have made him exceedingly rich without counting the millions he has made playing golf throughout his career. He is guaranteed his place in the pantheon as one of the greatest golfers of all time.

Along with Arnold Palmer and Jack Nicklaus he built the foundation of the modern game and changed the way that golf professionals were perceived and rewarded. He is one of only four players to have won the Grand Slam of British and US Opens, the Masters and the US PGA Championship, and is the only man to have won the Open in three different decades. So why is he still charging round the world as if he was trying to make a name for himself? What makes Gary run?

'I honestly don't know. My daughter said to me the other day: "How have you lived like this for 40 years? I couldn't last a week.' It's not possible for anyone of my age to put in more hours than I do. I suppose part of the reason is that I came from a very poor background and that taught me not to take anything for granted. If you have nothing and then get a taste of honey, it becomes a habit.

'The other day when I was leaving home in South Africa one of my grandchildren said me: "Why are you going away, grandad? Come back to my house with me." I had a little weep. But how do you achieve anything without sacrifice? George Bernard Shaw said complete happiness on earth would be eternal hell and I think he's right. I've got into the routine of striving.

'But, for the first time, I'm thinking of easing up. I shall play my last Open at St Andrews in the year 2000. That's where I played my first Open in 1955 so it will be a fitting end. Then I'll retire to my stud farm and spend time with my grandchildren. Of course, I'll still continue to design golf courses and travel the world a bit,' he said. In fact what Gary Player intends to do when he retires is just one full-time job instead of the five or six he has at present.

Player's plans have been made the more attractive by what has happened in recent years to the country of his birth. As South Africa's most famous sportsman during the time of apartheid he became a particular target for protest. When he played the US PGA at Dayton, Ohio, in 1969 he was guarded on the course by more than 50 policemen. Three officers slept in his house at night. During the tournament protesters threw telephone directories at him as he swung, rolled golf balls on to the green as he putted and sprayed ice in his eyes as he walked from green to tee. He lost by one shot to Ray Floyd.

'It was the greatest tournament I ever played in my life,' he said.

'The athlete is not responsible for the government. I wanted to explain that I couldn't go in with a gun and change the way things were. But now I treat all of what happened to me in that time like I do a missed putt. I don't look back.

'What I see now in my country is a bloody miracle. I really did believe that I would see snowballs in hell before I would see Nelson Mandela in a Springboks shirt being cheered by Afrikaners. Mandela is my great hero. I've been around royalty and mixed with presidents and prime ministers and the like but I have never met anyone with Mr Mandela's humility and effortless knack of doing the right thing. There is nothing false about him.

'You know the thing I'm proudest of? I never travelled on anything other than my South African passport. I could have changed but I was a South African and proud of it. I was offered a million pounds to go and live in America. I turned it down. I believed it was my job to help change what was wrong. Nowadays it amuses me when people say that a government of black men will fail. What about when the country was governed by white men? They didn't make a very good job of it, did they?'

He forks out about £500,000 a year to pay for the education of 400 black children at a school he built near his home.

'People ask me if I'll go to some godforsaken place. I don't really want to go but I tell them I will if they pay towards the school,' he said. 'It's very rewarding work. You have to imagine what it's like to see kids who live in a mud hut, who never even sat on a toilet seat, coming to school and using a computer and going to university.

It's like. . . ' He thought for a minute for a proper comparison. 'It's like winning the Open,' he said.

It says something for his resilience and self-belief that when he became the oldest man ever to make the cut at the last Open he actually thought he could win the tournament. 'I know that one day a man aged between 50 and 60 will win the Open. I lost it by three shots a round, including a 77, and I played bloody well for that 77, let me tell you.

'But what St Andrews brought home to me was how the equipment has changed the game. Technology is making golf courses obsolete. There is no such thing as a par five. On a calm day at St Andrews John Daly or Tiger Woods could probably drive six par fours. There are two bunkers on the ninth originally put there for the drive that nowadays players are clearing with six-irons.

'Daly is good for the game. Fine golfer. Woods has that something special. I played a round with him recently and he asked me what was wrong with his swing, and I told him his swing was perfect and all he had to concentrate on was getting the attitude right. It's what goes on between the ears that makes the champion. Call it dedication, positive thinking, concentration, application or, in my case, loving adversity.'

I asked him what loving adversity meant.

'Let us say it is God's plan to sometimes give you a hard time. Why should we always assume that everything will be perfect in our life? But in adversity some people start drinking, lose confidence and disappear. The trick is to make yourself accept adversity as a part of life, like happiness. Jack Nicklaus had the best mind of anyone who ever stepped on a golf course.

'He wasn't the best striker of the ball. Weiskopf was better, so were Hogan and Sam Snead. But no one had a better mind than Nicklaus. When I first started I was advised by one or two pros to save myself the heartache and take up another occupation. They looked at my swing and thought it unorthodox. But it's not the swing that counts.

'Look at Daly's swing. It's not possible. He's made of rubber. Look at Jack's swing – flying right elbow. Arnie's – flat. Doug Sanders – he could swing inside a telephone booth and not break a window. In the end it's all in the head.'

He should know. There have been more naturally gifted golfers, more graceful athletes, more glamorous stars than Gary Player. But few have matched his remorseless energy and immutable will. It has all, as he admits, been achieved at the expense of what the rest of us would call a normal family life. There is another ingredient which he is anxious to talk about.

'Do you know what Arnie, Jack and I have in common? Great wives. Nowadays all you hear about on the tour is divorce. The three of us have great wives. We can't claim we know how to pick 'em. Truth is, it's a miracle.'

The object of his wonderment – his wife Vivienne – was sitting in the hall surrounded by several heaps of luggage. As she surveyed the scene she shook her head and smiled ruefully. 'Here we go again,' she said.

29th July 1995

·48·

GEORGE POPE

—

1911–93

THE DEATH of George Henry Pope caused barely a ripple in the national press. Where it was noted it stated that Pope, the Derbyshire all-rounder whose career was interrupted by the war, died peacefully at his home aged 82. Those who knew him and played against him will mourn a much more considerable man than can be dismissed in a few lines.

He was a magnificent all-round cricketer and there can be little doubt that had it not been for the war years he would have played for England many times. In 1938 *Wisden* said of him: 'Good judges forecast a brilliant future for this tall, hard-working cricketer who personifies the true spirit of the game.'

On his return to county cricket in 1947 he joined forces with Cliff Gladwin, Bill Copson and a youngster called Les Jackson to form one of the best seam attacks ever possessed by a county side. Pope's come-back only lasted a couple of seasons but in his last – 1948 – he became the first player to reach the double, taking 100 wickets at 17.24 and scoring 1,152 runs at an average of 38.40. He went into the leagues, first Lancashire and then Yorkshire, where he didn't so much play cricket as conduct master classes.

When you look back at your sporting life you remember the key figures in its development. In my case they were my father, Webb Swift, who taught me cricket at school, and George Henry Pope. The difference between my father, Webb Swift and Mr Pope was that the first two were on my side and the other was not.

What I learned from Mr Pope was achieved the hard way, which is to say facing him at Bramall Lane on a grassy wicket and Pope armed with both a new ball and a tame umpire. 'How's Mabel's bad leg?' he would ask the umpire. Flattered by the great man's concern for his sickly wife, astonished he should remember her name and her rheumatic joints, the umpire was bound to give sympathetic consideration to Mr Pope's appeals for lbw.

He was also influenced, as was the batsman, by George Henry's non-stop commentary on proceedings. He would rap you on the pads, look ruefully down the wicket and say to himself: 'Nice little leg-cutter that George. Just did a bit too much, perhaps. What do you think, Mr Umpire?' And the poor besotted creature was bound to agree, as he invariably did the next time Mr Pope struck the pads and this time bellowed a demand for lbw.

When you played against Sheffield you actually took on Mr Pope's XI. He ran things. It would start in the dressing room before the game began, when he would visit to greet our professional. A gentlemanly gesture you might think. In fact it was designed to put the fear of God up the opposition. Our professional at that time was Ellis Robinson, late of Yorkshire and Somerset and an old sparring partner of Pope's.

'Fancy thi' chances, Ellis?' Pope would enquire. 'Tha' nivver could bowl,' Ellis would reply. 'Looks a bit green out there. You might be lucky to get fifty,' George would say. 'We'll see,' said Ellis, 'I just might give thi' some stick today.' On one occasion Pope bowled us out for under 50, taking eight wickets in the process. Ellis survived unbeaten with a dozen runs. As he took off his pads in the pavilion he uttered the immortal line: 'Nivver could bowl, that Popey.'

The point about facing George Pope was that it was the ultimate examination for any young cricketer. There were times when he would tell his team: 'I could bowl out England on this track.' It was not an idle boast.

He had a relaxed action and a high delivery and total command of line and length. He bowled outswing and inswing, snapped the ball back from outside off stump and had a lethal leg-cutter. He learned the leg-cutter from the great S F Barnes. When he retired Barnes settled in Derbyshire and asked if he might sometimes have a net at the county ground. Sam Cadman, the Derbyshire coach, said he could do so if he showed a young promising quick bowler called Pope how to bowl the leg-cutter.

So the great man taught Pope what he knew but made him first promise that he would not tell anyone else until he (Pope) had retired from the game. George kept his promise and it wasn't until after his retirement that he told the young Alec Bedser what Barnes had taught him. Thus are life's mysteries handed down.

He loved playing against Yorkshire and delighted in telling the story about batting against Hedley Verity with the redoubtable Brian Sellars standing intimidatingly close at silly mid-on. Pope, who was a formidable striker of a cricket ball, decided to remove the threat. He went down the wicket to Verity and hit him ferociously through midwicket, just missing Sellars. The Yorkshire captain became angry. 'I think you deliberately tried to hit me then,' he said, accusingly. 'Just stay where you are Mr Sellars and you'll be in no doubt about the next one,' said Pope.

George Pope played once for England, against South Africa in 1947. Many who were less talented played a lot more games for their country, and George Pope knew it. His legacy is that there is a generation of young cricketers – now getting on in years – prepared to testify that he was the best bowler they faced. He was a master of his craft and not many of us will go to our graves with that as our epitaph.

1st November 1993

SIR MATT BUSBY

———

1909–94

H E WAS a tough old cock, a mighty man. Two days before he died, I lunched with George Best and talk turned, as inevitably it would, to Sir Matt. Of all the players he employed, none spent more time with him than George Best.

Often, they would meet in the manager's office, where the conversations tended to be one-sided and consist of enquiries about the footballer's health and rumours about sightings in various pubs, the two subjects being inter-related.

There were many people around in those days eager to inform on George Best, most of the stories placing him in the Brown Bull, a favourite pub where the first pop star of soccer held court. George remembered that Sir Matt could never get the name right. 'What's this I hear about you drinking at the Black Pig?' he would ask. Widest of the mark was the Blue Parrot, nearest was the Brown Cow.

It was funny, but as George said, you were never quite sure with The Boss, who liked now and then to hide behind a mask of avuncular naivety. It was often his way of defusing the situation, of making an unpleasant task – such as reprimanding a player because someone ratted on him – more acceptable.

He used the technique shrewdly. When Nobby Stiles was kicking lumps out of the opposition Matt persuaded us he did it not because it might be a tactical ploy, but because he was short-sighted and not able to focus properly on his opponent. It was a mark of his genius that we believed him.

Similarly, when United in their European Cup winning year looked out of it in Spain against Real Madrid, he told the players at half-time: 'Just keep playing football.'

George remembered: 'We were getting stuffed, expecting and deserving a bollocking, and The Boss just tells us to keep on playing football. Unbelievable.' In the second half, United rallied and won.

The last time I saw him at Old Trafford was just before Mr Ferguson had fine-tuned the team to a point where Sir Matt would purr with satisfaction. It wasn't a good game and as we drank a cup of tea at half-time Matt suggested we would be better employed talking about football for the rest of the afternoon. And we did. He talked, I listened.

He reminisced about George, Bobby, Denis, Tommy Taylor, Duncan Edwards, Carey and Delaney, and you were reminded of the man's unique contribution to the game and his unswerving dedication to the simple faith that no matter what the theorists and coaches did to stifle talent, it could all be undone by one stroke of an artist's brush.

He never changed his style, his manner or his fundamental belief in the virtues of family life or the comfort of religion. Among the tracksuits and the frenzy of the modern game he appeared a venerable figure, but never old-fashioned. He treated tragedy and triumph, fame and despair in the same level-headed, steadfast manner. He was a very remarkable human being.

24th January 1994

·50·

BOBBY MOORE

———

1941–93

THE OBITUARIES were the sort reserved for monarchs. Those who knew and loved him would not have settled for less. He, looking down from the Pantheon, would be surprised and slightly bashful.

Bobby Moore knew how good a player he was, although he never boasted about it. What he never fully understood – and neither did a lot of people until he died – was the deep affection the British public felt for him.

He faced fame toe to toe and stared the impostor down. He might have been a superstar, a genuine working-class hero and a shy man, but he confronted public scrutiny in both good and bad times with the honest and clear gaze of a man who is not easily frightened. For all his celebrity he moved easily at street level dealing with the genuine and the crackpot in the same even-tempered manner.

When he was told he was dying he was just as calm and unflinching. Even those who knew and thought perhaps he might want to off-load his concern found him the same unperturbed, affable man, always eager to deflect personal questions with a cascade of enquiries of his own.

'All right, Mike?' he'd say, 'Mary okay? Boys all right? What you up to nowadays? What about the telly? Mary working? Seen Tarby? How's the golf?'

By the time you had finished telling him your problems you had forgotten what you were going to ask him in the first place. He had the most wonderful bedside manner. If there was an inner anxiety, a turmoil (and God knows there must have been at various times in his eventful life), he never let on.

It was the same with his football. His detachment from the hurly-burly was disdainful. He always looked like a king among commoners. Then, when there came a champion worthy of his attention, like Pele, we saw proof, if ever it be needed, that he was one of the greatest footballers of all time.

Nowadays, when very average footballers are being sold for millions of pounds, it is interesting to speculate what Bobby Moore would be worth. At a time when players like Gascoigne, who are allegedly role models, behave outrageously and yet are still pursued by sponsors and a media (who ought to know better) eager to stuff their pockets with notes, what riches would await a man like Moore, who not only looked and played like a hero, but behaved like one?

It is interesting to be reminded that Bobby Moore and the rest of his '66 team were paid £1,000 each for winning the World Cup, particularly when you consider that the FA's tax bill for the event exceeded £1 million.

The captain of the next England team to win the World Cup will drive home in a platinum Rolls Royce, over a silver drawbridge, across a moat of liquid gold. But I doubt he'll be a hero like Bobby Moore.

I am glad I saw him when I did, when the England shirt was pristine and not daubed with commercial graffiti, when there was still honour in the game, style and, most of all, humour. The lasting image of that time will always be Moore, slim as a reed, holding aloft the trophy at Wembley. It was the moment the boy from Barking became the golden icon of the Sixties.

He had a wicked sense of humour and when he wanted could be as hard as the best of them. We played together in a charity game when the opposition decided it might be fun to kick Elton John into the nearby supermarket car park.

Bobby had a word with the culprit, who stupidly decided not only to ignore his advice but to try kicking the great man. The foolish behaviour led to his early and permanent departure from the pitch, not that he knew what hit him. Nor did the referee.

Before the game I had taken instruction from my captain as to how I should play. 'Wide on the right, Parky, and when I get the ball you set off running the way I point,' he said. The first time he put the plan into operation he released me with a daisycutter inside the full-back and diagonally to the corner flag.

It meant a gallop of 50 yards to get there and when I did I was too knackered to get the cross in. In the next 20 minutes Mr Moore deliberately delivered seven or eight more passes to the identical spot. By the end I was on hands and knees, hoping for a miracle, like a passing taxi.

Shamefully, I have to recount that I was finally removed from the pitch by the trainer after being ill near the corner flag. This greatly amused Mr Moore, who was also much taken by the report in the local paper, which said: 'Parkinson responded feebly to intelligent prompting by Bobby Moore.' It was meant as a barb. In fact, I have been considering having it for my epitaph.

Writing all this, and remembering as I write, I keep recalling the time Dame Edith Evans was dying and her biographer and friend Bryan Forbes broke the news that she was seriously ill to one of his daughters. 'But she won't die, though, will she daddy?' the daughter said. 'Why not?' Bryan asked. 'Because she's not the type,' said his daughter.

That's what I feel about Bobby Moore. All of us will have a chance to pay our respects at the memorial service. I only hope they can find a hall that's big enough.

1st March 1993

THE THANKSGIVING

When we gathered at Westminster Abbey to pay tribute to Bobby Moore it was only the second time in the Abbey's history that there had been a thanksgiving service for an athlete. You could win some money on who the other one was. I said W G Grace, C B Fry, Jack Hobbs. The answer is Sir Frank Worrell.

There were similarities in the two men. Both were magnificent athletes and impeccable sportsmen; both were inspiring captains leading their countries at significant and historical moments; both died too young.

Comparisons fall apart when we look at how West Indian cricket embraced Worrell and how English soccer turned its back on Moore. Worrell became the ambassador for West Indian cricket abroad and an honoured member of its inner sanctums at home. Moore was largely ignored by the Football Association.

One of the greatest players we have produced was never asked by the people responsible for running English soccer to make a contribution in either a coaching or advisory capacity. Because they are mediocre men they are frightened of greatness. Modern soccer, in all its turmoil and angst, is what they have created. Moore and the rest of us deserve better. They don't.

Looking round the Abbey I felt proud and thankful to belong to the generation of the World Cup winners. It seemed to me there were real heroes about. Proper men, too. When I looked at the Boys of '66 I remembered them in the days before soccer shirts were defiled by advertising, when the game still belonged to the fans and not the merchandising men. In those days there were agents lurking, but they weren't the puppet masters they have become, nor were the players their witless accomplices.

Not only was the game more entertaining, it was altogether more wholesome.

Bobby Moore's service brought together all of us who lived through that moment in the history of English soccer. When we gathered at the Abbey and looked around us, what we realized was that we didn't know at the time how lucky we were.

Let us, for instance, suppose that in 30 years' time another England footballer is celebrated at the Abbey. I'll bet the congregation would not supply the pool of players like I had to choose from. Apart from the Boys of '66 I could pick George Best, Rodney Marsh, Jimmy Greaves, Franz Beckenbauer, Johnny Haynes, Colin Bell, Mike Summerbee, Bob Wilson, Ian St John, Terry Venables.

When we talk of great players we must remember the company they keep and in the case of Bobby Moore he only mingled with the best. Before the service, waiting in the cloistered garden, Bobby Charlton was nervous. He had to make a speech and it wasn't that he didn't know what to say but whether he would do justice to his friend. 'What would you like people to say about you, Bobby?' I asked. 'That I was a good player,' he said. 'Then that's all you have to say about your friend,' I said.

Later, what he said was perfect and moving because of its simplicity. Jimmy Tarbuck was looking for the illuminating anecdote. One he didn't tell but which summed up Bobby Moore perfectly was the occasion Mike Summerbee, a stern competitor, reduced Frank Lampard, the West Ham full-back, to a crumpled heap with a ferocious and illegal tackle. As he turned away from his skulduggery he was confronted by Bobby Moore. What he said was: 'Now that wasn't a nice thing to do, was it, Mike?' And Summerbee skulked away from the scene of the crime, feeling awful.

It is the function of heroes to make the rest of us feel small.

5th July 1993

·51·

CEC PEPPER

—

1918–93

CEC PEPPER spent most of his career in English League cricket but there was never any doubt about his roots. He was a dinky-di Aussie, a turbulent man and one of the best all-round cricketers Australia has ever produced. I base that judgment on what my eyes told me and the evidence of Keith Miller, who rang shortly after Cec had died to say that in his view you could rank Pepper with Benaud and there were those who thought that Cec might have the edge.

Miller reckoned Pepper's flipper was the best ball he saw in his entire career. 'It skimmed off the pitch at you,' he said. Pepper, like Miller, was nobody's lapdog. Perhaps he lacked Miller's effortless charm which is why, when he had a run-in with Don Bradman in 1946, it proved to be terminal.

Pepper was a stalwart of the great Australian Services team and played against South Australia at Adelaide when Bradman made his come-back after the war years and injury. Early in Bradman's innings Pepper caught him in front and appealed for lbw. The umpire rejected the appeal, whereupon Pepper asked the umpire just what a bowler had to do to get a decision against Bradman in Adelaide. The umpire reported Pepper and he was left out of the Australian team to tour New Zealand later that year. Cec packed his bags and came to England where for the next 20 years he enlivened proceedings with his great talent and huge competitive spirit.

Pepper became one of the legendary figures in league cricket in the North of England. On one occasion, having bowled an over of leg-spin, flippers and googlies at a batsman who had not the slightest idea what was happening, he said after the sixth ball: 'It's alright lad, you can open your eyes now . . . it's over.'

When he became an umpire there were those who wondered if he might curb his tongue on the field of play. He didn't. For one who suffered at the hands of officials both as a batsman and bowler he showed little sympathy for his fellow professionals once he changed sides. Before a game he was officiating at in Essex, Bruce Francis, a fellow Aussie, was chatting to Cec about the season and happened to remark he had been dismissed lbw 16 times. When Francis came in to bat he had hardly got moving before he was struck on the pad. 'That's 17 times, Bruce,' said Cec, sticking his finger up.

My favourite story about Cec Pepper is the one that also sums up the great love/hate relationship at the heart of an Ashes series. When Cec was terrorizing umpires in the Lancashire League he came across George Long who didn't say much but was not to be tampered with.

Cec kept appealing for lbw and George kept turning him down. Pepper's grumbling intensified and began to include observations involving the umpire's antecedents and possible illegitimacy.

At the end of one particularly abusive over even Cec thought he might have gone too far. He walked with George Long to square leg trying to explain that when he called his parentage into doubt he wasn't being personal, merely exuberant.

Indeed, as Cec explained, accusing someone of being born out of wedlock is a compliment of sorts in Australia. George Long said: 'Nay, Cec lad, don't worry your head about it. Up here we like a man that speaks his mind.'

Thus blessed and thinking that George might be entertaining thoughts of adopting him, Cec returned to the battle. His first ball of the next over struck the batsman on the pads. 'Owzat, umpire!' bellowed Pepper. 'Not out, you fat Australian bastard,' said George Long, with calm authority.

29th March 1993

·52·

FRED PERRY

—

1909–95

THE LAST time an Englishman took the men's title at Wimbledon the old king was a lad. It was the year Golden Miller won the Grand National, Elgar died, Bonnie and Clyde were shot and the Queen Mary was launched. It was also the year that Fred Astaire started dancing with Ginger Rogers, John Dillinger was bumped off and a song called *I Only Have Eyes For You* was top of the pops.

The man who won Wimbledon in 1934, then won it twice more before turning pro, is still, at 84, a formidable figure. Fred Perry is tall, square-shouldered with a boxer's nose. The handshake is firm and strong. You come to the conclusion that when he was younger he must have been a handful.

He is a legend, one of the few people I have interviewed who can point to a statue and say: 'That's me, up there.' It gives him great satisfaction to walk past the statue at Wimbledon and imagine those long-gone committee men spinning in their graves.

Fred Perry and Wimbledon have been together for a long time, but they were hardly made for one another. He was the son of a Labour politician, a chippy young man with a quick temper and a ready tongue. The All England Club and the Lawn Tennis Association were the caretakers of a tradition which dissuaded the likes of young Perry playing on their manicured turf. When he won his first Wimbledon in 1934, beating Australian Jack Crawford, Perry heard one committee man say to his opponent: 'This was one day when the best man didn't win.'

Today the eyes rekindle at the insult. 'I was born the wrong side of the tramlines for some at Wimbledon. I was too brash, aggressive for their tastes. It was a class-ridden set-up. I can still get angry when I think of the shabby way I was treated.

'All those hatchets have been buried now. We've got the statue, the Fred Perry Gates. I've always loved Wimbledon, the place, the event. If someone said: "Fred, you've got one more set left before you die," I'd choose the Centre Court at Wimbledon. That would be lovely.'

It would do him a favour if someone carved under his statue the plea: 'Don't Ask' in response to the question he has fielded ever since winning Wimbledon: How long do we have to wait for another champion? If Fred Perry knows he isn't telling. 'You trying to do me out of a job? Do you think I'd be here working at Wimbledon if there had been a winner after me?' he said. It was a joke, but like all the best ones it has an element of truth.

Nonetheless, jaded though it might be, the question remains a good one. Why, oh why, have we not had another Fred Perry for 60 years? He offers a few clues: 'You have to want it so much you can taste it. I did. You have to do it yourself. You are on your own. I had problems with my stamina, kept losing in the fifth set. I went training with the Arsenal football team, Cliff Bastin, Alex James, Joe Hulme. Eventually I was running 10 miles a day. Only lost one five-setter after that.

'Players today send their coaches to look at opponents. No good. Have to do it yourself. I used to study my opponents, not just the way they played but tell-tale mannerisms. When Bunny Austin got nervous he'd walk round in circles, Von Cramm used to get two little pink spots on his cheeks when he was worried.

'Jack Crawford normally wiped his hand down his trouser leg. When he was feeling the strain he used to wipe it across his shirt. When you see giveaway signs like that, you go.

'Bill Tilden taught me a lot. He never gave you what you wanted. One day he would talk to you, next day he would ignore you. He gave the impression that he was doing you a favour by turning up. You couldn't take your eyes off him. That's important. On court they should be looking at you.

'During knock-up I'd always say, loudly: "Anytime you're ready" to my opponent. A decision made by you, so they're watching. If my opponent made a brilliant shot and regained the spotlight there was the fly-in-eye ploy. You make out you have something in your eye. It brings the focus back to you. Surreptitious gamesmanship, I think you could call it,' he said.

Perry turned pro after winning his third Wimbledon title. The next time he came to England with fellow pro Ellsworth Vines they were given leper status by the LTA. So they played at the Empire Pool, Wembley, Bournemouth FC and the Town Hall in Edinburgh. As a tennis professional he lived and worked in America and the voice you hear on commentary nowadays owes more to San Francisco than his native Stockport. When he reminisces about his life in America in the Thirties you understand how much the world has changed.

'I was invited to play in the Los Angeles Championship. Jokingly I said to the organizer I would play if he arranged a date with Jean Harlow. On the eve of the tournament there was a dinner and dance at the tennis club. They sent a limo for me. It took me up into Beverly Hills where the stars lived.

'I went into this mansion and there, standing at the top of a wonderful staircase, dressed in a slinky black dress, was Jean Harlow. She asked where I was taking her and I said to the tennis club. She said: "Forget it. Let's go on the town." I said I didn't think I could afford it. She laughed and said when she went out MGM publicity paid the bill.

'We went to every night club and restaurant in town. It was the most wonderful, glamorous evening. I got back home at eight in the morning.' He paused, smiling at the memory. I chose the next question carefully. 'Did it affect your tennis?' I asked. 'I won,' he said.

For a while he ran the Beverly Hills Tennis club and the stars were his friends. He met Bette Davies, Paulette Goddard, Cary Grant, Randolph Scott, Clark Gable, Marlene Dietrich. 'None of 'em could play,' he mused. 'But was Dietrich very beautiful?' I asked. 'Oh yes,' he said.

It was a glittering lifestyle. One day he arranged a match, Great Britain versus the USA. The American team was Ellsworth Vines and Groucho Marx. Fred Perry and Charlie Chaplin turned out for Britain. That evening music for dancing was provided by the Benny Goodman Quintet. Perry had a screen test. 'I was dressed in tails. I had to open a door; I walked into it. End of film career,' he said.

It was an age of evening dress, fox-trots and elegance, where the professional sportsman was judged as much for his appearance off court as his style on it. The players milling around the lobby of Fred Perry's London hotel in tracksuits and trainers are the children of the revolution starred by Perry and a few others.

I wonder if they ever pause to consider what they owe this man as he picks a fastidious path through them? I wonder what he thinks of the tribe he spawned? 'Difficult when you get very old to put yourself in their shoes. The dress looks sloppy, doesn't it? But then that's the fashion. What do they keep in those big bags they carry around? Money? It's a case of too much, too soon, for many of them.

'What concerns me most of all today is the racket technology. The technology dictates the way the game is played. I think there's a case for going back to wooden rackets for men because there aren't any touch players any more. They've gone and that's sad for the spectators. I'd keep the modern rackets for the women. They've made a significant difference for the better in women's tennis.

'But the game still excites me. I still get the same thrill I always did when I pass through the gates at Wimbledon. The only difference between now and when I was a player is that nowadays I know I'll feel the same way coming out of Wimbledon as I did going in. I've been very lucky. The job the hobby, the hobby the job. Not many people can say that.'

It means he never thinks of retiring because he would only do in retirement what he does now he is working, namely follow the tennis. The trick is to keep going as long as he can. He's had heart surgery. 'They used part of a pig in the operation. Sometimes I grunt a lot,' he said.

He is looking forward to meeting the other members of the 1933 Davis Cup side at Wimbledon today. They are all still alive. Pat Hughes is 90, Bunny Austin and Harold Lee both 87, Perry 84 and Raymond Tuckey 77. They conquered what was considered to be an unbeatable French team. It is Perry's favourite moment from a crowded life.

What sustains Fred Perry and gives him a future in his old age is that every Wimbledon he moves among people who regard him not as a fossil but as a sage. He earned the honour not simply by winning at Wimbledon all those years ago, more by the way he has conducted himself since. What he demonstrates for the benefit of today's players is how to behave like a champion.

Getting there is often the easiest part, staying on top is harder. In the end the record will show that Fred Perry did both in great style.

26th June 1993

·53·

DANNY BLANCHFLOWER

1926–93

WHEN I heard that Danny Blanchflower had died I tried to remember the last time we met. I thought it had been at Wentworth Golf Club five or six years ago when we talked about his days at Barnsley and laughed a lot.

It wasn't until I saw the newsreel of him sick and infirm at his testimonial that I realized this was the last occasion I saw him. I had deliberately exorcised the memory. The dreadful illness which made him frail, dimmed those marvellous eyes, muddled that keen mind, was distressing to behold. It was also inappropriate. He was a hero, a god, so how could he possibly be stricken like an ordinary man?

Blanchflower illuminated my youth. He, like Tom Finney, Johnny Kelly, Wilf Mannion, defined for me a game of high technical skill, graceful athleticism and often vivid imagination. It was also played with a great deal of humour and sportsmanship. They were the finest role models a boy could wish for.

Blanchflower's was the most persuasive example of all because the rest were but occasional visitors to my youth, whereas, for two marvellous seasons, Blanchflower was a part of it.

Barnsley bought him from Glentoran in 1949 for £6,000. He played his first game against Rotherham United and we had to admit that we'd seen nothing like him. What was also obvious was that he wouldn't stay long at Barnsley; he was destined to move on to the highest levels of the game.

Whenever he turned out for the Tykes it was something of a special event. Every game was a farewell. He rarely let us down. Even in his springtime he was a footballer of great technical quality and maturity.

The first thing you noticed about Blanchflower was his balance, which enabled him to survive the sternest challenge and, added to his marvellous close control, gave him the luxury all great players share, that of playing in their own private space at their own tempo.

He was one of the best passers of a football I ever saw. He skimmed, stroked, chipped and curved passes all over the field with a quarterback's feel for weight and trajectory. He had a disdain for defending. It wasn't that he was a shirker or lacked physical courage, simply that he believed it was an area of the game better left to the players who enjoyed doing it.

At Barnsley, the mugging of visiting forwards was done by Danny's midfield partner, the incomparable Skinner Normanton. At Tottenham, in more illustrious company, Dave Mackay did the same job on Danny's behalf. Beauty and the Beast.

When, later on in life, I came to know Danny Blanchflower, he often talked about his days at Oakwell. He remembered that when he first arrived for training he imagined that the soccer would be a lot more cerebral than he had played in Ireland.

In his first practice game he encountered Skinner without knowing anything of his reputation for what can best be described as an uncomplicated approach to soccer.

As Skinner approached Danny with the ball at his feet, Danny quickly considered all the tricks that might be employed to beat him: would Skinner give him the body swerve, would he use the feint inside, might he waggle his foot over the ball daring Blanchflower to guess which way he was going?

As it was, Danny ended up flat on his back with Skinner's studmarks up his shirt front as Skinner walked through and over him. It was a suitable introduction to his new club and his midfield partner. It might have been worse because Danny told me that Skinner was once sent from the field by his manager during a practice game in which he inflicted serious damage on a team-mate.

If Barnsley gave him his first taste of football in England, it also allowed him a valuable insight into the way our soccer clubs treated their players in the Fifties.

After training in the morning the Barnsley players spent most afternoons playing snooker in a local hall. During a poor sequence of results, the manager received complaints from the fans that he was allowing his players too much time playing snooker when they ought to be practising football. As a gesture he summoned his players to the ground in the afternoons, which merely meant they played snooker at the club instead of the snooker hall.

Blanchflower asked for the ball. He was told he couldn't have one because over-familiarity with the ball would deaden his appetite for it on Saturdays. He replied, famously, that if he didn't see the ball during the week he wouldn't know what it looked like on Saturdays.

He was accused of being a trouble-maker and transferred, without much ado, to

Aston Villa. He sat in the kitchen of the hotel with a cup of tea while the chairmen of the two clubs haggled over a price in the dining-room. He was treated like a piece of meat and the affront lit a fire in him which burned and raged for the rest of his life.

He had a fine contempt for directors of football clubs and throughout his career never lost an opportunity to larrup them for what he considered their ignorance of the game and lack of understanding of players and managers. He was the most eloquent advocate of the beautiful game and its most passionate defender. He could talk the leg off an iron pot and, at his best, write with real style and imagination.

Sadly, he lost his war against the Philistines, otherwise he would not have been such a ghostly, marginal figure in the game he adorned long before he was rendered unemployable by his ghastly illness. It was unseemly and unutterably sad that such a proud and independent man should be sustained by charity at the end of his life.

Those of us who enjoyed his company, read him, watched him play will understand the significance of Danny Blanchflower. He was an important man in the history of football. He never compromised his own vision of how the game should be played, never lost his disdain for those who couldn't tell the difference between success and glory.

A lifetime in football taught him the valuable lesson that the difference between winning and losing, success and failure, is balanced on a razor's edge.

After defeat in the 1958 World Cup in Sweden, when he captained his country, he wrote: 'In the highly intensive world of professional football the sun rises and sets with alarming suddenness. The world turns over every 24 hours, but not with the smooth astronomical rhythm that compels our planet. It just gives a quick, impulsive spin and the character who has been basking in the summit sunshine unexpectedly finds himself clinging desperately to the South Pole with cold, bare fingers.'

With hindsight, that statement becomes an awful prophecy when applied to the last wretched years of his life. Reading the many generous obituaries about him I wondered how, for the last decade or so, the world became so neglectful of a man of such obvious quality. The sadness of it all is that often we only tell our heroes how important they are when they can no longer hear.

13th December 1993

·54·

GAVIN SMITH

—

1919–92

Gavin smith died last week. He was 73 and had been retired from his job as hospital porter for nearly 10 years. Before that he was the licensee of a pub and before that, in his golden youth, he ran like the wind down the right wing for Barnsley.

He was so swift he needed an arresting parachute to prevent him colliding with the crowd. He was the one they built the gate in the wall for so that he could continue his fastest gallops through the terraces and out of the ground before pulling up in the car park.

He loved cutting inside and scoring goals. They were always spectacular, often causing the Green 'Un to report: 'Smith's explosive shot bulged the net behind the hapless custodian.' He was much helped by a young Irishman called Danny Blanchflower whose ability to pass behind defenders gave vivid challenge to Smith's acceleration.

As if this wasn't enough of a feast, on the other wing was Johnny Kelly, who dawdled, tricked and conned his way through defences. He was a pickpocket of a player, Smith a battering ram. One of his greatest moments came in the '45–6 season when Barnsley played Newcastle United in the FA Cup. In the first leg, in front of 60,000 at Newcastle, Barnsley lost 3–1. The return leg was played at Barnsley the following Wednesday and I stood with my father in the rain along with 27,000 other supporters for our view of players like Ernie Taylor, Joe Harvey, Albert Stubbins and Jackie Milburn.

The interest in the game was such that the local pits had sanctioned a day off with a notice which said: 'In order that the management may have knowledge of the number intending to be absent on Wednesday afternoon, will those whose relatives are to be buried on that day please apply by Tuesday for permission to attend.'

We won 3–0 and not too many went down the pit the next day either. Gavin Smith scored the second goal, racing through the defence, cutting in and smashing the ball past King. It was poignant recalling that day of noisy crowds and silent pits at a time when the politicians have decided we no longer need a coal industry.

When I was growing up the link between club and mine was irrevocable. Not only did the pit provide the spectators but it also employed the players. They shared a common experience with the people who came to watch them on a Saturday afternoon. The relationship was deep and complete. It defined the character of clubs like Barnsley.

The ground told you what to expect. As you breasted the hill from the bus station it sat there guarded by slag heaps. The streets of weatherbeaten stone houses came right down to the main gate. There was a time when all I wanted in life was to save enough money to buy the house nearest the players' entrance and live there until I died, preferably with Hedy Lamarr.

The pits also provided a certain kind of player. He was likely to be medium height, of sturdy build and uncompromising in the tackle. In my time at Barnsley the wonderful Skinner Normanton epitomized the breed. But there were others. In fact, they were in unending supply. All you had to do was to peer down any pit shaft and whistle and one came up, ready to go to work.

Things have changed, soccer has become homogenized. A few years ago when Allan Clarke was player-manager at Barnsley, I went to see them play at Reading. We lost 7–1. It was one of the saddest days of my life and Mr Clarke wasn't too chuffed either. The worst insult came with Reading six goals up when a Barnsley fan shouted to a perplexed Clarke: 'Why doesn't tha' put Parky on?'

I was not surprised to read that the next week Mr Clarke took his players down the local pit to remind them what hard graft was really like. Mr Machin, the present manager, will soon be in the situation where there won't be a pit to take his team down even if he wants to. What will also disappear is a sporting tradition which enriched the lives of those lucky enough to experience it.

It is possible to glamorize the realities of life in a mining community, but it is not possible to invent the humour, drama, colour and enchantment provided by soccer teams like Barnsley in the days when they were suckled by the community they served. In future years when my grandchildren visit their ancestral home there will be little left of what I have described. The slag heaps will be landscaped, the stadium an all-seater and the car park where Gavin Smith used to finish his runs will be a hotel and leisure centre.

Smith and Blanchflower, Kelly and Baxter, Skinner and Tommy Taylor, Cec McCormack and Gordon Pallister will be ghostly figures in a forgotten landscape. My grandchildren will be told that it was ugly and grimy in those days. I want them to know that it wasn't pretty, but we made the best of it and, on looking back, it had a terrible grandeur.

19th October 1992

JIMMY BAXTER

—

1925–94

The trouble with nostalgia nowadays is that it starts with the invention of the video tape. Everything that went before is left to old men on park benches and grandads telling stories.

The major misconception of the television generation is that if it isn't on video it didn't happen. 'The 100 Best Goals Ever Scored' is a misnomer. It is, in fact, 'The 100 Best Goals Ever Seen On Television', a different proposition altogether.

It does not, for instance, include the goal scored by Jimmy Baxter in the third round of the FA Cup at Leeds Road, Huddersfield, in January, 1947. I have written of Baxter before. He was what journalists used to delight in describing as 'a ball-playing inside forward'.

He was so frail he looked like he ought to be placed in the care of the local authority. His physical condition was attributed to stunted growth brought about by an addiction to Woodbines. Such was his habit he would light up at half-time in the dressing room. When he left Barnsley and joined Preston North End the cameras visited Deepdale to capture Tom Finney for *This Is Your Life*. Baxter was discovered lying in the team bath having a smoke.

In those days Huddersfield Town played in the First Division. They had a team built around the incomparable talents of Peter Doherty. He was as good a player as I ever saw; inventive, combative, tireless. When he joined Raich Carter at Derby the two of them, all too briefly, formed one of the great inside-forward combinations.

At Huddersfield Doherty played alongside Vic Metcalfe, a stylish left-winger of great skill with a left foot so accurate and reliable it should have been used to deliver registered post. Jimmy Glazzard was the centre forward. There wasn't much of him but what there was consisted mainly of forehead flattened through years of contact with sodden leather footballs aimed by Metcalfe's left boot.

The score was 3–3 with 10 minutes to go when Baxter scored a goal of such wit and imagination it has remained in my mind ever since. He was about 30 yards out and dawdling on the ball, as players were allowed to do in those days, when he looked up and spied that the Huddersfield goalkeeper, Bob Hesford, had strayed from his line. Baxter flicked the ball up and lobbed it goalwards. It had the height and trajectory of a sand wedge hit high and soft to the pin.

As soon as the ball left Baxter's boot Hesford knew he was in trouble. He started back-pedalling with his eye on the ball until he reached the point where the angle of his head went beyond the point of balance. Then he toppled into his own net, arms flailing like a man falling backwards over a steep cliff. He arrived over the goal line at about the same time as Baxter's lob.

I couldn't begin to count the number of goals I have seen scored since that January day all those many years ago, but none remains so clear in my mind. I think it had something to do with the tempo of the moment, the fact it seemed to happen in slow motion. It was artful and clever. It was also witnessed by a child madly in love with soccer, many years before the taste of the game became sour on his palate.

What I also remember about that day is that as Barnsley battled to hang on and win the match a fan presented the Barnsley goalkeeper with an alarm clock so that he might put it in the back of the goal along with his cap and gloves and know how long there was to go. It was a charming and humorous gesture and typical of an age before soccer lost its innocence.

Not that Jimmy Baxter was a babe in arms. He was no oil painting. Indeed, he played the aforesaid game at Huddersfield with a broken jaw, unknown to his team-mates, who couldn't tell there was anything wrong by looking at him. As he only weighed just over nine stone, any lump appearing on his person was taken as a welcome sign that he was putting on weight.

He was physically so unlike an athlete that if he played today he would be in regular demand by shrewd television casting directors. Imagine him in those television commercials where the Gary Linekers of the game are seen eating cornflakes and looking brimmingly healthy.

Consider the fun to be had if the Lineker figure said to camera: 'If you don't eat your cornflakes then this is what can happen,' and we see Jimmy Baxter, looking like he is on his last legs, wolfing down bacon, eggs and fried bread with a full ashtray on the table next to the bottle of brown sauce.

There's little doubt that if Jimmy Baxter turned up at a club nowadays and asked for a trial he would be shown the door. If they let him inside he would fail the medical. It would be a grievous mistake because he was a tough little so-and-so who could mix it with the biggest and the roughest.

I once saw him topple Derek Dooley in spectacular fashion at Barnsley. A couple of weeks before I had seen Dooley at Hillsborough terrify the Middlesbrough defenders into giving him the freedom of the park. For those who never saw him play, Dooley was a tall and strong centre forward who feared no man and had the single-minded thrust of a rat up a pump. He scored 62 goals in 61 appearances for Wednesday before he was so tragically injured and forced to leave the game. He was greatly assisted in his goal-scoring feats by a considerable footballer called Redfern Froggatt who would send Dooley careering towards goal with meticulous and inviting long passes. There was nothing Dooley liked more than a straight gallop on goal and there were few 'keepers around who relished the prospect of facing 13 stone of highly motivated bone and muscle.

When Sheffield Wednesday came to Barnsley, our 'keeper, Harry Hough, threw himself at Dooley's feet and suffered a broken arm. Shortly after, our centre-half confronted Mr Dooley and thereafter spent the rest of the game doing a passable imitation of Long John Silver.

It was with his team reduced to nine men that Baxter, having already scored two goals, decided to come to the rescue.

I am not going to swear to what happened next but let me tell you what I think I saw. Baxter, who had dropped deep to look after Dooley, gained the ball near the corner flag in his own half of the field and invited the centre-forward to advance. As Dooley approached, arms outstretched, hemming Baxter in, the little man stepped over the ball and headed Dooley in the goolies. There were some who later claimed that Baxter was so small he had to jump to make contact, but that is clearly fanciful.

Over the years I have replayed the incident over and over in my mind and the only conclusion I can be sure of is that whatever happened caused Dooley to lose interest in proceedings for quite a time. Then, as now, the referee didn't see anything and even had he done so I doubt if he would have believed it.

Had Baxter played in the video era I have no doubt that he would have featured in a large chunk of tonight's programme. Similarly, as part of tonight is also devoted to goalkeepers and their foibles, I have little doubt that several custodians of my youth would have featured strongly, particularly a Barnsley keeper called Pat Kelly, who regularly patrolled his goal-mouth while walking on his hands. One day an enterprising opponent tried a shot from his own half having seen that Kelly was upside-down on the penalty spot. Kelly saw the ball coming and caught it between his knees.

Now you can believe that or not. The point is I was there and you weren't and neither was a television camera. The trouble with video evidence is that it stops people elaborating on past events. It means that my children won't be able to wax nostalgic to their children like I did to them.

You might regard this as a more honest approach and therefore a healthier state of affairs. I don't. The trouble with a newsreel approach to life is that it denies romance. It is also death to the imagination.

30th May 1994

·56·

CEC
McCORMACK

—

1922–94

S HORT OF Peter Tatchell outing Sir Bert Millichip it is difficult to imagine anything that could significantly add to soccer's present list of problems. What the game needs is a good scrubbing, top to bottom, every nook and cranny, and even then a de-lousing.

Everyone in football has a part to play in its reformation because everyone has contributed to its downfall. The managers and directors have encouraged and participated in a bung culture and have allowed the yobs to dominate the terraces and prosper on the field. The players have shown little or no enthusiasm for persuading people from the view that the game is played by over-paid thickoes and the media have constantly failed in their duty by making heroes out of monsters and celebrating mediocrity both in play and behaviour.

The entire mess is presided over by the FA, which fiddles while the game does the same thing, with George Graham leading the string section and playing a different tune. There are exceptions, of course, decent and honourable men who are concerned about the game and see the need for drastic action. At present they lack a sheriff and the bad guys are winning.

In the days when bungs were no bigger than the toe cap on a player's boot and George Graham's 'gift' would have bought the entire England soccer team plus Wembley Stadium, we had a centre forward at Barnsley, Cec McCormack, who was as good at his job as any I have seen.

He joined us from Middlesbrough in 1951 and it must be said there were a few who, when they saw him, wondered if the manager hadn't made a mistake. There wasn't much of him, he was short and frail-looking with wispy blond hair.

In those days centre forwards were big bullocking men with foreheads like Herman Munster and legs that would comfortably support a full-size billiard table.

They were put on earth to kick centre halves and to fill the net with footballs and goalkeepers. Their reputations were such that when they walked down the street people stepped aside to let them by and they never paid to get into the local dance hall.

So it was a shock when we saw Cecil McCormack. He answered our doubts by scoring 33 goals in 37 League games, setting a club goal-scoring record that still stands. He was skilful, graceful and two-footed. He wasn't big enough to dominate in the air but, as he said, he used his head for thinking with.

Anyone who watched Barnsley in that period will tell you about the day McCormack scored five against Luton Town. Bernard Stretten, who played for England, was in goal. Syd Owen, who also won a cap or two, was centre half.

Forty years on and I can still see McCormack's third goal as he flowed past two defenders and drove the ball into the roof of the net. The net did 'bulge', the goalkeeper was 'a hapless custodian'. All the clichés of the day were confirmed and remain in my mind.

No one knew him well. I followed him once from the ground to the snooker hall and waited outside but it started to rain so I went home. It was said he liked a drink and that he would sometimes tell the dressing room he fancied scoring a goal or two today, and was always as good as his word.

He went as soon as he came. We transferred him to Notts County, where he played alongside Tommy Lawton. We sold him for £20,000 and a young lad called Tommy Taylor took his place. McCormack emigrated to Canada, where he played with the Toronto All Stars. That was the last I heard of him until I was told the other day that he had died.

I always tell people he was one of the best and I mean it. I remember the line in the Barnsley programme that summed him up: 'Against West Ham McCormack scored his customary goal.'

20th March 1995

57

SKINNER NORMANTON

1926–95

SKINNER NORMANTON died peacefully aged 68. Between 1947 and 1953 he played 134 times for Barnsley and ended his career with a brief spell at Halifax. He retired to his garden where he grew sunflowers and turned out occasionally for the local team when they were a man short.

Sydney Albert Normanton was a local legend when he played at Barnsley. He was the hard man of the side, the minder for ball-playing colleagues of delicate disposition. There wasn't much of him but every ounce counted. He was destructive in the tackle, as unrelenting as a heat-seeking missile in pursuit of the enemy.

If I close my eyes I see two images. The first is a still photograph with Skinner posed in the manner of the day, arms folded and one foot on a leather football. His hair was short and wavy, parted near the middle and rigid with Brylcreem, and his legs were as sturdy as pit props with bulging shinpads and bulbous toecaps that glowed with dubbin and menace.

My second memory is more like a black and white film of the time with Skinner taking a penalty in a Cup tie and running from the halfway line before toe-ending the sodden football which became a blur as it passed the motionless goalkeeper, crashed into the underside of the crossbar and rebounded on to the back of the goalkeeper's head and into the net.

The goalkeeper was poleaxed and took several minutes to recover and it wasn't until much later that the iron crossbar stopped quivering from the impact of the shot. For a while it hummed like a male voice choir.

He was a local celebrity. Mothers would tell their children to stop mucking about or they would send for Skinner. He gained a wider audience many years after he retired when I first wrote an article about him.

I don't know what it was about the article that captured the imagination. I think it might have been the name. If you wanted to invent a local football hero of the time, someone who worked in the pits during the week and spent Saturday afternoons kicking lumps off the opposition you'd invent a man called something like Skinner Normanton.

Whatever the reason, his fame extended far beyond his beloved Oakwell. There used to be a Skinner Normanton Appreciation Society in Kuala Lumpur, and I have been asked about him during all my travels throughout the world. There was something in the name that was irresistible to Brits living abroad, particularly when they were feeling homesick for Saturday afternoons and kick-off time.

Many people believed him to be a mythical character like The Great Wilson of the *Wizard*. I remember Yorkshire Television producing him as a surprise guest on a programme I was doing in Leeds. They brought him into the studio and announced him in triumphant fashion as if they had found Lord Lucan or were about to produce the Loch Ness monster on the end of a lead.

He was smaller than I remembered and was wearing a blue suit with a nipped-in waist. The hair was as immaculate as ever and he looked like he was going to church. I had never seen him in his Sunday best. When he spoke his voice was soft, the manner modest, even shy.

It was difficult to convince people that this gentle and diffident man had at one time put the fear of God up any member of the human race who didn't wear a Barnsley shirt.

He played at a time when the game drank deep from its tap roots and although there were many more skilful and talented than he there was no one who better represented what you were up against if you took on a collier from Barnsley.

I was thinking that they ought to name the new stand at Barnsley after him. The Skinner Normanton stand would be a constant reminder that no matter how much we merchandise the modern game we must always remember what it is we are really selling.

Nowadays they talk of image. There was a time, when Skinner was a lad, when it had a soul.

1st May 1995

58

HAROLD LARWOOD

—

1904–95

Long before I ever met him I knew him well. My father told me he was the greatest fast bowler that ever drew breath and paid him the ultimate compliment of hero worship by copying his run to the wicket. Jack Fingleton, who also knew what he was talking about, said he was the best fast bowler he ever faced. He was, said Fingo, 'the master'.

Harold Larwood was a giant in my imagination, a legendary figure whose bowling frightened the greatest batsman there has ever been (and a few more besides) and in doing so created a political brouhaha of such resonance it echoes still, 60 years on.

When I first saw him standing outside a Sydney restaurant in 1979, he looked like one of the miners who would loiter around the pub on Sunday mornings waiting for the doors to open at midday.

He seemed uncomfortable in his suit, as if it was his Sunday best, his trilby hat was at a jaunty angle and he was smoking a cigarette which he cupped in the palm of his hand as if shielding it from a wind.

He was medium height with good shoulders and the strong, square hands of someone who had done some shovelling in his life as well as bowling. My father, in heaven at the time, would have been delighted with my impression that he and his great hero were peas from the same pod.

On the other hand, I had expected something altogether more substantial, someone more in keeping with the image I had of a man who terrorized opponents and whose fearsome reputation was such that at one moment in time governments were in thrall as he ran in to bowl.

In all of sport there never was a story to match the Bodyline saga. At its heart was the ultimate sporting challenge: a contest between the two greatest players in the world. In 1932–33 Donald Bradman was in his prime, the finest batsman of his generation, or any other before or since. Harold Larwood was also in his pomp, the fastest bowler in the world and about to prove himself the most lethal and unerring there has ever been.

The impresario of this world title contest was Douglas Jardine, the captain of England, patrician, implacable and a terrible snob who treated Australians with a contempt he never bothered to conceal. The story that unfolded around these three characters had everything except sex and a happy ending.

I was tempted to say it would have made a marvellous soap for television, except one was produced and a right mess they made of it.

The controversy stirred by Bodyline pursued Harold Larwood all his days. It changed him from a cricketer into a hunted man who hid away in a sweet shop in Blackpool before being persuaded by Jack Fingleton to seek a new life in Australia, where he ended his days surrounded by his large family in suburban Sydney amid the accents that once denounced him as the devil.

It was Jack Fingleton and Keith Miller who arranged my meeting with Harold; Bill O'Reilly was there too; and Arthur Norris and Ray Lindwall, so you could say I was in the best of company. There were so many questions I wanted to ask but dared not lest I turned what was a friendly lunch into a press conference. In any case, in that company I was superfluous to requirements except as a witness to what happened.

We sat at a round table on a spring day in Sydney. We all drank wine except Harold who said he was a beer man. 'Always had a pint when I was bowling,' he said. 'We used to sneak it on with the soft drinks. A pint for me and one for Bill Voce. You must put back what you sweat out,' he said.

'I hope you weren't drunk when you bowled at me,' said Jack Fingleton. 'I didn't need any inspiration to get you out,' Harold Larwood replied. Jack said of all the bowlers he faced Larwood was the fastest and had the best control. 'He was a very great bowler. Used to skid the bouncer. Throat ball,' said Jack.

Larwood took the compliment and said: 'You might not have been the best batsman I bowled against but you were certainly the bravest. I could hit you all right but you wouldn't go down. You weren't frightened, not like one or two I could mention but won't.'

Tiger O'Reilly said he was once sent out to bat against Harold when the ball was flying about, having been instructed by his skipper to stay at the crease at all costs. He was endeavouring to follow these instructions and was halfway through his backlift when Larwood bowled him a ball he sensed but did not see. 'I felt the draught as it went by and heard it hit Duckworth's gloves,' said Tiger. Being a sensible fellow he decided on a new method which, as he described it, involved his standing alongside the square leg umpire with his bat stretched towards the stumps.

'It was from this position,' said Tiger, 'I was perfectly placed to observe a most extraordinary occurrence. Larwood bowled me a ball of such pace and ferocity that it struck the off bail and reduced it to a small pile of sawdust.' When I first told this story a reader wrote to say that what O'Reilly claimed was clearly impossible. I wrote back informing the reader that O'Reilly was Irish and heard nothing more on the matter.

Jack Fingleton told Harold Larwood: 'You didn't need to bowl Bodyline. You were a good enough bowler to get anyone out by normal methods.' It was the first time during our luncheon that anyone had mentioned 'Bodyline'. Until then, the word had ticked away in a corner of the room like an unexploded bomb. Harold smiled. 'I was merely following the instructions of my captain,' he said. He produced from his jacket pocket a yellow duster and unfolded it to reveal a silver ash tray. The inscription said: 'To a great bowler from a grateful captain. D. R. Jardine.' The lettering was faint from nearly 50 years of spit and polish.

Jardine was the Field Marshal of Bodyline, Larwood his secret weapon. Jardine was the strategist, Jardine the assassin. I think it wrong to portray Larwood as the unwitting accomplice as some have done. It underestimates his strength of character, denies his intelligence and, most of all, does not take into account his determination to show Bradman and the rest of the Aussies who the boss really was.

But whereas Jardine fully understood the consequences of what he planned, Larwood was never likely to begin to fathom the undercurrents of intrigue created by his captain's strategy. They did for him in the end.

At our lunch, Harold recalled the day in 1933 when an Australian supporter accosted him and said: 'I hope you never play cricket again.' Harold Larwood replied: 'How dare you say that when cricket is my life, my job, my livelihood?' It wasn't too long before his critic's wish was granted and Harold Larwood, who thought he had been playing cricket for a living, wondered if he might have been mistaken.

After Jardine's team had thrashed the Australians, Harold Larwood, who was injured, went home ahead of the main party. He told me he realized he was to be made the scapegoat when he arrived in London to be confronted by a mob of journalists without any help from the MCC, which left him to his own devices.

Before reaching London, after his ship had docked in France, Larwood had been joined by his Nottinghamshire captain, A. W. Carr, who he took to be his official escort. Carr quizzed him about events in Australia and Larwood answered candidly as he would to his skipper. It was only when they arrived in London and Harold found himself on his own that he realized Carr had been working for a newspaper.

Harold said he arrived in Nottingham by train in angry mood in the early hours of the morning, to be greeted with brass band and a hero's welcome. Ordinary cricket lovers had no time for the political arguments taking place between the governments of Great Britain and Australia. All they cared about was England bringing home the Ashes and, as far as they were concerned, the man who did the job was Harold Larwood.

He enjoyed his celebrity for a while and capitalized on it. There was talk of making a movie and he went to Gamages store in London for a week to demonstrate bodyline bowling to an admiring public. For the week of personal appearances he earned five times more than he was paid for the entire tour of Australia.

He told us that the worst moment came when he was asked to apologise for the way he had bowled. He refused. 'I had nothing to be ashamed about,' he said. He never played for England again and he had only a few more seasons with Notts. Disenchanted, he bought a shop in Blackpool and didn't even put his name above the door in case it attracted rubber-neckers.

It was here that Jack Fingleton found him in 1948 and persuaded him to emigrate. Jack, who also worked as a parliamentary reporter and knew his way around the corridors of power, pulled a few strings and arranged that the prime minister of Australia, Ben Chifley, be on hand to greet Harold when he arrived.

Mr Chifley was a dinki-di Aussie with an ocker accent. After introducing the two men, Jack left them to have a natter. Ten minutes later, he was joined by the prime minister. 'He's a nice bloke but I can't understand a word he's saying,' he said to Jack. Ten minutes later, Larwood appeared. 'It was nice of the prime minister to see me, but I wish I knew what he was on about,' said Harold. So Jack Fingleton sometimes interpreted for two men who both thought they were speaking English.

Harold laughed as Jack told the tale. 'And I still haven't lost my accent,' he said. And he hadn't. 'Coming to Australia was the best thing that happened to me. I've been very happy here. I was signing in at a golf club some time ago and came to the bit where they ask you where you come from and my friend suggested I put Nottingham down in the book. I told him my home was in Sydney and pointed out I had lived in Australia longer than their best fast bowler, Dennis Lillee.'

We lunched together twice more before he became housebound because of his blindness. I called to congratulate him on being awarded the MBE in 1993. I didn't tell him it was 60 years overdue. Like elephants, the establishment have long memories and small brains. With Harold gone, only Bradman remains of the key protagonists in the Bodyline story. Neither man has told the whole truth, choosing to keep to themselves what they really thought about each other.

In that sense, the story has no ending and both men will be remembered for what we don't know about them as they will for their deeds on the field of play. Between them, the Boy from Bowral and the Lad from Nuncargate played out a story that will forever interest lovers of cricket and social historians looking for clues about the attitudes and mores of that time.

I was lucky to meet Harold Larwood and treasure the memory. I never saw him bowl, but my father did and Jack Fingleton, too. I think Jack should have the last word. 'One could tell his art by his run to the wicket. It was a poem of athletic grace, as each muscle gave over to the other with perfect balance and the utmost power. I will never see a greater fast bowler than Larwood, I am sure of that. He was the master.'

24th July 1995

OTHER
HEROES

—

No book about my sporting heroes would be complete without a tribute to my father. He taught me how to play sport, but most of all he taught me how to appreciate the humour and enjoyment to be had from watching and playing a game.

I have included an interview I did with Wilfred Rhodes in the Sixties because he was my father's hero as well as one of the greatest cricketers that ever lived. I resisted the temptation to alter the tense of what I wrote and change an interview into an obituary.

The fact is that good men like Wilfred Rhodes and John William Parkinson live on in the memory of those fortunate enough to have known them.

·59·

WILFRED

—

Wilfred Rhodes, 1877–1973

Wilfred Rhodes is in his nineties and still a young man. It was my grandfather who first told me about him. He once walked the 30 miles to Bradford to see Rhodes play and he never forgot it.

Rhodes didn't let him down. 'He took six or seven wickets that day without breakin' sweat and I said to a bloke sitting next to me: "How's tha' reckon he'll do in t'second innings?" and he says, "How's tha' know?" and he said, "If Wilfred does thi' once he'll do thi' again. He's spotted thi' weakness tha' sees and tha' bound to be Wilfred's next time round." And he was right tha' knows. Next innings he did t'same. Ah, he was a good'un Wilfred. Tha' could walk 30 miles and reckon on him doing summat.'

Throughout his career Wilfred Rhodes specialized in always 'doing summat'. When he retired from the game he had scored 39,802 runs and taken 4,187 wickets. Only ten batsmen in the history of the game have scored more runs and no bowler has come within a thousand wickets of Rhodes. Only George Hirst is within two of his 16 doubles of 1,000 runs and 100 wickets in the same season, only Tich Freeman within six of his 23 years of taking 100 wickets, and no one else has ever twice made over 2,000 runs in a season and three times taken over 200 wickets.

As Sir Neville Cardus wrote: 'The man's life and deeds take the breath away.' His career began with him playing against W G Grace in Victoria's reign and ended in the Thirties when he played against Bradman. He played first-class cricket for 32 years, surviving every changing fashion in the game, shrugging off every potential challenger to his crown. Even today, at the age of 90, the crown is still his.

There are, I suppose, more stories about Rhodes than any other cricketer. He has attracted many faithful chroniclers. My favourite tale, because it reveals the rare respect which Rhodes commanded from his fellow professionals, is told by Cardus. To illustrate Rhodes's known mastery of exploiting sticky wickets, Sir Neville tells of Charles McGahey, the old Essex player, going out to bat on a sunny day at Bramall Lane, Sheffield. As McGahey walked out to face Rhodes and Yorkshire the weather changed. Looking over his shoulder at the darkening sun McGahey said, 'Ullow! Caught, Tunnicliffe; bowled Rhodes. . .O.' And so it was, both innings.

I never saw Wilfred Rhodes play cricket. He had been retired 17 years when I saw my first Yorkshire game but I fancy I knew more about his deeds than I did of the other players who took the field that summer's day in 1947. My grandfather and my father had crammed my young head with tales about him. I first saw him at the Scarborough festival. Play had not started when he entered the ground. He was blind and being led. As he walked by the crowd stood and doffed their hats and said, 'Ayup, Wilfred lad,' and he nodded and said, 'Ayup.' I measured off my youth with visits to Scarborough to see the festival and gaze in awe at Wilfred Rhodes.

And later, much later, when my job gave me the excuse, I dared to sit with him. He was listening to the cricket and talking to Bob Appleyard. Jackie Hampshire was batting and he struck a ball massively over the square leg boundary, his bat making a sound like a hammer hitting an anvil. Wilfred stopped his discourse. 'I'll bet that went some way,' he said. Appleyard said: 'Six over square leg. Jackie was sweeping.' Wilfred said scornfully, 'Sweeping. That nivver was any sort of shot. Once I was listening to television and a cricketer was coaching youngsters how to sweep. I had to switch it off.'

I remembered that Rhodes, after retiring from the country game, had coached at Harrow and asked him if he enjoyed it. 'It was all right,' he said, 'but them young lads were overcoached when they came to me. Tha' could always tell what they do, allus forward, ever forward. I used to run up to bowl and not let go and theer they'd be on t'front foot, leg stretched down t'wicket. And I'd walk up to 'em and say, "Na' then lads wheers tha' going? Off for a walk perhaps." '

He shook his head sorrowfully, 'Tha' knows one thing I learned about cricket: tha' can't put in what God left out. Tha' sees two kinds of cricketers, them that uses a bat as if they are shovelling muck and them that plays proper and like as not God showed both of them how to play.'

I remembered how strange it seemed that he, the quintessential Yorkshire professional, the man who 'laiked proper' and not for fun, should teach cricket at one of the temples of the amateur game.

'Lads were all right,' he said. 'I liked them, we got on well. It was t'others, t'masters I couldn't get on with. They allus thought they knew more than me. I told one of 'em one day he'd been interferin' and I said, "Tha' can't know more about this game than me tha' knows," and he said, "Why not?" and I said, "Because if th' did tha'd be playing for England and I'd be doing thy job teaching Greek."'

Listening to Rhodes one is transported to a world where cricketers wore sidewhiskers and starched the cuffs of their shirts; a game of gentlemen and players, separate entrances, attitudes as different as night and day. Because his mind sees them clearly he introduces you to Trumper and Ranji and Grace and Gregory and

Armstrong and Plum Warner. He can conjure up cricket in Victorian England, in the First World War, through the Depression years to the 'Golden Thirties'. He is a walking history of the game, blessed with a fabulous memory and the unequivocal attitude of one who is certain of what he says for the simple reason that he was there when it happened. When Wilfred Rhodes tells you that Bradman was the best bat that ever lived and that S F Barnes was the best bowler, only the foolish would dare argue.

'It's a thinking game is cricket. If tha' doesn't use thi' brains tha' might as well give up. When I took up batting serious and opened wi' Jack Hobbs in Australia, a lot said I couldn't bat. But I thought about it and decided that t'best way to go 'bout t'job in Australia was to play forward. In that trip I made one or two (including a record opening partnership of 323 with Hobbs which still stands) and one day I'm going on t'tram to t'ground and Duff, t'Australian cricketer, sits next to me and starts chatting. He said, "Tha' knows tha' baffles me Wilfred," and I said, "How come?" and he says, "Well tha's got all these runs on this tour and yet tha' can't bat. Tha's only got one shot." And I said, "Ay, and that's all I need out here." Same with bowling, too, although you could say I was more gifted than most at it. But I still used to think 'em out. Batsmen used to say about me that I could drop a ball on a sixpence. Now that's impossible, no one can do that. I could probably hit a newspaper, spread out at that. But point is they used to think I could hit a sixpence and I used to let 'em keep on thinking and that way they were mine.'

During our talk he riffled through the years, illuminating forgotten summers with his yarns, breathing life into cricketers long dead. About M A Noble, the great Australian all-rounder who captained his country at the turn of the century, he said: 'That Noble was a good 'un. Used to bowl his quicker one with his fingers straight up t'seam. He nivver got me.' On Geoffrey Boycott, who played for England 70 years later: 'I said to him one day, "Does tha' cut?" And he said, "A bit," and I said "Remember not to do it until May's finished." '

He lives with his daughter Muriel and her husband Tom near Bournemouth. He still enjoys his good health, takes a daily walk and listens to the radio. During the cricket season he keeps in touch with the game by occasional trips to Lord's where he meets old friends eager for a yarn. His encyclopaedic mind is fed daily by fresh facts on cricket read to him from the papers by his daughter and son-in-law.

He doesn't miss a trick. I once wrote a story for the *Sunday Times* about an incident concerning W G Grace. During a gentlemen versus players fixture at Lord's Schofield Haigh, the Yorkshire player, asked the good doctor's permission to leave the field early on the last afternoon so that he might journey back to Yorkshire. Permission was granted. On that last afternoon, as the time for Haigh's departure and Grace's century drew nigh, Grace hit an easy catch towards Haigh. As Haigh awaited the ball the Doctor shouted: 'Take the catch and you miss the train.'

Not being daft, Haigh missed the catch and in consequence was home in Yorkshire when he wanted to be.

Shortly after writing the story I received a letter. It simply said: 'That story you told about Schofield Haigh was true. I know because I was the bowler.' It was signed: Wilfred Rhodes. I still have it. I wouldn't swap it for a gold pig.

It's not everyone who gets a letter from the gods.

·60·

MY OLD MAN

—

John William Parkinson, 1903–76

I was never told fairy tales as a child. Instead I heard about Larwood's action and Hobbs's perfection. Before I ever saw him play I knew Len Hutton immediately, and the first time I witnessed Stanley Matthews in the flesh I knew which way he was going even if the full-back didn't. The stories of these gods, and many, many more besides I heard at my father's knee.

He was a remarkable man with a marvellous facility to adorn an anecdote. It was he who invented the gate, complete with attendant, which was built in honour of a Barnsley winger who could run like the wind but didn't know how to stop. At the end of one of his gallops the gate would be opened and the winger would career through and out of the ground to finally come to a stop halfway across the car park. Or so Dad said.

It was he who told me of the full-back whose fearsome sliding tackles carried him into the wall surrounding the ground, causing the spectators to start wearing goggles at home games for fear of being blinded by flying chips of concrete. Frank Barson, he assured me, once ran the entire length of the field bouncing the ball on his head, beat the opposing goalkeeper and then headed his final effort over the cross bar because he'd had a row with his manager before the game.

Moreover, the old man swore he managed to see Len Hutton's 364 at the Oval by convincing the gate attendant that he was dying of some incurable disease and his last wish was to see Len before he took leave of this earth. I never swallowed that one until once at a football match where the gates were closed I witnessed him convince a gateman that he was a journalist and I was his runner. I was seven at the time, and it was the very first occasion I watched a football match from a press box.

Apart from being a fairy-story teller he was one of the best all-round sportsmen I have come across. He loved any game, and as soon as he took it up he played well. I never saw him play football, but I have been told that he did a fair imitation of Wilf Copping. As a cricketer he was a quick bowler with an action copied from his great hero, Harold Larwood.

He had a marvellous agility and a sure pair of hands near the bat, and as a batsman he was a genuine No. 11 who often didn't know whether he'd play left- or right-handed until he got to the crease. Not that it made much difference.

Of all games he loved cricket the most. He judged everything and everyone by the game. The only time I ever saw him lost for words was when someone confessed they neither knew nor cared about cricket. Then he would shake his head sadly, baffled that a great part of his world – for cricket was surely that – could mean so little to any other sane human being. Last season a friend and I took him to Headingley and sat him behind the bowler's arm and he never moved all day. We brought him pork pies and sandwiches and good Yorkshire beer, and he sat under his native sun watching Lillee bowl fast and he was the happiest man on our planet.

You always knew where my old man would be on any cricket ground: right behind the bowler's arm. Moreover, if you ever lost him, or he lost himself – as he often did, being born without a sense of direction – you simply asked the whereabouts of the nearest cricket ground and there you would discover the old man sitting contentedly awaiting the arrival of his search party.

In his younger days his favourite holiday was a week at Scarbro' – which he reckoned had the best beach wicket in Britain – or Butlin's, not because he particularly cared for the idea of a holiday camp, but because of the sporting competitions. He used to enter the lot and normally came home with a couple of trophies for snooker or running or the mixed wheelbarrow race. He entered everything and anything and owed much of his success to his ability to talk an opponent to death. I once heard an irate tennis opponent say to him: 'Doesn't tha' ever shut thi' gob?'

'Only when other people are talking,' said my old man, with a disarming smile.

When he finished playing he took up coaching, first the local youngsters and latterly his three grandchildren. They, like me, are left-handed batsmen. Not because God made them so, but because the old man's theory was that not many players like bowling to left-handers. His other theory, based on a lifetime's experience, was that fast bowlers are crazy, so he determined to make at least one of my sons a slow bowler.

The consequence of this is that I once had the only eight-year-old googly bowler in the northern hemisphere. At ten he added the top spinner to his repertoire and when he was twelve the old man's face was a picture as his protégé beat me with a googly and then had me plumb in front of the dustbin with one that hurried off the pitch and came straight through.

The old man's name was John William, and he hated John Willy. If anyone addressed him thus when he was playing in his prime, the red alert went up and the casualty ward at Barnsley Beckett Hospital could look forward to receiving visitors.

He's been dead for many years now, but I still think about him because he was a special man and I was lucky to know him. He was a Yorkshireman, a miner, a humorist and a fast bowler. Not a bad combination.

I only hope they play cricket in heaven. If they don't he'll ask for a transfer.